The Naturally Elegant

HOME

The Naturally Elegant

HOME

Environmental Style

JANET MARINELLI

WITH ROBERT KOURIK

PRINCIPAL ILLUSTRATIONS BY JEFF WILKINSON

LITTLE, BROWN AND COMPANY

Boston Toronto London

FIRST EDITION

Library of Congress Cataloging-in-Publication Data

Marinelli, Janet.
   The naturally elegant home: environmental style / Janet Marinelli with Robert Kourik. — 1st ed.
      p.   cm.
   Includes index.
   ISBN 0-316-54612-7
   1. Interior decoration — Environmental aspects — United States.   2. Gardens — Environmental aspects — United States.   I. Kourik, Robert.   II. Title.
NK2002.M37   1992
728′.37047 — dc20   92-13887

10 9 8 7 6 5 4 3 2 1

RRD-OH

Design by Janis Owens

Published simultaneously in Canada by Little, Brown & Company (Canada) Limited

PRINTED IN THE UNITED STATES OF AMERICA

ACKNOWLEDGMENTS

One thing that should be clear to anyone who reads this book is that a naturally elegant home in Los Angeles is quite different from one in Miami or my hometown, New York. Many thanks to Robert Kourik for sharing his expertise on environmental living in the water-short West. My friend Jeff Wilkinson was a joy to work with. His wonderful drawings speak for themselves; his architectural insights made this a better book.

Editors are the unsung heroes of publishing, and this is especially true of my crack team of editors at Little, Brown: Ray Roberts, Dorothy Straight, and Kit Ward. They, along with Donna Peterson and Ellen Bedell of the Production Department and designer Janis Owens, made the book read well and look good. The *House Beautiful* editors back in the 1940s who published a series of ground-breaking articles on climate-wise house design were also an inspiration.

Many of my colleagues in architecture and horticulture went out of their way to supply me with information and advice, especially Mark Feirer and Eileen Bellantoni of *Fine Homebuilding*, Linda Yang of the *New York Times,* photographer Peter C. Jones, Richard Kashmanian of the U.S. Environmental Protection Agency, Gordon Bock of *Old-House Journal,* and Robert Corbett of the National Appropriate Technology Assistance Service. My Brooklyn Botanic Garden colleagues Barbara Pesch, Steven Clemants, Lucy Jones, and Stephen Scanniello were a big help.

I can't thank Elvin McDonald enough for his encouragement early on, and for steering me to our mutual agent, Carla Glasser, who's great at working out the details. Carla's husband, attorney David Glasser, helped put my mind at ease. Thanks to Joe Iannuzzi, who let me borrow his lap-top computer, I was able to get out of the sweltering city and put my body at ease as well while still meeting my deadline.

Many thanks, too, to the architects and landscape designers featured in these pages, who met my repeated requests for time, drawing, and photographs with grace and good humor.

A special hug and kiss go to my husband, Don Hooker, and my parents, Gilda and George Marinelli, for their savvy criticism, love, and support.

CONTENTS

PART THREE

*Designing and Remodeling the
Naturally Elegant Home*

PART FOUR

Designing a Naturally Elegant Garden

The Naturally Elegant

HOME

INTRODUCTION

In March of 1845 Henry David Thoreau began an experiment on an uninhabited tract of land on Walden Pond, near Concord, Massachusetts. "I went to the woods," he wrote in *Walden* (1854), "because I wished to live deliberately, to front only the essential facts of life, and see if I could not learn what it had to teach, and not, when I came to die, discover that I had not lived."

The first thing he did was to build a house. With a borrowed ax, Thoreau cut and hewed rafters, studs, and timbers from some "arrowy white pines" on the site. He bought a shanty from a railroad worker and recycled its boards. He dug a root cellar "where a woodchuck had formerly dug his burrow, down through sumach and blackberry roots." He moved in on the Fourth of July. Before the onset of winter he built a fieldstone chimney, shingled the exterior, and plastered the walls. For the next two years he strove to "live deep and suck out all the marrow of life."

These last words have become a kind of American mantra. Something about being American makes many of us want to live close to nature and "suck out all the marrow of life." Well, maybe not all of it: over the past ten years we've been trying to figure out just how much marrow we can take.

In the 1970s we thought we knew the answer. Flush with a new environmental fervor, some of us decided to go "back to the land" — my friend and consultant Robert Kourik, for example — to live on farms or in the woods, to grow food in organic gardens, to compost all organic wastes (even bodily wastes, in waterless toilets), and to convince the rest of the country, in Robert's words, "of the virtues and healing powers of, the magic surrounding, and the essential ecological need for" the self-sufficient life.

While Robert was making compost in California, I was making trouble at my typewriter in Washington, D.C. America was in the throes of an energy crisis. Coast to coast, motorists were curled around street corners waiting for a tank of gas, muttering about the

prospect of yet another summer with air-conditioners locked at 80 degrees. The time was ripe for serious talk about alternative energy plans, and by God, I wouldn't be left out. I blasted what were then known as "hard-path" schemes to produce more energy. One of my favorite targets was the Solar Satellite Power System — sixty satellites forming one squat constellation in the evening sky, gathering sunlight twenty-four hours a day, converting it to electricity and then to microwaves, and finally beaming it down to huge antenna farms on earth to power an unfathomable number of Cuisinarts, Salad Shooters, and electric hot-dog cookers. At the same time I tirelessly touted "soft-path" solutions that emphasized *conserving* energy, solutions such as the solar house.

Lo and behold, within a few short years we succeeded in convincing the country that living the environmental life meant shivering in the dark in the proverbial cave. What was more, we also began to suspect it ourselves. It was one thing to point out that every time America flushed, five or six gallons of water went down the tubes; it was quite another to begin each day with a trip to the composting privy. It was one thing to rhapsodize about solar houses, and quite another to live in a solar house that sent you scurrying for the bikini at noon and the down parka at night.

Over the years we've mellowed. Self-sufficiency is no longer the goal. Sure, a few people have managed to fashion more or less self-reliant lives. But most of us want a more expansive, more cosmopolitan, more — dare I say it? — *convenient* life.

■ Natural Elegance

One of the most glaring faults of the environmental home of the 1970s was its rather narrow definition of style — or its complete lack thereof. Back-to-the-land houses were rag-tag, makeshift, and make-do. Solar houses had a strident science-fiction look. However, in the past ten years or so, largely outside of the national media spotlight, architects, gardeners, and scientists have been collaborating with nature to create a new environmental home, a naturally elegant home.

According to *Webster's,* the word *elegant* means "characterized by dignified richness and grace." The new environmental home embraces elegance and blends into its "dignified richness and grace" a measure of ecological attunement. Natural elegance celebrates biological diversity and bioregional style. North America, like other continents, comprises a number of bioregions. Just south of the polar ice cap is the Arctic tundra, an expanse of permafrost and mostly low or dwarf shrubs, lichens, and mosses. Beneath that is a vast area of deep green coniferous forest that sweeps in a giant crescent from Alaska across Canada. This is the boreal forest. As it dips into the northern reaches of Minnesota, Michigan, New York, and New England, its conifers mingle with sugar maple and other deciduous trees. A related forest flows down the spine of the Appalachians as far as North Carolina.

Another vast coniferous forest covers the western third of North America. It includes the lush, moss-draped rain forests of the Pacific maritime forest, the sunny stands of ponderosa pine and quaking aspen in the Rocky Mountains, and the groves of giant sequoia in the Sierra Nevada. These are among the most magnificent forests in the world.

The eastern half of the United States is dominated by deciduous trees. The eastern deciduous forest bioregion includes most of New England and the Middle Atlantic states and skips across the Appalachians to the Ohio River Valley. Its colors change dramatically with the seasons. A sprightly yellow-green in spring, it matures to a deep green in summer and explodes into a fireball of color in autumn before settling into an iridescent winter gray.

South and east of the deciduous forest is the bioregion often called the coastal plain, an area of salt marshes, cypress swamps, and pine forests. This bioregion includes much of what is still called the Deep South, but it also extends north and east as far as the pitch-pine barrens of New Jersey and sweeps around the bottom of the Appalachians into eastern Texas and up the Mississippi River Valley as far as southern Illinois.

Although northern Florida is deep in the southern pinelands of the coastal plain, on the southern tip of the state is a splash of flora related to the tropical forests of southern Mexico, Central America, and the Caribbean islands. Edging the coast is a forest of stilt-rooted mangroves. In South Florida the land flattens out and is covered with broad, shallow rivers thickly populated with saw grass. These immense sedge prairies, or everglades, are occasionally interrupted by raised clumps, or hammocks, of dense tropical forest.

West of the Appalachian Mountains, deciduous forest gives way to open woodland, or savanna, and eventually to prairie. While humid climates support forests and dry climates support deserts, the prairie thrives on a moisture level somewhere in between the two. Unlike deserts, grasslands have a solid ground cover of vegetation; unlike forests, they feature

Environmental houses of the 1970s were often defiantly anti-style. The naturally elegant home celebrates biological diversity and bioregional style. Rustic twig furniture enhances the sense of living in the eastern deciduous forest.

This house is suited to the splash of tropical flora on the southern tip of Florida. Like the houses of Florida's early settlers, it is raised to get above the dampness and catch the breeze.

With its majestic saguaro cactus, this Arizona home is unmistakably of the Sonoran Desert.

open space and endless vistas. The grasslands of North America are generally divided into the tall-grass prairie of the Midwest, where rain is comparatively plentiful, and the short-grass prairie of the drier Great Plains.

West of the prairies is the intermountain region, a vast area of arid western North America sandwiched between the Rocky Mountains and the Sierra Nevada. All four deserts of the United States fall within its boundaries. The Great Basin Desert spreads north from Utah and Nevada. Its northernmost reaches comprise the sagebrush steppes of eastern Oregon, southern Idaho, and western Wyoming, an area of austere beauty dominated by sagebrush, saltbush, and grasses. The Mojave Desert straddles the boundaries where California, Nevada, and Arizona meet and extends into the extreme southwestern corner of Utah. Unlike the Great Basin Desert, the Mojave is dotted with cacti and yucca, and annual flowers explode into a short-lived kaleidoscope of color in spring. One yucca, the Joshua tree, is synonymous with the Mojave Desert to travelers and Western movie fans.

The Chihuahuan Desert, which occupies a

relatively small area of southern New Mexico and the Texas Panhandle but drives a wedge through the heart of northern Mexico, is North America's largest desert. The tall, columnar, often many-armed saguaro cactus dominates the horizon of the Sonoran Desert bioregion of western Mexico, Arizona, and extreme southern California. The southern coast of California is blanketed with chaparral, a type of dense scrubland that develops in regions that have mild, wet winters and extremely dry summers.

Each of these bioregions has a unique climate, plant community, and visual character. These features should suggest a distinctive design for the naturally elegant house and its garden, and should contribute to their sense of place.

Sometimes natural elegance is invisible. Its subtle beauty requires inference, study, and interpretation. In nature, dead trees are alive with owls and woodpeckers; nothing is wasted. In architecture as in nature, frugality can be the most refined form of elegance. For example, a well-designed graywater system is hidden from view yet efficiently recycles shower, bathtub, and laundry water to make the landscape flourish.

Low maintenance is another hidden elegance. In the 1970s, high maintenance was the Achilles' heel of environmentally sound houses and gardens. Solar houses that required constant opening and closing of shades and vents to function properly and hot compost piles that demanded frequent turning are but two examples of the onerous features of circa 1970s environmental homes.

In sharp contrast, computers constantly adjust temperature and humidity in the new generation of solar houses and automatically kick on backup heating systems when necessary. In the seventies "ultra-low-flush" toilets, which use a mere 1.6 gallons per flush, were difficult to find, expensive ($400 or more), and odd-looking. Now there are dozens of ultra-low-flush toilets available in designer colors and familiar shapes, and some cost as little as $100.

The Natural House Tradition

Frank Lloyd Wright was North America's first great bioregional architect. The lines and masses of his Prairie houses are made for the American grasslands. Wright wrote that his first Prairie house "began to associate with the ground and become natural to its prairie site" — vast, flat, horizontal. The houses' horizontal lines were punctuated by vertical elements — massive chimneys, tall casement windows — just as the prairie horizon is accented by an occasional tree.

Sounding downright Thoreauvian, Wright declared that the naturally elegant home — he called it "the natural house" — would help liberate Americans from the stale traditions of Europe by awakening in us "the desire for such far-reaching simplicities of life as we may see in the clear countenance of nature." So that we could more clearly see nature, he merged the inside and the outside through large expanses of glass, and he did away with many interior walls. Wright and other Prairie architects further fused building and landscape by using materials that were indigenous to the Midwest, such as limestone and oak.

Around the turn of the century, as these midwestern architects were declaring their independence from Europe, Jens Jensen and other Chicago designers were developing a new language of landscape design for the prairie states. It, too, celebrated the horizontal, and reflected a keen understanding of the ecological and aesthetic personalities of native plant communities in the grasslands.

Today's new generation of environmental homes has also been inspired by the natural character of the house's region, as well as by the site itself — not by imported notions of architectural style. In the naturally elegant home, the house and garden are linked to each other and to the bioregion, restoring architecture and horticulture to their rightful place in the larger ecological community.

What else do these houses have in common?

Because decades of intensive development since the heyday of Jensen and Wright have reduced the native landscape to patches and fragments that are few and far between, the naturally elegant home takes great pains to preserve that landscape. The floor plan is pushed and pulled to save a tree or rocky outcrop or arroyo.

But the naturally elegant home does more than preserve nature; it celebrates it. Windows artfully frame views, and sunspaces bring the

Frank Lloyd Wright was America's first great bioregional architect. At Fallingwater, in Pennsylvania, Wright linked building with nature by using native rock: the boulders in front of the fireplace seem to be part of the streambed that runs under the house. Photograph: Ezra Stoller/Esto.

Left: Believing that people should live close to nature, Wright did away with many interior walls and merged inside with outside by means of large expanses of glass. In the Jacobs house in Wisconsin, he further fused house and landscape through the use of limestone, which is indigenous to the Midwest. Photograph: Ezra Stoller/Esto.

The naturally elegant home does more than preserve nature; it celebrates it. The breezeway of this California ranch house by William Turnbull Associates artfully frames the view.

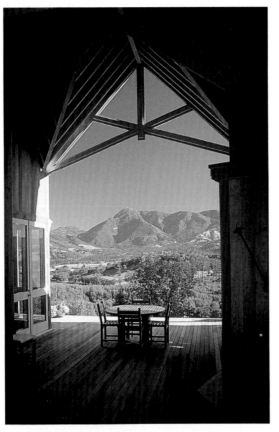

outside in and send the inside out. Outdoor "rooms" further blur the distinction between nature and architecture, allowing us to "suck out the marrow of life" whenever we want to.

A naturally elegant home is attuned to the local climate in natural, energy-conserving ways. Unlike the environmental house of the 1970s, it conserves energy but is not dominated by energy concerns. Daylight is allowed to flood the home, reducing the need for artificial lighting. The new environmental home is positioned to capture solar heat passively, without the rickety collectors that once littered rooftops; high levels of insulation and energy-efficient appliances conserve the wood, oil, natural gas, and other precious fuels that are used for backup heating and cooling.

The naturally elegant home is made of materials that don't threaten the health of the inhabitants and the manufacture of which causes a minimum of pollution. Ideally, the materials are also sustainable — that is, they will last as long as it will take nature to replace them in

The wood on the windows of this Northwest home by architect James Cutler is Douglas fir, one of the towering conifers that dominate the region's magnificent forests. Photograph: Peter Aaron/Esto.

Above: Because the native landscape has shrunk to patches and fragments that are few and far between, the naturally elegant home is designed to preserve as much of it as possible. This sod-roofed house in northern California displaces a minimum of coastal meadow.

Right: From its insulation (derived from seawater) to its wood finishes (made from rosemary and berries), this house by architect Paul Bierman-Lytle eschews toxic materials. A wooden spiral staircase winds up to the tower, which affords panoramic views of this island off the South Carolina coast.

The naturally elegant home must often re-create nature. This bur-oak savanna in Illinois — the work of landscape designer P. Clifford Miller — is as vibrant and colorful as an English flower border.

the wild. Materials native to the bioregion reinforce the connection with the natural world; recycled Douglas fir woodwork in a Northwest home echoes the towering Douglas firs of the area's lush forests, for example.

The naturally elegant home is also designed to smoothly integrate water conservation, recycling, and natural food production into our hectic everyday lives. Edible landscapes challenge the notion that landscaping is purely ornamental and demonstrate that beauty and practicality are not mutually exclusive. In the kitchen, one of the most critical spaces in the ecologically sensitive house, herbs grow in sunny bay windows, and handsome built-in cabinets discreetly store glass, aluminum, newspaper, plastic, and other recyclables. With its graywater system, low-flow showerhead, and ultra-low-flush toilet, the bathroom is the center for water conservation in the naturally elegant home.

Left: Wildflowers, including the vivid orange California poppy, are woven into a tapestry with garlic and other vegetables. Edible gardens such as this one challenge the notion that landscaping is purely ornamental and demonstrate that beauty and practicality need not be mutually exclusive.

Above: The naturally elegant kitchen is designed to smoothly integrate recycling and natural food production into our busy everyday lives, and to once more make suppertime a feast for all the senses.

■ The Naturally Evolving House

In his 1954 book *The Natural House,* Frank Lloyd Wright advised readers who were looking for a place to build a home to look anywhere but the city. "The best thing to do," he wrote, "is go as far out as you can get. Avoid the suburbs — dormitory towns — by all means. Go way out into the country — what you regard as 'too far' — and when others follow, as they will (if procreation keeps up), move on." But now there is no more "on" left. Today the naturally elegant home must not only commune with nature, it must often *re-create* it.

Fortunately, we're learning not only how to avoid doing ecological damage, but also how to *undo* it once it's been done. In places where the natural landscape has been decimated — which in the United States is almost everywhere — native plant communities are being restored. Ecologists and gardeners are learning how to put back the pieces, how to restore natural processes so that nature can heal itself and get on with the business of evolution.

What's more, since the days of Frank Lloyd Wright and even since the 1970s, new technologies — from superwindows to superinsulation — have enabled us to build homes that are ever easier on the environment. Thanks to the emphasis on aesthetics in recent years, they don't assault our sensibilities, either. Some architects are using these new technologies to create a new indigenous architecture, a twenty-first-century vernacular. Their homes have all the emotional warmth of natural materials and homespun architectural traditions, and they are responsive to the local climate. Yet they also have all the comfort and convenience we've come to expect from our surroundings. One traditional technology has been elevated to high-tech status in the work of David Easton (see pages 10 and 76), who builds handsome rammed-earth houses. As builders in arid areas have been doing for centuries, Easton constructs his homes from soil, but he adds cement and compacts the mixture between

knock-down plywood forms with power tools. The result is an earth-walled house that's easier and cheaper to build. An emerging generation of technologies — photovoltaics, or solar electricity, for example — guarantees that the naturally elegant home will continue to evolve.

One thing we have not learned is that big homes aren't necessarily better. The average American house continues to grow, even as the average household shrinks. The famous Levittown house of the 1950s had 750 square feet of living space. By 1989, according to the National Association of Homebuilders, the average single-family house was about 2,000 square feet. The houses we lust after are even larger. Ironically, many of the environmentally sensitive houses that purport to conserve resources as a matter of principle are conspicuously large. As architect and author Witold Rybczynski has written, in the era of the two-career family, there is another, nonenvironmental price to be paid for the bloated floor plan. Big houses mean more time spent on

You need not start from scratch to have a home that is both environmentally sensitive and beautiful. The renovation of existing houses is the ultimate form of recycling — especially if, like this Connecticut Colonial, they are redesigned in a way that makes them more energy-conserving and more in tune with nature.

Above: The rammed-earth villa has the emotional warmth of natural materials and homespun architectural traditions, yet at the same time it has all the comfort and convenience we've come to expect from our homes.

Right: Bioregional style for the California chaparral: as builders in arid areas have been doing for centuries, David Easton constructed this elegant rammed-earth home from soil.

cleaning and maintenance — or else more money, and there's something un-American about domestic help.

Diminutive dwellings such as the Wharton house on page 48 are proof that small can be quite elegant. Small is easier and also more affordable. One of the criticisms leveled against environmental architecture is that it's too expensive for anyone except the truly rich. But it doesn't have to be that way. Many of the new houses, such as those illustrated on pages 94–103, are economical to build. And because they're designed for the local climate, they save on fuel bills and are more economical to maintain than conventional houses. Thanks to bioregional design and the new climate-wise building technologies, there's a naturally elegant home for almost every budget.

We still have a lot to learn about designing naturally elegant homes for the city. Most of the houses featured in this book are in the suburbs or even farther from the urban core,

as planners like to call it, but many of the ideas discussed here will work in the town house as well as in the country house. As a New Yorker, I know only too well that densely populated areas have their own environmental pluses and minuses. On the plus side is being able to walk to the store and walk to work. Noise — especially those confounded car alarms — is at the top of my list of minuses. Figuring out how to live close to nature without compromising privacy, not to mention security, and even coming up with a way to keep plants from "disappearing" from your garden — if you *have* a garden — are additional challenges. They are a subject for a separate volume.

Part I of this book looks at the history of the natural house and provides a snapshot of the naturally elegant home in the 1980s and early 1990s. State-of-the-art houses and gardens across the continent are featured in part II.

But you need not start from scratch to have a home that is both environmentally sensitive and beautiful. Indeed, the construction of every one of the more than 100 million homes in the United States required wood, brick, concrete, or other materials. The manufacture of these materials required energy and resulted in air and water pollution and other environmental damage. More energy was needed to transport them to the site and put them in place. And if the house were to be torn down, it would take still more energy to demolish it and haul away the materials, probably to an already overburdened landfill. Whether it's called renovation, remodeling, retrofitting, or restoration, the preservation of existing houses is the ultimate form of recycling. And if the homes are redesigned in a way that makes them healthier, more energy-conserving, and more in tune with the natural environment, the ecological benefits will be that much greater. Parts III and IV of this book give you the nuts-and-bolts details on how to transform your house into a naturally elegant home for the 1990s and the next century.

TOURING THE
Naturally Elegant Home

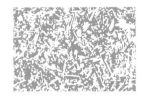

CLIMATE AND SITE

"As Dignified as a Tree in the Midst of Nature"

Lacking mechanical heating and cooling, vernacular houses had to be responsive to the local climate. This Massachusetts saltbox has a two-story windowed south side to catch the sun and a low-sloping back roof turned to the prevailing winter winds. The chimney forms a thick masonry core that warms the rooms.

For close to two years, from October 1949 through June 1951, each issue of *House Beautiful* featured disquisitions on climate and house design. The series was the culmination of a ground-breaking twenty-seven-month study. More than aesthetics was at stake.

In an article entitled "So You Think You're Comfortable!," which launched the series, *House Beautiful* challenged its readers to consider how often they reached for a sweater, had a sudden urge to kick off their shoes, or lunged for a paperweight to keep bills from scattering when the windows were open — all signs of a house that was uncomfortable because it was oblivious to climate. In America, rooted in Puritanism, it is seen as a sign of character to accept the pinpricks of discomfort, the editors noted. Yet, they argued, not only is discomfort not good for the soul, it's bad for the body: "A bad house is a drain, like constant under-feeding." A professor of public health at Yale was quoted at length on how grippe, pneumonia, strep, and other germs thrive in the very dry or moist air of the uncomfortable house. But the coup de grace was the observation that those areas of the United States with the most easily controlled climates had not only the healthiest citizens but also the highest per capita incomes.

The magazine commissioned eight outstanding scientists to study the climates of the principal population centers of the United States, from Phoenix to Philadelphia to Miami, and report on what each climate meant in terms of human comfort. It then commissioned climate-sensitive house designs from leading architects.

Interest in climate-sensitive design began to snowball. The prestigious American Institute of Architects serialized the material in its bulletin. Top weather scientists met in 1950 in Washington, D.C., for the first federally sponsored conference on climate and building. *Progressive Architecture* soon joined the chorus, publishing Jeffrey Ellis Aronin's *Climate and Architecture,* which it called "the first book to *do* something about the weather."

And that, suddenly, was that. By the mid-1950s, climate consciousness was out, and cheap energy was in. The ensuing period of cheap and plentiful fossil fuels charted the course of domestic architecture for decades.

■ Weather Returns to Architecture

The first English settlers in North America brought their idea of a house with them — usually the "half-timbered" house, with exposed wooden framework and wall spaces filled with brick nogging or wattle and daub (a kind of primitive basketry held together with mud, clay, or plaster). This kind of house worked well in England, where summers are cool and winters mild, but it was not suited to the bone-chilling winters and stifling summers of the Northeast. The North American climate — or rather *climates* — made short shrift of any preconceived notions about building a house.

In North America we have almost every sort of climate there is. In Seattle or Vancouver the climate is quite English, but New York and Washington, which are at the same latitude as the south of Italy, can get so hot and humid you'd think you were in Amazonia. Arizona and the Baja are like the Persian Gulf. Iowa has the sort of Russian winter that wrecked Hitler and Napoleon, and parts of the United States and much of Canada get colder still.

Lacking central heating, air-conditioning, and other domestic technologies, the first Eu-

Far left: In the Desert
Southwest, where the days
are hot and dry and the
nights are cool, Spanish
settlers modified an ancient
Arab construction tech-
nique and built houses
with thick adobe walls that
soak up solar heat, keeping
interiors cool during the
day and warm at night.
The sand-toned cement
plaster coating on the exterior walls protects the
adobe block.

Left: The antique fireplace
in this restored adobe
home takes the chill off the
cold desert nights. Today,
energy-efficient paddle fans
are a part of the cooling
strategy.

ropean settlers had to get to know their climates intimately and make those climates work
for them. Today we romanticize the old
houses of Nantucket and Charleston, New Orleans, and Santa Fe. But there was nothing
whimsical about the ceiling heights in these
houses, nor about the slope of their roofs, nor
about their wraparound porches. New England "saltboxes" were built with a windowed
two-story side to catch the sun and a low-
sloping back roof turned to the prevailing winter winds. Chimneys and fireplaces formed a
thick central core of masonry that retained
heat and radiated it to surrounding rooms.
The sod houses of the Great Plains had well-
insulated walls and roofs, and they were even
more climate-proof when they were built partially underground. Spanish settlers in the Desert Southwest, where the days are hot and dry
and the nights are cool, modified an ancient
Arab building technique and constructed flat-
roofed, thick-walled adobe houses with rooms
aligned in a quadrangle around a portal, or
sheltered porch, that opened onto a central
courtyard. The portals provided shade, and the

thick adobe walls soaked up solar heat, keeping the houses cool during day and warm at
night. Even city living was dictated by climate:
the elegant Charleston, South Carolina, town
house was oriented so that its two-story colon-
naded piazza, or side porch, could catch the
prevailing summer breeze.

Between 1850 and 1950, central heating, electricity, evaporative cooling, and finally air-
conditioning (first known as "man-made
weather") became mainstays of the American
house. Climate was forgotten for nearly a century. Spanish villas proliferated on Long Island, and saltboxes were marketed in Texas.
For one brief interlude, *House Beautiful* tried
to convince the public that a lack of knowledge about climate and its effect on our houses
was the biggest impediment to human comfort: for example, expanses of south-facing
glass had become chic, but the new air-
conditioners were still pricey, meaning that
many Americans were baking in summer. The
debate was forgotten, however, as cheap electricity in the 1950s and '60s made air-
conditioning a middle-class amenity. Cheap oil

and gas also meant that we could keep our houses warm in winter no matter how flimsy the walls were.

In 1973, when the OPEC embargo sent oil prices through the roof, climate awareness returned with a vengeance. This time the issue was not "discomfort" but rather "energy efficiency." Homeowners rushed to install storm windows, turned down thermostats, and for a few summers even kept air-conditioners set at a previously unthinkable 80 degrees. Engineers and architects began to take a serious look at houses powered by alternative sources of energy — especially the sun.

■ Let the Sun Shine In

Around the time *House Beautiful* was arguing that climate should be a major design determinant in the American house, researchers at the Massachusetts Institute of Technology were building the first fully documented solar houses under the auspices of the Cabot Solar Energy Conversion Project. The fourth and final solar house built under the project was constructed in 1956 in Lexington, Massachusetts. The house had a flat-plate collector mounted on a south-facing roof tilted toward the sun. Water was heated by the sun as it cir-

culated through the collector and was then stored in a 1,500-gallon insulated tank in the basement. Heat from the water tank was transferred to the air by a heat exchanger and distributed throughout the house by a blower and ducts.

This and a handful of similar dwellings, largely forgotten during the late 1950s and the 1960s, became the models for the solar houses of the 1970s, when solar home design took a gigantic leap forward. But too many of these houses offered little in the way of pleasing design or emotional warmth, with their awkwardly pitched roofs, hulking collectors, massive walls of masonry or water, and harsh glint of glazing everywhere. What was worse, they didn't work particularly well.

The high-tech collectors, pumps, and fans of the so-called active solar houses of this period often proved cranky and unreliable. Designers turned instead to passive solar systems that, in the words of a song from a popular 1960s musical, "let the sun shine in": the south side of passive solar houses was wall-to-wall glass for this very reason. These homes utilized only the natural laws of thermodynamics to collect warmth and coolness and circulate them through a house; there were no moving parts, no pieces of high-tech solar hardware, no automatic controls. However, inadequate air cir-

Below: Nestled in the picturesque Potomac River valley, this passive solar-cooled house is surrounded by an outer lattice "porch house" sheltered by a translucent roof. Multilevel exterior decks, shaded by the latticework and cooled naturally by the breeze, encourage outdoor living and sleeping during Virginia's sultry summers. Architect: William Turnbull Associates.

Right: When the high-tech collectors, pumps, and fans used in active solar houses of the 1970s proved unreliable, designers turned to passive solar systems. This Connecticut house is oriented toward the sun for passive solar heat gain. The trellis on the west side of the house provides privacy and cooling shade.

Architects Ford Powell & Carson used a time-honored technique to moderate the violent Texas heat: they designed this San Antonio house around a courtyard and added a fountain for evaporative cooling.

culation was a chronic problem, resulting in areas that were either too hot or too cold for comfort. Other passive designs relied on unwieldy glassed-in walls of concrete, adobe, brick, or water — in drums or tanks — along the house's south side to collect and store solar heat. (The masonry versions are known as trombe walls, after Dr. Felix Trombe, one of the developers of the design.) Early water walls made from metal drums inevitably leaked, and both trombe and water walls competed for precious floor space.

To top it off, it wasn't uncommon for temperatures in early passive solar houses to vary from 55 degrees in winter to 85 degrees in summer. The houses were difficult to regulate — like a boat whose sails had to be constantly trimmed. Blinds and shades needed to be ad-justed and windows and vents opened and closed in order for the solar systems to function properly.

Although early solar houses did manage to harness the sun, they were still largely oblivious to climate. Much attention was paid to capturing solar heat, but not nearly enough to keeping it in. Walls, roofs, and windows were often poorly insulated, which meant that even more unsightly collectors and more glazing was needed to compensate for heat loss. And most passive solar houses weren't very good at cooling.

In 1979, experts convened in Washington once again, for the first climate and architecture conference in almost thirty years. During the decade that followed, architects finally began to design houses that not only take ad-

The traditional Arab wind tower meets modern engineering in Beth and Carl Hodges's home in the Arizona desert. As the water at the top of the tower circulates, it evaporates, cooling the air. The cooled air, which is moist and as much as twenty-five degrees cooler than the air outside, falls to the bottom of the tower and is dispersed into the rooms.

Mary Otis Stevens drew on the villas of Italian Renaissance architect Andrea Palladio in designing this New Hampshire house. The house is built into a south-facing slope for winter protection and solar heat gain. The east and west wings further insulate the central octagon and main living space. Highly insulated walls also help keep the interior at fifty degrees or warmer throughout the heating season.

Below left: Like the traditional Florida Cracker-style house, this home is built on stilts to raise it above the dampness and insects, and topped with a cupola for ventilation. Galvanized steel roofing reflects heat away from the interior. The fireplace, faced with native limestone, warms the house during the occasional winter cold snap.

Below right: Set in a hardwood hammock on Florida's Gulf coast, the house has a deep roof overhang to keep rain off the wrap-around veranda. Construction was confined to a small area to safeguard the native vegetation.

vantage of the sun but are suited to the climate in other ways as well. New Texas houses, for instance, combine deep overhangs, extensive cross-ventilation, galleries, arcades, and other means of combating the area's violent heat. At the same time they rely on basic passive solar technique: proper orientation to the sun, some south-facing windows for solar heat during the cool months, and enough thermal mass to store it — usually discreet ceramic tile floors on a concrete slab. The well-insulated skin of the structure works with the thermal mass to moderate extremes in temperature.

In an increasing number of areas, active solar systems have been making a comeback. Solar hot-water heaters have improved over the years and are now becoming commonplace. Photovoltaic cells, which convert sunlight into electricity, are already cost-effective in remote locations and other areas where the cost of electricity is high.

Other new technologies are currently enabling architects to design houses that are ever more finely tuned to the local climate. In Florida, engineers and designers have improved on

the traditional Cracker house, named after the early Florida settlers. These houses were built on stilts to raise them above the dampness and insects; a cupola on top allowed the warm air inside to rise and escape as cool outside air entered, ensuring a constant movement of air through the house — critical for comfort in such a humid climate. A wide veranda that wrapped around all or part of the house provided cooling shade. One high-tech improvement to this commonsense design is the radiant barrier, a layer of reinforced aluminum foil built into the walls and roof. This innovation restricts the transfer of solar heat indoors by reflecting it back outdoors. The radiant barrier blocks an astonishing 95 percent of the solar heat that would otherwise be radiated down by the roof and absorbed by the insulation, eventually heating up the house.

The rediscovery of climate adds a sense of proportion to the naturally elegant home. Huge heating systems, whether powered by the sun or by fossil fuels, no longer must strain to maintain comfort in a house ill suited to its locale. It also adds a sense of place, tying a new dwelling to its environment and, more often than not, to the architectural heritage of the area.

■ An American House

The rediscovery of climate has gone hand in hand with a new kind of regionalism known as bioregionalism, which draws on past houses and new technologies but looks beyond them, at the land itself. When designing houses, an increasing number of architects are taking their cue from the character of the site and its surroundings. To preserve a steep, rocky, heavily wooded slope overlooking Lake Pawtuckaway in Nottingham, New Hampshire, architects Gail Woodhouse and Ken MacLean designed one house as a line of connecting spaces that stair-step, between hemlocks, down toward the lake. The need to preserve giant saguaro cacti, jojoba, acacia, and ironwood trees dictated the placement of architect Les Wallach's home at the base of Tucson's Catalina Mountains, while Wallach's desire to protect the arroyo, or desert wash, that bisected the site led to the design of the house itself — two separate spaces joined by a bridge spanning the chasm.

The La Luz housing development designed by Albuquerque architect Antoine Predock rises from a ridgetop like an abstract modern version of the mesas that surround it. *New York Times* architecture critic Paul Goldberger described Predock's buildings as "deeply ingrained in the traditions and spirit of a place[,] yet unlike anything we have seen before."

Indigenous materials enhance the sense of place in the naturally elegant home. Built of sun-baked adobe made partially from soil excavated on site, La Luz is linked culturally to the pueblos of the region's indigenous peoples and geologically to the Rio Grande Valley, which it overlooks. The Texas houses of Frank Welch, Chris Carson, Lawrence Speck, and others are built with limestone from the hill country west of Austin, terra cotta–colored tiles from west of San Antonio, flooring of mesquite from the state's arid south and west, and tawny brick from Mexico.

In the naturally elegant home, the sense of time is as important as the sense of place. Suf-

In designing houses, an increasing number of architects are taking their cue from the character of the site and its surroundings. Antoine Predock's La Luz condominiums, in Albuquerque, New Mexico, rise from a ridgetop like an abstract modern version of the mesas beyond.

To make the most of the Pacific Northwest's unrelentingly gray skies, architects Morgan & Lindstrom designed a house with a roof-over-the-roof, made of translucent panels.

Underneath the translucent roof of the house on Bainbridge Island, two long corridors with skylights bathe the interior with soft light. When the grayness is punctured by the sun, the entire roof lights up, and the house is suffused with solar energy.

fusing a house with daylight not only conserves energy that would otherwise be used by artificial lighting but also enables the inhabitants to follow the sun in its arc from dawn to dusk. The quality of light is also celebrated. In the Pacific Northwest, for instance, rain is seemingly incessant, punctured only occasionally by rays of sun. To make the most of the region's unrelenting gray skies, the architectural firm of Morgan and Lindstrom designed a house in Bainbridge Island, Washington, with a roof-over-the-roof covered with translucent fiberglass panels; underneath, two long corridors with skylights bathe the interior with diffused light. When the sun erases the grayness, the effect is spectacular: the entire roof lights up, and the house is flooded with solar energy.

The naturally elegant home is a dwelling that is a part of nature, not apart from it. It evolves from its site, climate, materials, and function as a shelter in much the same way that a shell or a nest evolves from similar imperatives.

The natural house, Frank Lloyd Wright wrote, should grow from its site, out of the ground and into the light, "as dignified as a tree in the midst of nature." This notion of organic design is one of America's enduring contributions to the history of Western architecture.

Since Wright built his first "natural house" around the turn of the century, this idea of organic building has been eclipsed by the Modern movement and more recently by Postmodernism, but it has never been entirely vanquished. The environmental crises of recent years are bringing the work of a new generation of organic architects into the national spotlight.

Frank Lloyd Wright's notion of organic design is evident in Jersey Devil's hill house on the northern California coast. The house is cut into the crest of a hill to present a low profile to Pacific storms. Its curved shape serves to deflect the wind and takes advantage of the panoramic view. A sod roof and fieldstone walls merge the house with its magnificent site.

Right: Following the contours of the ridge, the hill house wraps around a protected sunken deck on the leeward north side. The "snout" brings the sod roof gently down to the outdoor living area and shelters the main entrance. Photograph: Peter Aaron/ Esto.

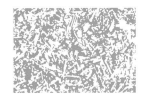

THE GARDEN

A Place for Us

In the naturally elegant garden, human habitat merges with the native landscape. The link between nature and daily life is restored.

This new environmental garden consists of two primary areas: a natural landscape toward the periphery of the property, and an edible landscape in the immediate vicinity of the house. The backbone of the naturally elegant garden, however, is its zones of native vegetation. In sparsely populated areas these may be huge tracts or smaller swaths of existing natural landscape. In more developed areas they may be small pockets of local flora around which the garden is designed. Where the last vestiges of wild habitat have disappeared, native plant communities can be restored.

In ever-increasing numbers, home gardeners are studying their local ecology for broad patterns and a plant palette. In the southern Appalachians, for example, North America's deciduous forest achieves its richest and most varied growth. Towering canopies of tulip tree, maple, buckeye, beech, and oak arch over understory species such as sorrel tree, with its drooping sprays of white summer flowers and its brilliant red-purple foliage in fall, and redbud, with its heart-shaped leaves and clusters of diminutive rosy-pink flowers in April. Showy shrubs such as *Rhododendron canescens,* an exquisite wild azalea with masses of fragrant white flowers, provide a procession of color from early April to mid-November. The rare and beautiful oconee bells and other woodland flowers burst into bloom in spring, followed by lush ferns, adding a fourth layer to the forest community. Mosses blanket the woodland floor. This layered effect may reach its pinnacle in the southern Appalachians, but it is typical throughout the eastern deciduous forest, and gardeners are striving to re-create it.

Gardeners in the Midwest, meanwhile, are re-creating native prairie on 50-by-200-foot city lots as well as on 200-acre rural estates. These prairie gardens change dramatically with the seasons. In midsummer, four-foot-tall rattlesnake master and purple coneflower form a dramatic display of rose and white against a canvas of airy midheight prairie grasses such as side oats grama.

In Arizona, the site of rapid urbanization, Steve Martino, a landscape architect with a keen interest in desert flora, has created some of the most beautiful gardens ever produced by an American designer. They are desert gardens, framed by such Sonoran Desert natives as the giant saguaro and the squiggly, multistemmed ocotillo. Select plants from the nearby Chihuahuan Desert and other, similar climates are added for accent and color.

Left: This five-acre Sonoran Desert garden designed by Steve Martino is on Usery Mountain, elevation 1,850 feet. Outdoor patios follow the natural descent of the hillside on a series of levels. Around the pool, the bold pads (or leaves) of prickly pears form living sculptures.

Right: Located between two arroyos, the garden is inspired by the character of the desert wash, where plants are dense and lush. Blooming in the foreground is the chuparosa or hummingbird bush. (For more on the garden, see page 180.)

In this garden outside Sun Valley, Idaho, designed by Robert Murase, indoors and outdoors are merged with exquisite detailing: the walls and floors of the terrace are formed of the same aggregate as those inside the house, but with a slightly rougher texture.

Near Sun Valley, Idaho, landscape architect Robert Murase has created an unforgettable garden of native rock and colorful drifts of naturalized flowers, which fades out to wilder patches of grass and yarrow. The garden forms a transition between the elegant terraces that flank the south side of a striking solar house and the surrounding sagebrush steppe.

What these diverse bioregional gardens have in common is this: they are designed to enhance the sense of place, to blend easily into the surrounding native vegetation, and, in many instances, to restore what once flourished. Culturally, the naturally elegant garden alludes to the native landscapes that greeted the pioneers and that have for centuries imbued America with its sense of limitless possibility; biologically, the garden provides a sanctuary for species that are fast disappearing from our land and our lives.

Gardeners already play a largely unrecognized role in the preservation of some species — *Franklinia alatamaha,* for example. This spectacular small tree, which offers white blooms in late summer and round, nutlike fruits that cling to the branches after the leaves fall, was collected along the banks of the Altamaha River in Georgia in 1770 by botanist John Bartram. Just twenty years later, *Franklinia* could no longer be found in the wild, but thanks to Bartram's efforts, the species survives today in gardens up and down the East Coast.

The ecological role played by gardeners is destined to become even more important in the future. While wildernesses in North America and around the world continue to shrink, compromising the biological diversity of the planet, garden acreage is increasing. If the widely predicted global warming does occur, this acreage will become crucial. The natural ranges of many plants will shift radically and rapidly northward, but some species may not be able to migrate quickly enough to keep pace with changing conditions. Scientists — and gardeners — may have to help such plants along by nurturing healthy populations in backyards as well as on public lands throughout the northern reaches of their ranges.

Indeed, home gardens have a potential as ecological sanctuaries that is just beginning to be explored. In professional journals, conservation biologists — those who specialize in the preservation of native plants and animals — are starting to flesh out proposals for a system of ecological reserves in bioregions around the world. Each bioregion would include a core area with minimal human activity (like a Yosemite), ringed by areas whose level of development would increase in relation to the area's distance from the undisturbed core. The outermost areas might be subject to timber harvesting and other kinds of resource extraction, for example, or housing development.

In such a land-use system, homeowners in sparsely populated regions of the West, especially areas surrounding national parks and for-

The bent brow of the spectacular solar house hovers over a garden of native rock, wildflowers, and scrub. The garden eases the transition from elegant terraces to the surrounding sagebrush steppe.

Left: A five-acre site in Lake Forest, Illinois, designed by P. Clifford Miller, celebrates America's disappearing tallgrass prairie. In the front garden, a sea of black-eyed Susans blooms.

Right: In the back garden, Miller restored a wet prairie area that was overrun by woody plants. The walkway leads to a pond he created where the vegetation was too degraded to recover. (For more on the garden, see page 176.)

The naturally elegant garden wouldn't be complete without some healthy homegrown food. This formal edible landscape was once a parking lot. Sage, dill, savory, and other herbs tumble onto the paths that divide the garden into sixteen symmetrical planting beds.

ests, would be discouraged from tampering with the native vegetation on their property. In most of the eastern United States, where no large undisturbed ecosystems remain, the few surviving natural fragments would need to be preserved and surrounding areas restored so that eventually there would be large, self-sustaining tracts of natural landscape. Because suburban backyards blanket the East Coast from Boston to Richmond and beyond, home gardeners would obviously play a major role in the restoration effort.

▪▪ A Tasteful Way to Landscape

The naturally elegant garden would not be complete without some healthy, homegrown food. For decades, the only link to the age-old rhythms of agriculture for the vast majority of Americans has been the produce section of the supermarket. Food has become simply another commodity, like dog food or detergent. We've lost all sense of depending on the land for daily sustenance. The typical garden, if it includes vegetables at all, banishes them to a corner of the backyard, the way old living-room furniture is moved unceremoniously to the basement to make way for trendier decor. However, a new kind of vegetable gardening called edible landscaping allows us to complete the natural cycle of gardening and cooking and restores food to its rightful place — around all the walls of the home.

Like the classic kitchen garden, the edible landscape can be elaborately geometric, with intersecting paths, symmetrical box-edged beds, rose arbors, and topiary standards. These formal edible landscapes are more common in the East, where they descend from the colonial kitchen garden, itself a descendant of the dazzling culinary gardens of eighteenth-century Europe. In many areas, a new, naturalistic kitchen garden is evolving. It eschews straight lines and mingles vegetables, culinary herbs,

Above: One of the many striking combinations includes (*clockwise from left*) Lady's mantle with its dainty chartreuse blooms, purple catmint, and tricolor sage.

Right: Designed by landscaper Andrew Hogan for his family's home in Greenwich, Connecticut, the formal herb garden, with its intersecting pathways and geometric planting beds, harks back hundreds of years to monastic gardens in which culinary herbs were mixed with others grown solely for their beauty or fragrance. (For more on the garden, see page 189.)

edible and ornamental flowers, fruit trees, and shade trees in lush profusion.

Whether formal or naturalistic, edible landscapes contain a cornucopia of unusual edible plants: the sculptural, lime-green, and tasty 'Romanesco', a member of the broccoli and cauliflower family; the short, well-behaved 'Garden Beauty' nectarine tree, with its hot-pink springtime blossoms; the pineapple guava with its succulent, tropical-tasting petals and fruit; the ornamental kales, which come in a spectrum of pastel pinks, blue-greens, light green, and creamy white; the magnificent Mediterranean herb lovage, with its distinctive flavor, like pungent celery with a hint of lemon and anise.

In their own gardens, homeowners can nurture a food-producing landscape without dangerous pesticides or fertilizers made from precious fossil fuels. Besides being chemical-free, an edible landscape's bounty is the freshest and most nutritious produce possible. No amount of money at the fanciest gourmet market can buy a salad as fresh and vitamin-packed as one that is tossed with a light vinaigrette dressing just moments after being gathered.

In a Sonoma County, California, garden, one of the new edible landscapes, wisteria shades the windows from the hot sun and perfumes the air with its fragrant blooms. Below, alpine strawberries mingle with violets, coralbells, and other flowering perennials.

The informal design eschews straight lines and mingles vegetables with culinary herbs, edible and ornamental flowers, fruit trees, and shade trees in lush profusion. In the foreground are artichoke and rock rose; drought-tolerant 'Lady Banks' rose blooms above. (For more on the garden, see page 192.)

At a site on Mount Desert Island, Maine, landscape designer Patrick Chassé edited nature, carefully exposing the rocky ledge to show where nature and foundation meet.

■ An Evolutionary Leap

As early as 1625, Francis Bacon asserted that the ideal garden should include "a heath or wilderness." It was one of the first recorded calls for a more natural landscape. The gardens of Bacon's day were highly formal spreads with knotted hedges and perfect symmetry. He described his new ideal, by contrast, as "nature imitated and tactfully adorned."

"Nature tactfully adorned" — statuesque trees on a sweep of velvety green lawn — is as good a description as any of the typical late-twentieth-century North American garden. This kind of manicured woodland may have been state-of-the-art natural landscaping in the seventeenth century, but it is nature much *too* tactfully adorned for an age whose natural verdure is being stripped bare.

The naturally elegant garden features nature *un*adorned — an exuberant tangle of bioregional form, color, and texture that changes year-round. The sun-splashed colors of the grasses and wildflowers that replace a portion of lawn in the prairie states are transformed each fall into glorious dappled honey-browns and Tuscan umbers. In winter, spiky seedheads poke through shimmering blankets of snow.

While the edible landscape celebrates nature at its most bountiful, the natural landscape respects nature at its least benign — dead trees and all. Glossy gardening magazines feature no photographs of dead or dying trees, yet in a garden with a dead limb or a decaying trunk, woodpeckers hammer away at gathered seeds, search for insects, or carve out protected nests; the meticulously pruned garden is diminished by its fastidiousness. Ian McHarg, professor of landscape architecture and regional planning at the University of Pennsylvania and one of the most eloquent contemporary thinkers on the relationship between human and natural environments, declared his preference for nature over gardens and their "illusory order" and "imperfect reassurance." "Nature," he writes, "contains the history of evolution of matter, life, and man. It is the arena of past, present,

and future. It exhibits the laws that obtain. It contains every quest that man can pursue. It tells every important story that man would know. Therein lies its richness, mystery, and charm."*

Even more charming for most of us is the fact that natural gardens require much less coddling than their more cultured counterparts. Once established, they thrive with relatively little maintenance. They require no more water than that which is provided by summer rains and winter snows. All the nutrients they need are supplied by the decay of older generations of plants and the soils in which they

*From "Nature Is More Than a Garden," in Mark Francis and Randolph T. Hester, Jr., *The Meaning of Gardens* (Cambridge: MIT Press, 1990).

Left: The rocky coastal ledge and surrounding spruce-fir forest are the "bones" of the natural garden.

Below: A circular driveway once severed the house from the forest. Chassé knitted the two back together with "native sod" — a combination of red-berried bunchberry dogwood, wintergreen, and haircap moss rescued from a blueberry farm. (For more on the garden, see page 173.) Photograph: Peter C. Jones.

grow. They demand no artificial protection from the pests to which the centuries have accustomed them. Ironically, what they often do need is protection from the invasive competitors — from the Norway maple in Middle Atlantic woodlands to the ice plant in the California chaparral — that four centuries of settlers have released in their midst.

Perhaps most important, in the naturally elegant garden we nurture nature, and nature nurtures us. We interact with nature on a daily basis, not just on two-week jaunts to some far-off national park. And in our own quotidian way, we try to balance human and ecological needs — one of the great scientific and philosophical tasks of our time.

In a 1989 essay on man and nature in *Restoration & Management Notes,* the journal for scientists who specialize in restoration ecology, editor William R. Jordan described his feelings as he walked through the Curtis Prairie and Wingra Woods in Wisconsin, two of the oldest restored ecosystems on this continent. He found himself thinking that they were some-

Right: In this island planting and around the house
on the outskirts of Austin,
landscape designer Stephen
K. Domigan scattered Yau-
pon holly, Texas persim-
mon, and other native
trees, as well as clusters of
indigenous shrubs, wild-
flowers, and a few exotics.

Below: East-central Texas is
a bioregional crossroads,
where the prairie, the
coastal plain forests, and
the Desert Southwest inter-
sect. Like the native landscape, the one-acre site
includes a diversity of habitats. Outside the master
bedroom, water tumbles
over rocks and flows into a
small aquatic garden.

how defective and less worthy than the original communities, which had covered the area for hundreds of thousands of years: "I would think about the nature writers I had read — Thoreau in particular — and his celebration of wilderness and the 'natural,' and I would wonder whether anyone would ever write a poem about a restored forest or prairie."

Since then he has come to see things quite differently. The restored ecosystem, he feels, is usually defective, but it is valuable nonetheless. Biologically, it may leave something to be desired, but as ecologists struggle to restore a natural community, it becomes — through human involvement — more aware of itself, and in this sense more fully realized. Jordan calls this a great evolutionary leap. Knowledge once locked in an undecipherable genetic code has been liberated by the human mind. "For all their defects," he writes, "our restored communities are the Walden Ponds and Yosemites of a new sensibility, and if we have as yet no books about them, no poems and hymns of praise, it is only because they have not yet found their Thoreaus and their John Muirs."

In the naturally elegant garden, homeowners are struggling to make this same evolutionary leap.

Natural plantings, including sword-leafed Spanish bayonet (*Yucca aloifolia*), were restored on a boulder-strewn slope behind the pool. The house is built of native limestone. (For more on the garden, see page 179.)

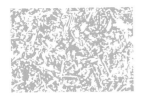

SUNSPACES AND OUTDOOR ROOMS

*Nature and
Architecture
Intertwined*

Around the turn of the century, when American designers rebelled against Victorian artifice — especially its overwrought, machine-made ornament — they turned to nature for inspiration. American residential architecture has been moving toward a marriage of structure and nature ever since.

In *Examples of American Domestic Architecture* (1889), one of the watershed statements of the era, Maine architects Albert Winslow Cobb and John Calvin Stevens railed against the architecture of the day, "flourishing, like some rank, luxurious weed, in concomitance with decaying public health." They expressed disgust at America's slavish imitation of the opulent structures "inflicted upon the world" by the corrupt tyrants, past and present, of Europe and the Orient. The primary mission of architecture in our society, they wrote, should be the provision of good houses for the people.

Cobb and Stevens held up as examples their own various houses in the Shingle Style, a style of "primitive simplicity" that came to dominate summer houses on the Northeast coast. These rambling timber structures were clad in wood shingles toned silvery gray by the weather. Built on foundations of native rock that seem to grow out of the rocky coastal

ledges, they have a dignified beauty that comes not from mere decoration but rather from pleasing shapes and graceful massing — and especially from the way the houses harmonize with the natural landscape.

It was turn-of-the-century furniture-maker-turned-publisher Gustav Stickley who popularized the new naturalism, bringing it to the American middle class from coast to coast. In his magazine, *The Craftsman,* he waxed eloquent on the relationship between architecture and nature: "Whatever connects a house with out of doors, whether vines or flowers, piazza or pergola, it is to be welcomed in the scheme of modern home-making. We need outdoor life in this country; we need it inherently, because it is the normal thing for all people, and we need it specifically as a nation, because we are an overwrought people, too eager about everything except peace and contentment."

This bit of *Craftsman* philosophy came in an article championing pergolas in American gardens. Stickley believed that the pergola — an arbor formed by a double row of posts or pillars with joists above, the whole covered with climbing plants — "epitomizes modern outdoor life, and its beauty [lies in its] simplicity of construction and intimacy with Nature." Every garden, he insisted, must have such a

Like its turn-of-the-century predecessors, this Shingle Style house on Cape Ann, Massachusetts, designed by Jonathan Poore, is built on a foundation of native granite that seems to grow out of the rocky coastal ledge. The rambling, shingle-clad structure fits comfortably on its site.

The handsome stonework is made up of rocks from the site.

living room outdoors, one that "[is] draped in vines, that gives us green walls to live within, that has a ceiling of tangled leaves and flowers blowing in the wind, a glimpse of blue sky through open spaces, and sunshine pouring over us when the leaves move."

From 1901 until 1916, when it ceased publication, *The Craftsman* published designs for simple farmhouses with pergolas, suburban stucco houses with wraparound pergolas, and bungalows with pergolas framing the approach to the front door. There were picturesque pergolas with cobblestone piers topped with rustic poles, and classical pergolas with turned wooden columns, plain or fluted, and trellised roofs. Stickley instructed his readers to choose materials from the local landscape, whether fieldstone or terra cotta, cedar, white pine, oak, or madrone, so that the house would harmonize with nature.

Turn-of-the-century architects did not stop with the pergola in their quest to link nature and daily life. Porches, courtyards, and terraces were furnished as outdoor living rooms. Open-air dining rooms were much admired and sometimes came complete with a fireplace that shared a chimney with the kitchen range indoors. Just as important was the "sleeping porch." Post-Victorians believed that fresh air was as important to the body as fragrant bowers, songs of birds, and a sky spangled with stars were to the spirit, and many period houses included a sleeping porch, or several, near the bedrooms on the first or second floor. Banks of windows linked indoor spaces with the outdoors, as did the use of natural materials both inside and out — from wood-shingled exteriors and richly colored wood paneling to slate roofs and floors.

One house design published in *The Craftsman* in 1909, billed as a "House with Court, Pergolas, Outdoor Living Rooms, and Sleeping Balconies," combines most of these features. A broad terrace runs across the front of the house and continues around the side, where it forms a porch meant to be used as an outdoor living room. In the indoor living

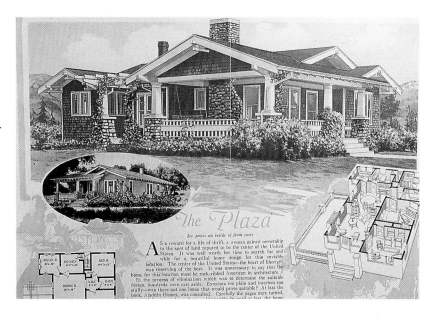

room, a square bay window with window seat looks out on the terrace, and double glass doors from both living room and entry hall "bring this part of the house into very close communication with the outside world." Beyond the living room are the dining room and kitchen, whose range shares a chimney with a fireplace on the back porch. From this porch one steps down into a courtyard surrounded by a sun-splashed, vine-festooned pergola. Double doors lead from the courtyard into a den, which also opens onto the entrance porch, via still another set of double doors. Upstairs, a bedroom has double doors leading to a balcony; there is an outdoor sleeping room, and a central hallway with a long window seat built beneath a group of windows that look out over the pergola and courtyard.

This house was designed for outdoor life in a mild climate such as California's. Already California had established its reputation as a place where there is a certain feeling of unity between house and garden, where the outdoors is simply an extension of the home. "Living so much out of doors," Stickley, a New Jersey resident, wrote wistfully, "Californians almost instinctively make the transition between outdoors and indoors as little marked as possible."

Early-twentieth-century architects strove to link nature with daily life. With its ample porch, its pergola festooned with flowers, and its natural materials, including stone and wood shingles, this house from the 1919 Aladdin Homes catalog is typical of its era.

This Baja beach house on the Sea of Cortez, designed by Jersey Devil, opens so completely to sea views and breezes that it is difficult to know where architecture stops and nature begins. The areas between the folding doors are breezeways.

While Stickley was defining a new architectural ethic for the middle class, brothers Charles Sumner and Henry Mather Greene were building "ultimate bungalows" (as their work came to be called) for California's cultural and intellectual elite. They embraced Stickley's ideals and pushed them even further. Their Culbertson House of 1903 was one of the first designs in which the pergola was treated as an extension of the house. In the Arturo Bandini House, also of 1903, Greene and Greene found their roots in California mission architecture; *The Craftsman* soon published a popularized version of their design, which was U-shaped, with a series of one-room-deep chambers arranged around a central courtyard enclosed by a pergola. By 1907, the Greenes had mastered all the elements of the California bungalow, including the porte cochere, or covered entryway for carriages (the post-Victorian version of the carport), the low-pitched roofs with long overhangs covering sleeping porches, and the multiple terraces.

■ The Struggle for the Window

Around the same time that Gustav Stickley and Greene and Greene were establishing a new architectural vocabulary on both coasts, Frank Lloyd Wright was building his low, earth-hugging Prairie houses for wealthy Chicago suburbanites. Wright believed that the citizens of a democracy deserved to live in something better than a "box." While architects of the Shingle Style did their part to break up the box, manipulating the floor plan to enable a house to fit comfortably on its site, Wright led a full-blown crusade against it. Like Stickley and the Greenes, he broke the box by using transitional spaces to link house with landscape. In the Ward W. Willits house in Highland Park, Illinois, for example, built in 1902, the living room gives way to its own enclosed terrace, and the dining room opens onto a covered porch; Victorian verandas have been transformed into modern outdoor rooms, making it difficult to know where the house stops and the outdoors begins. A porte co-chere also extends the house into the land-scape. Unlike Stickley and the Greenes, Wright made use of steel and glass to achieve this new ideal. Steel made possible wider spans and therefore more open spaces, while glass afforded a closer relation to the natural world.

In Wright's houses, opaque walls are replaced with long expanses of glass to bring the outside in and let the inside out. Wright even espoused the casement, or out-swinging, window as opposed to the traditional double-hung version, which he called the guillotine window. He considered the casement window much more "natural" because it associated the house with the outdoors and gave "free openings outward."

One reason Wright was enamored of glass was that truly transparent, fool-the-eye glazing was something new in his day. In Le Corbusier's view, "The history of architecture is the history of the struggle for the window" — and a struggle it was.

It wasn't until the middle of the nineteenth century that an even moderately transparent

glass became available. It replaced the crown glass of the Colonial era, also called bull's-eye glass because of the spiral-like pattern that showed where the glass had been attached to the glassblower's pipe. Even several inches out from the bull's-eye, crown glass was still thick and wavy, and it could only be cut into small panes.

Frank Lloyd Wright wrote that a profusion of glass affords "something of the freedom of our arboreal ancestors living in their trees" — a much more auspicious vision of twentieth-century life than that suggested by the box-like houses of the past. Expanses of glass are standard fare in the naturally elegant home, as demonstrated by this house in Santa Ysabel, California.

In houses of the energy-obsessed 1970s, greenhouses were often ugly add-ons intended primarily to capture solar heat. Today's sunrooms add elegant living space, for sunbathing in the dead of winter or watching a glorious sunset. Architect: Obie Bowman.

fect optically. Plate glass was first produced at a profit in 1883, right around the time when Frank Lloyd Wright began designing houses.

A profusion of glass, in Wright's words, afforded "something of the freedom of our arboreal ancestors living in their trees" — a much more auspicious precedent for freedom in twentieth-century life than the "box."

■ Expanses of Glass

The predilection toward naturalism continues in the late-twentieth-century American house. Expanses of glass are now standard fare. What's more, breakthroughs in glass technology since Wright's day have produced windows that are almost as energy-efficient as walls.

The late-twentieth-century dream house also borrows and adapts the Victorian tradition of the conservatory. In eighteenth-century Europe, "glasshouses" were used to grow tender plants such as orange trees that could not be grown year-round outdoors. A century later they were often attached to the house, in part so that the beauty and fragrance of flowers could enhance everyday living. Conservatories filled with rare and exotic plants collected from remote corners of the globe were also a status symbol, a backdrop for Victorian social life. But they were very expensive to heat and maintain, and gradually they fell out of favor.

Greenhouses and sunrooms — even modest versions — are a staple of the naturally elegant home. In the energy-obsessed 1970s, these sunspaces were often ugly, obvious add-ons intended primarily to capture solar heat and cut heating costs. In the past ten years or so, however, there has been dramatic progress not only in glass technology but also in greenhouse design.

Sunspaces ranging from exquisite, English-style conservatories to elegant redwood and glass structures are now used as mudrooms, places to stow wet shoes and umbrellas before entering the house. Attached greenhouses in

Cylinder glass was a Victorian innovation that required a small assembly line of workers. The process began with the usual glassblower's bubble, but instead of blowing the bubble into a wide globe, the blower let it hang down from his pipe and swung it over a pit as he worked, creating an elongated shape. A "gatherer" added additional glass, increasing the size of the cylinder. After the blowpipe was detached, the cylinder was allowed to cool and was then slit top to bottom and flattened out, or ironed, with a sort of wooden hoe. The outer surface of the cylinder, which was always larger than the inner one, inevitably wrinkled and puckered as the ironer worked; the finished product was more suited to a funhouse than to the natural house.

It took a full-blown industrial revolution to bring about the next revolution in glazing technology: plate glass. Molten glass was poured onto a large iron table, rolled smooth with a large roller, and allowed to slowly cool, until it emerged as a sheet of very hard glass of uniform thickness. Any marks caused by contact with the table and roller were painstakingly ground down and polished, resulting in glass that was brilliantly shiny and almost per-

Attached greenhouses are now often used as mud-rooms, places to stow wet shoes and umbrellas before entering the house. The double entries prevent home heat loss.

This courtyard garden in San Antonio, Texas, is closely associated with the house. Billowy shades keep out the scorching sun, while the fireplace takes the chill off in winter. Architect: Ford Powell & Carson.

kitchens are used to grow food, especially herbs. They're also used as double entries to prevent home heat loss. Annual vines and flowers clamber over the sunspaces in summer, when their heat-trapping ability isn't needed. Most important, the new sunspaces add beautiful living space — for sunbathing in the dead of winter or for watching the sun set year-round. In the naturally elegant home, nature supplants the fireplace as the focus of the living spaces.

Outdoor living, meanwhile, has spread far beyond California, and outdoor rooms range ever farther from the confines of the house. If the Eskimos have a dozen words for snow, late-twentieth-century Americans have at least that many for the spaces that ease the transition from human habitation to natural habitat: *porch, pergola, patio, arbor, balcony, terrace, veranda, deck, courtyard, gallery, gazebo, garden room.* Each expresses an exquisitely subtle distinction in degree of progression from inside to outdoors. The porch, for example, which first appeared in nineteenth-century America, is usually covered by a roof and often partially

Only a wall of glass separates the large screened porch from the main living area in this Laredo, Texas, house designed by Ford Powell & Carson.

Right: The Victorian-style veranda of this Napa Valley house by William Turnbull Associates is furnished with white wicker, flowers, and all the luxuries of civilization. It affords spectacular views of the vineyards and wild mountain scenery beyond.

Below: The handsome colonnade and rustic joists cast a shadow mural on the living-room walls of this house — a form of architectural ornament that changes from hour to hour and from season to season in the sun-drenched Desert Southwest. Architect: Ford Powell & Carson.

surrounded by walls, and is therefore closely associated with the house. It is furnished with upholstered chairs, tables draped in linen or chintz, and all the luxuries of civilization. The post-Victorian pergola, with its ceiling of joists and tangled leaves and flowers, is truly a transitional space. A mid-twentieth-century patio, by contrast, gives merely a suggestion of enclosed space and is even more closely linked with nature. A "floor" of clipped lawn or fieldstone and thyme may be all that distinguishes it as living space. The late-twentieth-century garden room may be defined by nothing more than the furniture that's brought there: a rustic wooden bench under the boughs of an ancient oak, for instance, or a twig chair in a tiny clearing in the forest.

Our need for nature and "the outdoor life," as Gustav Stickley put it, has become ever more urgent since the early decades of the century. The more urbanized our culture becomes, the more we crave some semblance of the natural in our homes and in our daily lives.

In the late-twentieth-century home, wooden decks are often used for outdoor living and to extend the house into the landscape.

A pergola is a transitional space that quite poetically eases the passage from darkness to light. Photograph: Peter C. Jones.

Outdoor rooms range ever farther from the confines of the house. Jack Lenor Larsen's Long Island garden room is defined only by the checkerboard ''floor'' of clipped lawn and stone and the furniture that's taken there.

THE KITCHEN

The Center of Daily Life

Grounded in memories of harvest kitchens, the naturally elegant kitchen repairs the ruptured link between us and the seasonal cycles of our agrarian past. Design: The 18th Century Company.

John Ford's classic film *The Searchers,* released in 1956, is set in 1868 Texas. Along with other Westerns, it has shaped our image of the ideal American kitchen, an image that still exerts a powerful influence on the way we organize and decorate this important room.

The Searchers begins with a shot looking outdoors into stark, blindingly bright mesa country from the cool, dark confines of a homestead house. The shot is framed by the rustic timbers that support the deep overhang of the front porch. In this scene, Ethan Edwards (played by John Wayne) returns home from the Civil War. He's greeted outdoors by his brother Aaron and his family, and the action quickly moves inside.

The family gathers around the long-absent Ethan in a mid-nineteenth-century Texas frontier version of the live-in Colonial kitchen — an all-purpose room where families lived, ate, worked, and socialized with guests. As the camera moves lovingly around the room, we feast our eyes on its snug mud-brick walls, thick wooden beams and sapling ceiling, wooden harvest table where dinner is set, shelves full of pewter, pottery, and foodstuffs,

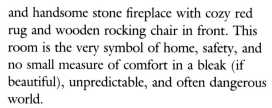

and handsome stone fireplace with cozy red rug and wooden rocking chair in front. This room is the very symbol of home, safety, and no small measure of comfort in a bleak (if beautiful), unpredictable, and often dangerous world.

We crave the same kind of comfort and emotional reassurance in our late-twentieth-century kitchens. "To liberate the kitchen for the nineties, we wanted it all — the latest technology embedded in the warm soul of a room, as welcoming and adaptable as the ancestral hearth of our imagination," wrote the editors of *Metropolitan Home,* a manual for the well-heeled "yuppie" life-style (about as far from frontier Texas as it gets), in a January 1991 article featuring a "dream kitchen" the magazine designed and built. "So we borrowed elements once reserved for living rooms — the soaring pitched ceiling, the cozy seating areas, the friendly face of windows that make the garden a live-in painting." This wish-list kitchen centers around an archetypal "harvest table" reborn as a modern work island. Suspended above it is a sinuous chandelier that marries Colonial style to halogen tech. In one cozy corner, two plump wing chairs sit atop a braided rug. A nearby banquette provides a comfy nook for doing homework or copying recipes. A homey pantry contains a colorful assortment of stainless-steel appliances and peanut butter jars, bottled water and garlic braids.

Grounded in memories of farmhouse kitchens, the room exudes all the emotional power of Home. But its state-of-the-art appliances and no-nonsense layout afford all the efficiency and ease that affluent citizens of the final decade of the twentieth century demand.

Why, after decades in which the kitchen looked more like a high-tech lab, has the room once again become the down-home hub of family life? A recent report in the *New York Times* offers a clue. According to the *Times,* even in this era of the two-career family and its breathless life-style, Americans still consider it important to eat their evening meal together. The period between work and bedtime is the

Left: The kitchen has once again become the down-home hub of family life. This roomy remodeled kitchen in a Connecticut Colonial Revival house features a nook for doing homework or copying recipes and a handsome bank of windows that connects the kitchen with the garden.

Below: In an age in which traces of nature are rapidly disappearing, we want kitchens that have an intimate relationship with the natural world. This kitchen, designed by Arne Bystrom, looks out onto Washington's Pacific coast.

only time many working parents have to spend with their kids, and much of this time must be spent on meal preparation and cleanup. Hence the trend of recent years: the living room and dining room are shrinking, while the kitchen is growing ever larger.

Metropolitan Home's kitchen also reflects an even newer trend: the rediscovery in the kitchen of our give-and-take relationship with nature. From the kitchen sink, ten-foot-high dormer windows afford a view of the outdoors, and a spectacular peaked and many-paned glass wall links the kitchen with the garden. In this sense, the late-twentieth-century dream kitchen is unlike the ancestral version in *The Searchers,* which was above all a profoundly sheltering space that protected the frontier family from the howling wilderness outdoors. In our own world, where traces of nature are disappearing rapidly, the have-it-all kitchen literally throws open the doors to the kitchen garden and the natural landscape beyond.

Today's ideal kitchen features luscious fruits and vegetables and fragrant herbs planted no farther away than the kitchen door. In the pots is *Citrus limon* 'Meyer'.

In a modern take on the old harvest kitchen, today's ideal kitchen features luscious fruits and vegetables and fragrant herbs that are no farther away than the kitchen door. In these fast-food times, when food preparation and mealtime are all but bereft of their former sensual pleasure, the sight and scent of herbs and fresh foods are yet another form of emotional reassurance.

The modern kitchen is also linked ever so closely with the local landfill. The naturally elegant kitchen is designed to break this link by making recycling as easy as possible. For example, the *Metropolitan Home* fantasy kitchen's roomy walk-in pantry encourages bulk buying, one way of eliminating wasteful packaging. Four slide-out bins under the sink provide plenty of room for cans, glass, and other recyclables. Shelves for newspapers are concealed behind another cabinet door.

A Revolution in Domestic Engineering

Compare the *Metropolitan Home* kitchen with one described by a New Englander at the end of the eighteenth century. The kitchen was large, he wrote, fully twenty feet square, with a fireplace six feet wide and four feet deep (in those days the fireplace served as both furnace and stove). On one side, the kitchen looked out upon the garden, "the squashes and cucumbers climbing up and forming festoons over the door." According to this early kitchen historian, it was the most comfortable room in the house, cool in summer and "perfumed with the breath of the garden and orchard; in the winter, with its roaring blaze of hickory, it was a cozy resort, defying the bitterest blasts of the season." Half a century later, many American kitchens included a comfortable inventory of chairs, table, cupboards, chests, dishes, plates, tankards, spoons, milk pots, and pottery. And the nearby kitchen gardens were compact plots laid out in exquisitely designed geometric patterns, sometimes edged with box and studded with topiary.

With the arrival of the Victorian era, however, this ancestral kitchen so close to our late-twentieth-century hearts was replaced by an unceremonious workplace hidden from public view and used almost exclusively by servants. Many Victorian kitchens were located on the ground floor or in the basement of the home, their grease and odors kept at a safe distance from the plushly upholstered parlor. Later in the nineteenth century, as servants abandoned domestic service for factory jobs, the kitchen became the housewife's domain, and the modern kitchen was born. "Domestic engineers" such as Catharine E. Beecher (author of *A Treatise on Domestic Economy for the Use of Young Ladies at Home and at School,* 1841) and, later, Christine Frederick (*Household Engineering,* 1923) sketched out the modern, labor-saving kitchen, specifying not only the most efficient placement of major fixtures such as the sink and stove, continuous work surfaces, and built-in cabinets for simplified cleaning, but also such practical details as the inclusion of drawers for towels and correct counter heights.

To Victorians, cleanliness was next to godliness. The late-nineteenth-century obsession with sanitation turned the kitchen into a cold and clinical place. Sterile white tiles and enameled metal cabinets replaced wooden wainscoting and cupboards, creating a chilly, laboratory-like atmosphere. Within the span of a generation, electricity revolutionized the kitchen, and ads touting the "all-electric" (and energy-wasting) kitchen were all the rage in women's magazines. By the 1970s, the kitchen had become a repository for electrical appliances such as the microwave, designed for quick processing of the overpackaged convenience foods that proliferated in supermarkets.

Today, as we rethink the very meaning of such words as *convenience* and *waste,* the kitchen is once again being transformed.

■ The Naturally Elegant Kitchen

The naturally elegant kitchen promotes both personal and environmental health. Fresh, nutritious — and pesticide-free — food grows indoors in attached greenhouses, on sunny windowsills, or in skylight gardens, as well as in the kitchen garden or edible landscape. Wholesome foods — sun-dried fruits, nuts, whole-grain crackers, and other tasty treats and staples — are invitingly displayed on shelves or in well-stocked pantries. Only materials that are as healthy as they are handsome are used to build and decorate the kitchen; in counters and cabinets, plastic laminates, plywoods, and other materials that release harmful fumes are giving way to locally produced ceramic and quarry tiles, slates, granites, solid woods, stainless steel, and terrazzo. Improved ventilation systems get rid of harmful pollutants, and heat-exchange systems conserve energy at the same time.

The new environmental kitchen is also a

In the kitchen of a restored adobe house, bioregional style is evident in the beautifully detailed old ceramic tile floor and the large windows, which admit ample daylight but have wooden shutters on some sides to keep out the blistering Arizona sun. French doors open the dining room (*below left*) to the outdoors. The ceiling of the adjoining hallway is covered with saguaro cactus ribs.

Above: Traditional Texas touches abound in this Laredo kitchen designed by Ford Powell & Carson: a fireplace, ceramic tile floors, a lazy paddle fan. The living rooms that wrap around the kitchen reduce the available natural light, so monitor windows were added to brighten the room.

Above, left and right: Coppery green and cream-colored glazed tiles made in Delores Hidalgo cover the countertops of this Baja kitchen and are arranged in an Aztec pattern on the backsplash. Outdoor dining in a covered breezeway makes the most of cross ventilation and the views.

In an early-eighteenth-century kitchen renovated by Nelson Denny, the cabinets are made of recycled wood.

center of energy and water conservation in the home. Kitchen appliances are as energy-efficient as they are sleek and stylish, particularly superinsulated, solar-powered — and totally quiet — refrigerators. Finnish dish-drying cabinets are becoming familiar fixtures above the sink and next to water-efficient dishwashers that do without energy-intensive hot-air drying cycles. Sun-ripened fruits and vegetables go straight from the garden to solar food dryers and ovens. Wood-fired ovens bake crusty, robust-tasting breads. Double or triple sinks make washing fresh produce easy, just as they did in older homes — only this time they're plumbed to graywater systems that whisk relatively unsullied wastewater to the garden.

Pantries encourage thrifty bulk packaging. Carbonated-water dispensers installed at the kitchen sink minimize the number of soda bottles that need to be recycled. Attractive built-in cabinets temporarily store cans, bottles, and other recyclable materials. In an increasing number of new homes, chutes, dumbwaiters, and horizontal conveyors effortlessly transfer these recyclables to containers in the garage or outdoors. Stowed under the kitchen sink are gleaming stainless-steel containers that temporarily store vegetable trimmings and other food scraps to be deposited on the backyard

compost pile or picked up by local sanitation officials. (The collection of compostables, or "wet wastes," will be the next frontier of municipal recycling.) A bit further in the future, under-the-sink "in-vessel" composters that grind up food scraps and turn them into compost for the organic garden will be as commonplace as garbage disposals are today.

In short, the naturally elegant kitchen is a nurturing space that is the center of family life; that eliminates the most laborious and time-consuming chores and at the same time conserves water, energy, and other precious natural resources; that resurrects suppertime as a feast of all the senses; and that repairs the ruptured link between us and the seasonal cycles of our agrarian past.

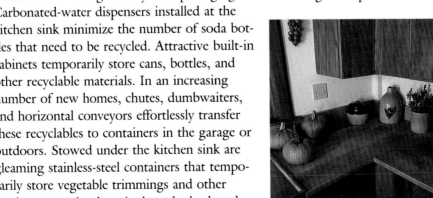

The modern kitchen is our
most direct link not only to
the food chain but also to
the landfill. Pantry shelving
in food writer David Goldbeck's kitchen helps save
on packaging by encourag-
ing thrifty bulk buying.

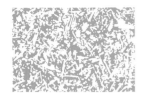

THE BATHROOM

A Space for Conservation — and Relaxation

The Europeans use the term "water closet" for the toilet, and the term is apt. Toilets account for more than one third of indoor water use. The bathroom as a whole represents up to 80 percent of domestic water consumption.

The first "bathroom" was the great outdoors. The slightly more civilized outhouse, which persisted until well into the twentieth century in rural areas of North America, afforded a degree of privacy if not of comfort, especially in northerly climes with their piercing winter winds. Nonetheless, the idea was the same: human waste was returned to the earth, not flushed into the nearest river. The many microorganisms that live in the soil digested the excreta and turned it into food for plants.

When people started settling in cities, elimination became a matter of high tech and high art. The first major monument to Roman engineering genius was, as Lewis Mumford put it in *The City in History* (1961), "the Cloaca Maxima, the great sewer, constructed on a scale so gigantic that either its builders must have clairvoyantly seen . . . that this heap of villages would become a metropolis of a million inhabitants, or else they must have taken for granted that the chief business and ultimate end of life is the physiological process of evacuation." In any event, public sanitation subsequently entered a dark age that lasted for two millennia.

The chamber pot was elevated to an art form in the hands of eighteenth-century cabinetmakers such as George Hepplewhite. The 1794 edition of Hepplewhite's guide included several designs, among them a "night table," or discreet cabinet, that opened to reveal a seat with a built-in receptacle, and a pedestal and vase that were supposed to be used in pairs in the dining room, one on each side of the sideboard. The vase was fitted with a spigot and contained ice water, but the pedestal was in actuality a cupboard for a chamber pot. Once the women had withdrawn for the evening, the cupboard was opened and the vessel was brought out for the convenience of the men.

As a sanitary device, the chamber pot in any

form left a lot to be desired. As there were no wastewater pipes in those days, and no sewers, the contents were disposed of, like all dirty water, in haphazard fashion — which often meant being tossed directly out of a window and onto the street. Witold Rybczynski writes in *Home: A Short History of an Idea* (1986) that the British slang for toilet, "loo," may have derived from this practice: it was the custom in eighteenth-century Edinburgh, before tossing sewage into the street, to shout "Gardyloo!," apparently the Scottish pronunciation of the earlier French warning "Garde à l'eau!" ("Watch out for the water!").

According to Rybczynski, the first commercial toilet was patented in 1778 by Joseph Bramah, a mechanically inclined cabinetmaker. Called the Bramah Valve Closet, it had the now-familiar water seal to prevent smells from pervading the room. But the water closet was slow to catch on until the advent of centrally supplied water and plumbing.

In the United States, municipal water and sewers arrived in the mid–nineteenth century. Cities boomed, overwhelming existing sewage-disposal systems. New York, Chicago, and San Francisco reeled from cholera and other sewage-related epidemics. The first comprehensive sanitary sewer system was constructed in Chicago in 1855; New York did not get such a system until 1886. Meanwhile, nineteenth-century advancements in molding large glazed drains and casting iron pipes made possible the tapping of distant supplies of relatively untainted water.

Public waterworks and the disposal of wastes in water went a long way toward eradicating disease. These innovations also led to domestic plumbing and the bathroom as we know it today — a compact, three-fixture space with the tub at one end and the sink and toilet placed side by side. This new arrangement was not only sanitary but also convenient: there would be no more frigid trips to the outhouse, no more hauling heated water to the tub. Water consumption, however, inevitably increased.

By the 1960s, sewage disposal was getting out of hand again. The sheer volume of waste from toilets and factories, not to mention the polluted runoff from farms, landfills, and city streets, was far exceeding the diluting and natural cleansing abilities of waterways. In 1969, the oily, chocolate-brown Cuyahoga River in Cleveland burst into flames. Lake Erie was pronounced dead.

Over the past twenty years, near-universal sewage treatment has dramatically improved water quality in a number of areas, but municipal officials are still struggling to remove some of the contaminants that pass through treatment plants into receiving waterways. At the same time, drought in the West, salt-water intrusion in the South, acid rain in the Northeast, and chemical contamination everywhere are making pure water an endangered resource. As we regard our water supplies with renewed respect, the bathroom — the nerve center of domestic water use — is being rethought.

The Search for an Environmental Commode

Throughout the 1970s and early 1980s, a small vanguard of environmentalists with lofty visions of a solar-powered, water-conserving society — one in which all nutrients, even those in human waste, would be recycled — championed the waterless, or composting, toilet. Such toilets don't require water for flushing and are supposed to turn human excrement into well-aged, pathogen-free compost that can be used in the landscape. A few staunch advocates are quite satisfied with their composting privies. But while waterless toilets may be necessary in areas where water supplies are extremely tight, for most people, the no-flush toilet is a less-than-elegant solution to the sewage problem.

In the past ten years, a new generation of environmental commodes employing the standard water seal has been refined. In these ultra-low-flush toilets, which use only 1.6 gallons per flush, the tank size and working mechanism and the shape and fluid dynamics of the porcelain bowl and goose-necked water trap have all been redesigned for water conser-

Fresh air and sunlight, two of nature's great cleansers and purifiers, abound in the remodeled bathroom of Becky Hollingsworth's forty-year-old Atlanta bungalow. The sun's ultraviolet rays act as a mild fungicide, while good ventilation is essential for expelling excess moist air. Design: Peg'O Interiors. Contracting: Design Development Construction.

A crackling fireplace is all that separates this bedroom from its adjoining bath. The shower is built around native boulders. A ten-square-foot skylight illuminates the entire room and affords views of the pine boughs above. Architect: Obie Bowman.

vation. And they come in enough shapes and designer colors to satisfy the most discerning buyer.

The new environmental bathroom also includes a low-flow showerhead. The standard showerhead gushes five to eight gallons of water per minute. The latest low-flow models with high-velocity pulsing jets, by comparison, use only one to three gallons a minute — and yet they offer the same invigorating torrent to which we've become accustomed. Bathroom sinks are fitted with faucet aerators, inexpensive devices that add air to the water to provide the same pressure with less water flow.

It is not only the fixtures that have been redesigned in the water-conserving bathroom, but also the plumbing itself. Since its arrival in the late nineteenth century, domestic plumbing has remained virtually unchanged. Every bathroom generates three kinds of water: fresh, clean water, which comes out of the tap while we wait for hot water; toilet water, which is referred to as blackwater; and the used water from the bathtub, sink, and shower, known as graywater. Traditionally, no distinction has been made among the three: all are routed straight to the septic tank or municipal treatment plant. A handful of forward-thinking communities, however, are now revising their plumbing codes so that the relatively unsullied graywater can be diverted to the garden to irrigate trees and ornamental plants. In the new graywater systems, ball valves send used water either to the septic or sewage system or to the landscape, where the soil's rich array of beneficial bacteria purify it. Trace amounts of dirt, oil, and soap in the graywater act as mild fertilizers.

Energy as well as water is conserved in the new environmental bathroom. Solar water heaters provide hot water for washing and bathing and conserve fossil fuels. Homes without adequate sunlight use energy-efficient on-demand water heaters. In these tankless heaters, only the water flowing through the hot-water pipes is heated, a change from conventional systems, in which a large tank of hot water must be heated constantly.

■ The Naturally Elegant Bath

The new environmental bathroom is as elegant as it is efficient. During the Victorian era, when the modern bathroom evolved, bathing was considered a necessary evil, certainly not a pleasure. Queen Victoria no doubt considered herself at the cutting edge of personal hygiene when she reportedly pronounced that she bathed once a month, whether she needed it or not. In America, it's still widely considered a sign of a weak character to take pleasure in the bath; when hot tubs became popular in California, they were written off as flaky. But the Scandinavian and Oriental notion that bathrooms need to be relaxing and pleasurable, not just functional, is spreading beyond California.

Above: In a growing number of homes, the tub or shower has been moved outdoors. A greenhouse provides partial shelter for this whirlpool bath in a cool Pacific Northwest forest.

Left: Tubs and showers cost far less than swimming pools and use less heat and water. This outdoor shower with an open pediment top was designed by Peter Gisolfi Associates for a circa-1920s Georgian-style house north of New York City.

Above: The blurring of the distinction between nature and architecture that is apparent throughout the naturally elegant home even extends into the bathroom, once the most private of rooms. This whirlpool bath overlooks the mountainous, fog-enshrouded Maine coast.

Above left: The owners of this Baja house, located a thousand miles south of Tijuana, at Punta Pescadero, can soak in the tub while watching the Sea of Cortez change color as the sun arcs across the sky.

Above right: Landscape architect Dick Guzauskas's garden shower, shaded by rustic latticework and surrounded by palms, is a lush oasis in the Arizona desert.

The small, standardized bathroom invented in late-nineteenth-century America is being replaced by two separate spaces: a toilet with commode and washbasin and another space for taking baths and showers. Unlike the typical bathroom with its claustrophobic tub and suffocating shower curtain, the evolving bathroom is a spacious living room that invites lingering. It's equipped with both a shower for cleansing and a tub for soothing soaking. The tub is designed with water conservation in mind; since the water is used for soaking only, it is not changed after every use but rather filtered and recycled.

The new bathrooms also look inviting, decorated with colorful tile or rustic stone for the wet areas and lots of wood, especially cypress, cedar, or other species whose natural fragrance is drawn out by the heat and moisture of the bath. The room is a natural setting for ferns and other moisture-loving plants.

Fresh air and sunlight, two of nature's great cleansers and purifiers, are important design elements as well. The ultraviolet rays in sunlight act as a mild fungicide, and good ventilation is essential for expelling excess moist air. Consequently, the naturally elegant bathroom

is designed with large, operable windows and sliding glass doors, which also offer spectacular views of the garden or surrounding terrain. Indeed, the blurring of the distinction between nature and architecture apparent throughout the naturally elegant home is well under way even in this once most private of rooms.

In a growing number of homes, tubs and showers have moved outdoors entirely. This is true even in cool climates, where they are used in all but the most frigid weather, or sheltered partially in a greenhouse. Outdoor bathing enhances the pleasures of the bath, allowing us to get back in touch with the open air, the sun, and, of course, the water. The tub or shower is often surrounded by sweet-smelling pines, herbs, or flowers.

Outdoor bathing is as sensible as it is hedonistic. Tubs, showers, and spas cost far less than swimming pools and use less energy and water. The plumbing is rigged so that instead of disappearing down the drain, the water is sent on to the garden. Besides, what makes more sense, after a day at the beach or some heavy-duty gardening, than taking an invigorating outdoor shower before setting even one sandy or muddy foot inside the house?

PART TWO

A PORTFOLIO OF

Naturally Elegant Homes

In the 1980s and early 1990s, environmental home design matured. In the 1970s, the emblems of environmental style — or, more to the point, *antistyle* — were ascetic A-frames and solar collectors perched precariously on roofs. These have now given way to homes that not only respect the natural world but also celebrate human creativity. The pages that follow feature houses from many different regions, from a Texas ranch house to an earth-walled California bungalow. They reflect the fact that many of the new environmental architects look back to indigenous houses, which were eminently suited to their locales, even as they look forward to space-age technologies and building techniques. In the Sun Valley house, for example, solar technology, homely and unreliable in the 1970s, has been elevated to flawless engineering and fine art. Also represented here are different schools of thought, from the new generation of organic designs first espoused by Frank Lloyd Wright to the new houses designed first and foremost to safeguard human health. Some of the houses are simple cottages, a few are downright luxurious, and most fall somewhere in the middle. No matter what their price, however, they are some of the best examples of contemporary environmental design. See parts III and IV for practical tips on how to make your own house and garden both environmentally sound and beautiful.

A HIGH-STYLE TREEHOUSE

Nottingham,
New Hampshire

Architects:
Gail P. Woodhouse
Ken MacLean
Amsler Woodhouse
MacLean Architects Inc.

A tiny gem of a house commissioned by the Wharton family, this compact abode makes the most of every inch and defers to its wooded lakefront site.

The spare, 1,200-square-foot structure stair-steps, between hemlocks, down a north-facing slope toward Lake Pawtuckaway in New Hampshire. The Wharton house is really three discrete spaces connected by a walkway leading to the lake. The owners are avid sailors with a liking for small quarters, and the design, with its three separate cabinlike spaces, keeps the scale of the house small. It also minimized damage to the sloping and heavily wooded site. In addition, this particular orientation provides spectacular views of Lake Pawtuckaway and the surrounding hemlock forest from every space.

At the top is the main house, with a walk-through kitchen that leads directly into the living and dining rooms, which extend out into the landscape. The double-height space includes a sleeping loft instead of a traditional bedroom; the effect is one of living in a treehouse. Below is the Wharton sons' house, a private space in which teenagers can blast the stereo or chat on the phone to their hearts' content. It, too, has its own sleeping loft. The string of spaces terminates in a screened porch. A glassed-in hallway links the three cabins to each other and to the landscape.

The eastern hemlock, with its short, flattened needles and its tiny brown cones, grows in dense stands in ravines and on north-facing slopes throughout the northern hardwood forest, which marks the transition between the deciduous forest of the eastern United States and the coniferous forest of Canada. The three structures comprising the Wharton house were inserted, just barely, between the hemlocks that crowd the site. Architects Gail Woodhouse and Ken MacLean modified the roof heights during construction and felled trees only as a last resort. The sons' house narrowly clears a nearby trunk. When the wind blows, each structure is brushed by hemlock boughs.

The sons' room has its own wood stove. This space can be closed off when not in use to save heat in winter. At the top is a sleeping loft.

The Wharton house is really three compact, cabin-like spaces that stairstep down a heavily wooded New Hampshire hillside, minimizing damage both to the slope and to the hemlock forest. At the top is the main living area, with a spacious sleeping loft instead of a master bedroom. Next is the sons' room, followed by a roomy porch. Each space has spectacular views of Lake Pawtuckaway.

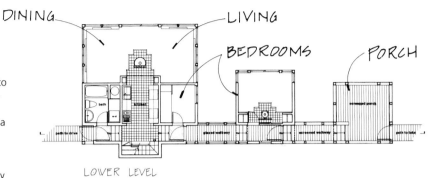

LOWER LEVEL

Above: In the main house, a walk-through kitchen leads to the many-windowed living and dining rooms. The handsome wood-burning stove is the primary source of heat.

Below: Like traditional New England dwellings, the Wharton house has a homey porch. At right is the glassed-in walkway that links the three cabins together and to the landscape.

The wood-frame construction and wood finishes harmonize with the house's woodland environment. On the exterior are white cedar shingles and stained pine trim; inside are stained poplar ceilings and oak, cedar, cork, and ceramic-tile floors. The homey screened porch and metal roof celebrate the local character of the houses of northern New England.

One of the most ingenious features of the house is its efficient use of space. Again, the architects took their cue from compact boat design, so everything doubles as something else. The treads of the three steps leading down to the kitchen from the front door, for example, flip up to provide storage for muddy boots. Two tubes that capture the heat that collects at the top of the main house and recirculate it do double duty as railings for the stairway up to the bedroom.

The same elegant frugality is also evident in the house's heating and cooling system. The sons' house and the porch can be closed off entirely in winter if they're not in use. Wood stoves heat the main house and the sons' house; electric heat is needed only as a backup. The heat the stoves generate is used efficiently: hot air trapped at the ceiling is recirculated to the basement, via fans and grille-covered openings in the floors. The house's compact shapes, open floor plans, and sleeping lofts take advantage of the centrally located stoves in winter and cross-ventilation in summer. In this densely forested setting, it seems most appropriate that the primary fuel at the Wharton house should be wood.   ∎

From foundation to finish, this house built for Linda Burnham epitomizes the painstaking attention to materials that has become a hallmark of environmental design in the 1990s. Each piece of lumber and each can of paint was subject to an environmental litmus test: Does it pollute the home and become a health hazard? Does it cause an inordinate amount of environmental damage when it is manufactured? Is it a renewable material — for example, a hardwood that is being grown in well-managed plantations, not one that is being overcut and therefore disappearing from the wild? Can it be recycled?

In many ways, the work of Paul Bierman-Lytle's design/build firm, the Masters Corporation, reflects the evolution of environmental architecture. In the mid-1970s, the company's primary mission was to design energy-efficient houses that didn't look as if they had been lifted from the set of a science-fiction film. These early houses married solar technology to tasteful design. It wasn't until the mid-1980s that Bierman-Lytle began to realize that his el-

egant solar houses were toxic. He and his colleagues were increasingly bothered by coughing and itchy eyes whenever they laid a floor or finished woodwork, and a number of studies indicated that common building materials were bothering the inhabitants of energy-efficient houses as well.

Linda Burnham's house, which doubles as an office complex for her work as a holistic health practitioner, is nestled in a forest in the Berkshires. Local woods such as maple, oak, poplar, and cherry have been used extensively, and all tropical hardwoods in the house have been approved by the Rainforest Alliance, an environmental group (see "Materials," pages 154–163). Pressure-treated lumber, which contains toxins, has been avoided. Wall cavities are filled with Air-Krete, a cementlike insulating foam that is less irritating to the lungs than fiberglass; Air-Krete is made from magnesium oxide, a naturally occurring mineral mined from seawater. Linseed oil, beeswax, and other natural coatings protect woods inside and out. The walls are colored with paints that contain

A CONSUMMATE HEALTHY HOUSE

New Marlborough, Massachusetts

Architect and Builder: Paul Bierman-Lytle, the Masters Corporation

The kitchen cabinets in this nontoxic house are made of solid cherry, glass, and formaldehyde-free plywoods. The counters are granite, not plastic laminate with formaldehyde-based glues. At right is a south-facing solarium.

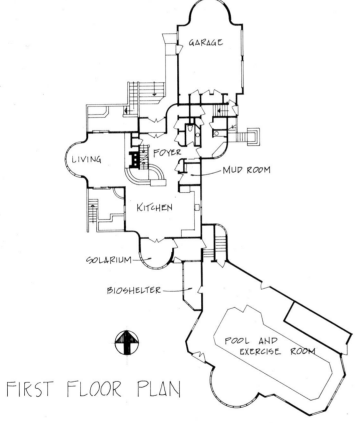

FIRST FLOOR PLAN

GARAGE

LIVING

FOYER

MUD ROOM

KITCHEN

SOLARIUM

BIOSHELTER

POOL AND EXERCISE ROOM

The Burnham house, in western Massachusetts, is made only of materials that will not pollute the home or become health hazards. In the bioshelter, at right in the photo above, fresh, pesticide-free food can be grown even during winter.

toxic to humans and all of which contribute to smog and other environmental ills.

Not only the finishes but even the furnishings pass environmental muster. The cabinets are made of solid cherry and glass and formaldehyde-free plywoods. The counters are granite, not plastic laminate with its formaldehyde-based glues. The floors are all-natural maple, vitreous tile, marble, and brick. The carpeting is 100 percent wool — wool that hasn't been treated with toxic pesticides, mildewcides, or stain guards. The carpeting is backed with natural jute.

A similar level of concern prevails throughout the house, not least of all in the ventilation system. A sub-slab venting system prevents buildup of cancer-causing radon gas. A heat-recovery ventilator exhausts stale air from the house and transfers its heat to fresh incoming air. Two state-of-the-art high-efficiency particulate absolute (HEPA) filters remove airborne particles of pollen, mold, dust, and dander, and an activated carbon pack absorbs combustion gases, formaldehyde, and other noxious vapors.

From the perspective of human health, this high-end house leaves nothing out. Its bioshelter (see page 121) is designed to yield fresh, pesticide-free produce year-round in a climate with a short growing season. Two large tanks filled with water enable the owner to engage in home fish farming; on the surface of each tank, lettuce, basil, and watercress are rafted, with their roots suspended in the water, absorbing the nutrients supplied by the fish. To promote healthy eating habits and thrifty bulk buying, the house also has a pantry and a spacious root cellar. To encourage exercise in this remote rural location where winters are long, the home is connected, by way of the bioshelter, to an enclosed lap pool.

In the kitchen, a recycling unit about the size of a dishwasher allows aluminum, glass, plastic, paper, and compostable food waste to be sorted, sped through chutes, and deposited outside in separate, labeled bags.

What's more, the house is designed to pro-

earth, minerals, and other natural pigments. These products either use lesser amounts of the biocides found in ordinary finishes (some of which are suspected carcinogens) or are altogether free of them. And they don't emit volatile organic compounds, some of which are duce a substantial amount of its own energy instead of draining it from the earth. About half of the home's energy requirement is taken care of by its highly insulated, supertight construction and passive solar design. Lots of south-facing glazing and a solarium off the kitchen capture solar heat, which is stored in tile floors and other kinds of built-in thermal mass and keeps the house warm well into the evening, when temperatures drop. A heat pump that extracts warmth from groundwater provides additional heat via hot-water baseboards and a radiant floor system, in which heat from pipes beneath the floor is radiated up and into the rooms. This combined heating system is divided into twenty-two zones. The temperature of each zone, as well as the lighting, humidity, and air quality, can be monitored and manipulated separately by a central computer system — a bit of discreet high-tech hardware that makes the ordinary thermostat seem downright prehistoric. ■

Below: Local woods including maple, poplar, and cherry are used in the bathroom and throughout the Burnham house. Beeswax and other natural coatings protect woods used on both the inside and the exterior.

Bottom: The ample windows in the living room afford views of the surrounding forest while admitting natural light. In this room and elsewhere, the walls are colored with natural paints that contain either none or less of the toxic ingredients found in conventional products.

AN UPDATED CRACKER HOUSE

Redland, Florida

Architect and Builder:
Jersey Devil

Above: A view from the screened porch to the stairway and the native slash pine and palmetto forest beyond. A pink flamingo guards the entrance.

Right: Florida's early houses were built on stilts to raise them above dampness and insects and to catch the breeze. Norma Watkins and Les Cizek's house is built above a ground-floor workshop. Hot air in the attic and inside the walls is expelled through roof vents and aluminum louvers — before it even enters the house. For longevity and minimum maintenance, the upper levels of this space-age Cracker house are sheathed in metal.

When the architects and builders pulled their Airstream trailers up to this future home-site in Redland, Florida, an agricultural area southeast of Miami named for its iron-rich soil, it looked like a jungle. Exotic Brazilian pepper trees, with their aerial roots and phenomenal growth rates, were overtaking long-needled native slash pines, palmettos, and silver palms. Before they could set up camp, the architects, who traditionally live on site when they build, had to hack away patches of pepper trees. It was a fitting introduction to the ferocious climate of South Florida, where wood rapidly rots, paints blister and peel, and hurricanes lash the coastline with regularity.

Florida's first European settlers coped with the heat and humidity by building their houses on stilts and crowning them with cupolas to vent away hot air. Inspired by the vernacular Cracker house, architect Steve Badanes of Jersey Devil (the design/build firm takes its name from the winged and cloven-hoofed mythic character that roams the pine barrens of southern New Jersey) came up with a design for clients Norma Watkins and Les Cizek, a writer and woodworker, respectively. To catch Miami's southeast breezes, Badanes raised the

two upper living areas and oriented them on a long east-west axis with generous roof overhangs for shade and screened porches to the east and west to capture views and act as buffers against the heat. These upper levels in turn shade a ground-floor workshop.

Jersey Devil's other inspiration was an open field several miles away, where General Motors tests the effects of the environment on automotive finishes. The location of this facility is quite telling, as the combination of blazing summer sun, stifling humidity, and heavy rainfall makes short work not only of Chevy paint jobs but of most building materials as well. For longevity and minimum maintenance, and because the owners love the metal roofs of the old, romantic houses on nearby Key West, the roof and the upper levels of this space-age Cracker house are sheathed entirely in metal. The roof is finished with sheet steel coated with an aluminum/zinc alloy to protect it from the pervasive salt that is an inevitable part of

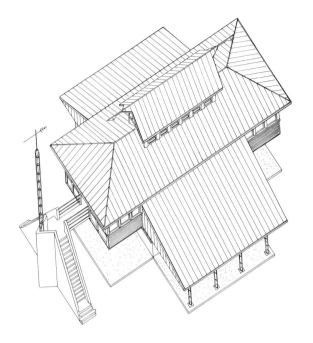

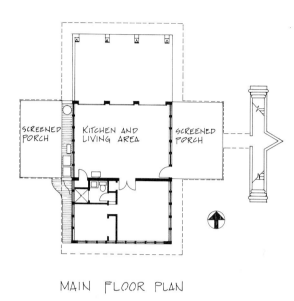

MAIN FLOOR PLAN

any coastal climate. For soffits, the architects used the snap-together aluminum panels found on most convenience stores, displaying their usual panache with offbeat materials. For siding, they chose the corrugated-aluminum panels popular with the makers of storage sheds.

Jersey Devil also employed the construction strategy advocated for the subtropics by the Florida Solar Energy Center, which has done extensive research on natural cooling techniques in a climate that sends most residents racing for the comfort of air-conditioning six months out of the year. Foil radiant barriers in the roof and most of the walls block the transfer of solar heat by reflecting it rather than absorbing and reradiating it to interior spaces.

In fact, the entire house is designed to breathe — critical for natural cooling in a hot and humid climate. Continuous soffit and ridge vents get rid of heat in the attic. Where it was impossible to use a ridge vent, the roof is vented through the walls with standard aluminum louvers. The inside of the house is vented with awning windows, which provide the most ventilation per square foot of glass; operable awning windows are located opposite each other to encourage cross-ventilation. Pad-

dle fans increase air movement when the air is still. To permit air to move up and out the loft windows and to encourage cool air to flow into the house from below, the floor of the loft is made of metal grating, which also allows more daylight to reach the lower floor.

A four-by-four solar collector on the south face of the gable roof takes advantage of South Florida's abundant sunshine and provides more than enough hot water for daily use. A built-in

Les Cizek's workshop has lots of awning windows for cross-ventilation and natural light.

The kitchen and main living area are sandwiched between screen porches on the east and west, which capture views and breezes and act as buffers against the heat. Warm air rises up through the grated ceiling and is constantly replaced by cooler outside air.

Above: Writer Norma Watkins's loft office has plenty of cooling paddle fans and awning windows for cross-ventilation. The floor grates and roof vents promote upward ventilation as well.

photovoltaic cell powers a small pump that keeps water cycling between the collector and the water tank.

Because the owners were convinced that they couldn't survive a South Florida summer without air-conditioning, a heat pump was installed to cool the house in unbearably hot and humid weather and to heat it during winter's short cool spells. Even during the insufferable summer of 1988, however, when the entire country wilted, Les Cizek and Norma Watkins reported that they slept soundly under a sheet, cooled by natural ventilation.   ■

On an eleven-acre site in the tiny rural town of Hogeye, Arkansas, sits a small masterpiece by Fay Jones, one of the most acclaimed former apprentices of Frank Lloyd Wright. In the Hogeye house, as in his other work, the architect has mastered the art of integrating structure with nature. Jones credits Wright and the principles of organic architecture — the need to relate a building to its site and to use and display materials honestly — with having had the greatest influence on his work. But while Wright's low-slung houses associate with their horizontal prairie sites, Fay Jones's buildings are masterworks in wood that soar above rustic stone bases, just as the oak and hickory forests rise from the rocky highlands in his native Arkansas.

Like other Jones works, the Hogeye house, a modestly priced, 2,300-square-foot frame structure, melds into the landscape. The house is at the edge of a sloping meadow surrounded by a forest of hickory, cedar, and oak. The native fieldstone base on the west side of the house is an artful rock outcropping; on the east side, the steep gable roof seems to lean into the hillside. Sliding glass doors leading to a fieldstone patio on the east side and a wooden veranda on the west ease the transition from architecture to nature.

The owners' request that their house reflect the rural life of the Ozarks while being both fuel-efficient and inexpensive also influenced the structure's design. Architecturally, the three-level house is a small barn resting on a rustic fieldstone base. According to Jones, the corn cribbing common to the area was the inspiration for the diagonal siding on the house's north and south sides. The posts and bracing were inspired by those in nearby tractor sheds. And two of the most dramatic visual elements of the house, the sixteen-foot-high, south-facing, diamond-shaped hayloft window and its narrower version on the north side, were likewise adapted from traditional barn design.

The Hogeye house merges with its site in other ways as well. Its cedar framing and cedar shake roof blend in with the muted colors of

A HOUSE IN THE ORGANIC TRADITION

Hogeye, Arkansas

Architect:
Fay Jones and Associates

An Arkansas house by Fay Jones, a former apprentice of Frank Lloyd Wright, is a small masterwork in wood soaring above a rustic stone base, much as oak and hickory forests rise from the surrounding rocky highlands.

This modestly priced house in rural Hogeye was inspired partly by local farm buildings. One of its most dramatic features, the large diamond-shaped hayloft window on the south side captures solar heat in winter and prevailing breezes in summer. Another, smaller hayloft window graces the north side.

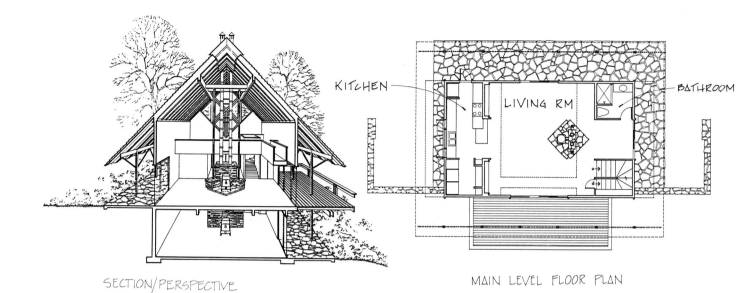

SECTION/PERSPECTIVE

KITCHEN   LIVING RM   BATHROOM

MAIN LEVEL FLOOR PLAN

surrounding tree limbs. Local fieldstone is used not only in the retaining wall on the west side but also for entry porches and interior stove-back walls.

Inside is a spare but soaring space — a full-height, gable-ceilinged living room. At the highest part of the ceiling is a ridge opening characteristic of many of Jones's works, inviting light from the sky into the house's inner reaches. The only enclosed room in the house is the second-story master bedroom, whose interior wall is pierced by a huge window that provides a view into the open living space and through the south-facing hayloft window to the meadow and forest beyond.

The centerpiece of the living space is a wood-burning stove, whose two floor-to-roof clay tile flues radiate heat throughout the space. The flues are strapped together at intervals and are flanked by two square and notched structural columns. The effect is one of a striking piece of sculpture visible throughout the house. Yet nothing in the Hogeye house is mere decoration. Its most visually ar-

resting elements — the hayloft windows and the central flues — are also its main engines of heating and cooling.

Indeed, the house's sole sources of heat are the wood-burning stove in the living area and another in the owners' basement study. The highly insulated walls and roof retain the heat. Fuel efficiency is also evident in the Hogeye house's natural cooling system. The deep overhangs of the large, sheltering roof provide shade, while prevailing southerly breezes enter and exit through the hayloft windows at the gable ends. Two ceiling fans create cooling air currents in summer and push warm air back down to the living space in winter. In summer, the owners fit wood frames covered with translucent fabric over the ridge skylight, reducing solar heat gain and producing a soft, diffuse light. That explains the ladder that runs all the way up the east side of the roof: the best way to stow the giant-legged ladder needed to reach the skylight was to leave it where it was.   ∎

Above: Inside, the Hogeye house is spare but elegant. Sliding glass doors leading to a fieldstone patio at left and a wooden veranda at right link the structure with the landscape. Local fieldstone is also used for the hearth and the stove-back wall.

Right: Nothing here is mere decoration. Clay tile flues provide floor-to-ceiling drama as they help to heat the house. In summer, wood frames covered with translucent fabric are fitted over the ridge skylight at top to reduce solar heat gain and cast a soft, diffuse light over the interior.

Left: The master bedroom upstairs is the only enclosed room in the house; its interior wall is pierced by a window that provides a view of the living space below and the south-facing hayloft window, meadow, and forest beyond.

AN ARBOR HOUSE

Zavala County,

Texas

Architect:
Lake/Flato Architects, Inc.

San Antonio–based architects David Lake and Ted Flato are at the forefront of a new Texas regional architecture that looks back to its roots — and beyond. Climate, terrain, views, and people's relationship to the outdoors are the new regionalists' fundamental concerns.

At this Rio Grande Valley site, as in most of Texas, the climate is ferociously hot. Summer temperatures top 100 degrees, and humidity from the nearby Gulf of Mexico intensifies the discomfort. To cope, the architects borrowed elements from local buildings, including screened porches, breezeways, and barn roofing. To capture breezes, the house is situated on a high spot on the Burke Ranch. The breezeways are positioned for optimum natural ventilation. Paddle fans promote cooling breezes when there are none; air-conditioning is used only in August, when temperatures don't cool down at night. Where it's not sheltered by a porch, the house is surrounded by an arbor topped by a leafy canopy of Mustang grapes for shade. The metal roof, insulated underneath, is ideal for a sun-baked climate: being thin, it doesn't store a lot of unwanted heat.

The traditional Texas touches are organized around an unconventional floor plan. The Burke Ranch house is actually a U-shaped compound linked by breezeways and arbors. Three self-contained spaces — two bedrooms and a living room/dining room/kitchen — are connected by wide, brick-paved outdoor rooms. Not only does this arrangement encourage cooling breezes, it also turns the house inside out to let the outdoors in. The breezeways replace indoor hallways, inviting nature into the heart of the home. They also allow for a variety of sheltered outdoor spaces where the owners can entertain with a minimum of formality. On the north side, accessible through handsome double glass doors in the living room, is a screened porch that sits in the shade all summer long, enjoying a tree-framed view. On the opposite side, buffered from the wind, is a leafy bower of a porch that becomes a sunny, protected place to eat or to bask in the sun when the weather turns cool.

The house is climatically attuned in other ways. All three structures are only one room deep, ensuring optimal cross-ventilation. In the main living area, Lake and Flato used the tallest windows they could find, then topped

For a ranch in the Rio Grande Valley, architects David Lake and Ted Flato designed a house that is stylish yet unpretentious — and eminently suited to the ferociously hot south Texas climate. The house is actually three self-contained spaces linked by breezeways and arbors.

them with operable clerestory windows, for openings a total of ten feet tall. These plus the tall double doors allow cool air to enter at ground level, while hot air rises and escapes on the opposite side of the lofty space. South Texas gets only ten or so freezing days a year, but an efficient shallow fireplace is set in a corner of the east wall to heat the living space when necessary. The house's highly insulated two-by-six stud walls retain the warmth.

Lake and Flato drew freely from buildings of nearby Rio Grande Valley towns for materials and scale. The house is built simply of relatively low-cost materials, with wood stud construction, concrete blocks, stucco, and industrial roofing. The thick stud walls allowed the architects to recess windows and doors, making the walls appear massive and imparting a sense of refuge from the area's violent heat. In the living room, the architects used "thick walls" — stucco-clad wood-frame interior walls — to create storage. The technique has

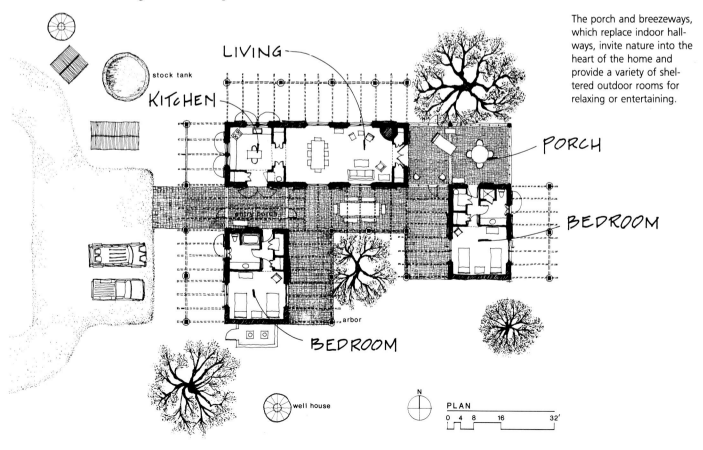

The porch and breezeways, which replace indoor hallways, invite nature into the heart of the home and provide a variety of sheltered outdoor rooms for relaxing or entertaining.

the added benefit of making the walls appear soothingly thick and protective. Simple, sturdy materials are used indoors: brick and sealed concrete floors and stained wood. Barn doors — a Lake/Flato signature — and heavy shutters can be rolled across the house's generous doorways and windows to keep out summer sun or winter winds, or for security when no one's home.

The Burke Ranch house takes tradition to intelligent extremes. Age-old tricks of construction have been employed to cope with climate in commonsense, energy-conserving ways. At the same time, the avant-garde use of self-contained spaces linked by breezeways and pergolas blurs the boundaries between indoors and outdoors and embodies a uniquely twentieth-century definition of shelter. Humble yet durable materials add to the sense of style while ensuring that the ranch house will grace its tough South Texas landscape for some time to come.   ■

Above: In the main living area, the architects used the tallest windows they could find, then topped them with operable transom windows for maximum ventilation.
In winter, the heat supplied by the efficient shallow fireplace is conserved by thick, highly insulated walls.

Left: Off the living room, on the cool north side, a screened porch offers shade all summer long, with a tree-framed view.

Right: Like the other spaces, this section of the house is only one room deep for optimal cross-ventilation. The bedroom's sturdy barn door can be rolled shut to keep out summer sun or winter winds, or for security when no one is home.

A DESERT HOUSE

Tucson, Arizona

Architect:
Les Wallach, Line and
Space

Filtering through the giant saguaro cacti, acacia, and ironwood trees that cover this magnificent Sonoran Desert site are views of Tucson, framed by the distant Santa Rita and Tucson Mountains. Bobcats and javelina roam the area. An arroyo, a conduit for runoff from violent summer storms, naturally bisects the site, studded here and there with boulders that the torrents of water have exposed over the centuries. To architect Les Wallach and his wife, Susan, the owners, it was clear that any building would have to defer to the natural beauty of the desert site.

The design of their house began with aerial photos and topographic and hydrological surveys. The northern reaches of the property offered the highest elevation, and the saguaros were spaced far enough apart there to leave room for the footprint of a house.

In the desert, any house that isn't oriented from east to west will be unbearably hot. Fortunately for the Wallachs, a south-facing house would also make the most of the views, which are captured through large expanses of glass. Deep roof overhangs shade the glazing on the south side, while wing walls that extend beyond the living space shade the west side from the fierce late-afternoon sun, which strikes the walls and windows just when temperatures are hottest. The wing wall that juts out beyond the roof on the southwest side (and that has a big opening so a giant saguaro can pop through) also shades the south-facing bedroom window from the low winter sun, which can heat up this side of the house even during the cooler months.

In the Wallach house, nature and structure are integrated. Trees grow through the building, while the building grows over the wash. The floor plan evolved around the arroyo,

Les and Susan Wallach located their Tucson house on a part of the property where the tall, columnar saguaro cacti were spaced far enough apart to accommodate its footprint. The shape of the house was pushed and pulled by the need to preserve the desert environment.

The house's broad, flat roof, which in places projects as much as twenty feet from the walls, casts cooling shade. It is punctured with ''sky holes'' that flood the house with daylight and frame views. The wing wall at left, which juts out beyond the roof on the southwest side, shades the master bedroom from the scorching sun.

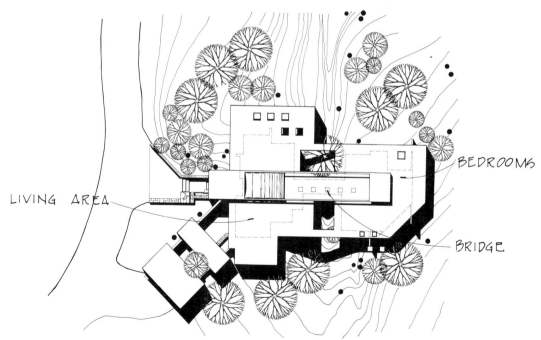

LIVING AREA

BEDROOMS

BRIDGE

ROOF PLAN

with the public areas — the entrance, kitchen, and living room — on the street side, linked to the private spaces by way of a bridge spanning the small canyon. The shape of the house was pushed and pulled by the need to preserve the desert forest. The construction, too, aimed at conservation: to spare the desert flora, the foundation was laid a small section at a time, making large stockpiles of materials unnecessary. To further minimize damage, the house was actually built from both sides of the arroyo; no construction equipment was allowed to breach the fragile chasm.

Another key to integrating the house with its surroundings is the broad, flat roof, which not only provides shade but also connects the two separate buildings and reaches out into the desert to extend the interior space. The roof, whose area is more than twice that of the house itself, projects out as much as twenty feet from the walls. Both inside and outside, it is punctured with "sky holes" ranging from four feet square to ten feet by sixteen feet, which flood the house with daylight and frame mountain views. Indoors and outdoors are also merged by the Douglas fir ceiling and concrete floors, which flow uninterruptedly through the glass walls and stretch outward, leading the eye to the mountains above and the valley below.

Beneath the sheltering roof are some exterior walls of native stone salvaged from a nearby construction project. Natural gray center-scored, split-faced concrete blocks complement both this stone and the rocky groundcover on the site. The exposed concrete masonry visually unites the outside with the inside, where it is used as a finish on some interior walls. The gray tones and rough texture of the split-faced concrete units are suited to the rugged site, while the gridlike pattern adds a human touch.

Also integral to the design of the Wallach house are spaces that ease the transition from inside to outside, which in the desert can be a shock to the senses. A gently lapping fountain beckons visitors from the blistering sunlight

The floor plan evolved around an arroyo. The "bridge" shown here spans the fragile chasm, connecting the bedrooms to the living spaces. As elsewhere in the Wallach house, the Douglas fir ceiling flows uninterruptedly through the glass, merging indoors with outdoors.

The living room's striking fireplace seems to float above the floor. The same natural gray center-scored, split-faced concrete blocks are used on exterior and some interior walls, visually linking inside with outside.

into the welcoming shade of the entry — and provides some evaporative cooling. Inside the house, further relief is provided by an energy-efficient, multizoned, two-speed, two-stage air-conditioner. The precious shade cast on the decks by the deep roof overhangs and the swamp coolers that employ evaporative cooling to temper the hot, dry desert air invite outdoor living, even deep in the heart of the Sonoran Desert.   ∎

Left: Among the kitchen's resource-conserving features are an adjoining pantry to encourage thrifty bulk buying and a gray-water system to recycle relatively clean rinsewater in the garden.

Above: In the master bedroom, the lack of windows on the long west wall keeps out the fierce late-afternoon sun, which strikes the house when temperatures are at their hottest.

A SOLAR MASTERPIECE

Sun Valley, Idaho

Architect:
Arne Bystrom
Solar Design:
Gregory Franta
Landscape Architect:
Robert Murase

The house's distinctive roof, a great creased plane, echoes the outline of the Sawtooth foothills beyond. The solar house is located at an elevation of six thousand feet.

For even greater energy efficiency, the house is protected by an earth berm on its cold north side. Passive solar design, along with the solar collectors suspended from the roof on the south side, provides about 70 percent of the energy needed to heat the house — no small feat in a climate where temperatures regularly plunge to twenty or thirty below zero.

In 1982, architect Arne Bystrom was approached by a San Francisco couple. They wanted a mountain house for their extended family, one that would combine the latest in solar technology with the warmth of richly detailed wood construction. The Sun Valley house that resulted is proof that, in the right hands, solar technology can be transformed into high art.

The site defines the form of the Sun Valley house, located at an elevation of six thousand feet. Nature and architecture, craft and technology are seamlessly integrated. The lines of the distinctive roof, a great creased plane, echo those of the rolling hills and mountains beyond. Huge redwood columns that fan open at the top to support the beams give the impression that the roof is held aloft by a dozen great trees.

The roof has been carefully designed to divert heavy winter snows — the snows that have made Sun Valley a world-class ski resort — away from the front entrance and terraces. The north slope is pitched to precisely match the angle of the sun at midday on the winter solstice. Every day, around midmorning, the sun begins to stream into the solarium that runs the length of the south side, stoking the passive and active solar systems, which together provide about 70 percent of the energy needed for heating and cooling — no small feat in a climate where winter temperatures often plunge to twenty or thirty below.

The sun striking the greenhouselike glazed south facade is stored in the house's concrete floor and walls. The glass is made of energy-efficient double glazing, with a thin layer of plastic and argon gas between the panes to keep warmth in and cold out. When the temperature in the sunspace heats up, the warm air that collects at the top is drawn into tubes and down to the rock bed beneath the floor, where it's stored until needed. Computer-controlled slat blinds and awning windows at the top of the glass wall automatically control sun and temperature. Also lining the south facade is an array of unusual evacuated-tube heat-pipe collectors, which are the key to the

ACTIVE SOLAR HEATING SYSTEM

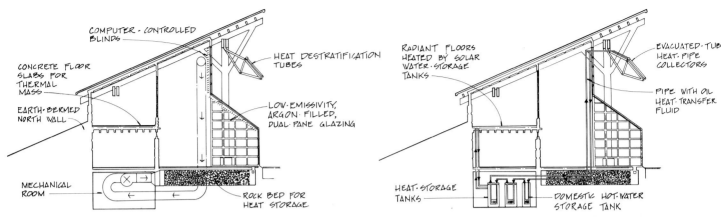

COMPUTER - CONTROLLED BLINDS

HEAT DESTRATIFICATION TUBES

CONCRETE FLOOR SLABS FOR THERMAL MASS

EARTH - BERMED NORTH WALL

LOW - EMISSIVITY, ARGON - FILLED, DUAL - PANE GLAZING

MECHANICAL ROOM

ROCK BED FOR HEAT STORAGE

PASSIVE SOLAR HEATING SYSTEM

RADIANT FLOORS HEATED BY SOLAR WATER - STORAGE TANKS

EVACUATED - TUBE HEAT - PIPE COLLECTORS

PIPE WITH OIL HEAT - TRANSFER FLUID

HEAT - STORAGE TANKS

DOMESTIC HOT - WATER STORAGE TANK

Sun Valley house's solar design and have been totally maintenance-free. These collectors work by transferring heat from air to a special oil. The oil circulates in a closed loop, delivering the heat to a series of water storage tanks that provide hot water for domestic use and feed into a radiant heating system built into the floor slabs on both levels. A gas-fired furnace serves as a backup energy source.

For summer cooling, a well-thought-out cross-ventilation system is augmented by the radiant floors, which are cooled with water from a decorative fountain in the courtyard outside. A mechanical evaporative cooling unit draws cool outside air from the north side of the building, along which the earth has been piled up, or bermed, to minimize winter heat loss.

Solar designer Greg Franta wasn't wild about the idea of installing windows on the north side, but Bystrom insisted on them because of the view. As a compromise, he specified windows that are even more energy-conserving than those in the glass-covered south facade. They have two layers of plastic and three spaces filled with argon. Heavily insulated "double roof" construction also protects against heat loss in winter and heat gain in summer. The owners, one of whom is trained as an electrical engineer, say the insulation and high-tech glazing perform extremely well, making the solarium comfortable even during the bitterest weather that winter can muster.

High-tech detail: the energy-efficient greenhouselike south wall and solar collector.

Architect Arne Bystrom is famous for his richly detailed wood construction, much in evidence in the kitchen and dining room. The furniture was also designed by Bystrom.

Bystrom and landscape architect Robert Murase collaborated from the start, and the Sun Valley house and garden grew together over several years. A series of concrete terraces tumble down the south side like a riverbed among planted stands of cottonwood, extending interior spaces into the landscape. The indoors and outdoors are merged with exquisite detailing. The walls and floors of the terraces are formed of the same decorative cement mixture used inside the house, only with a slightly rougher texture; the red tile banding in the floors likewise flows effortlessly outside. Redwood finishes both indoors and out are inlaid with fir. The cross-hatching first noted outside continues on the inside, and the design of the iron garden gates is repeated in the screen that surrounds the spectacular sunken fireplace, the focus of the living space.

The house's bent brow hovers above a garden of native rock, wildflowers, and grasses. The garden eases the transition from the elegant terraces to the natural meadow below and the Sawtooth foothills beyond.

(For more on the Sun Valley garden, see page 183.) ▪

Woodwork detail: garage doors and one of the huge redwood columns that fan open at the top to support the roof beams.

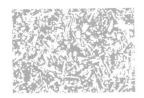

A ROCKY MOUNTAIN HOME

Evergreen,
Colorado

Architect:
Anderson Mason Dale

Built at an elevation of eight thousand feet, this is a house of one elemental wall, thirty-three feet high, 135 feet long, and two feet thick. The house leans against the great wall, erected at the base of a rocky cliff on a south-facing slope where ponderosa pines dot a meadow of grasses and occasional wildflowers.

A professional couple ready to retire asked architects Anderson Mason Dale to design a year-round house with living spaces that would capture the spirit and capitalize on the views of this remote mountain site near Evergreen, Colorado. The vistas include a commanding view of Mount Evans, which soars more than fourteen thousand feet on the Continental Divide. The owners also wanted enough bedrooms for frequent family visitors, a greenhouse, and a workshop, as well as an energy-efficient design to make the most of the abundant Colorado sunshine.

Anderson Mason Dale designed a house that celebrates the Rocky Mountains and incorporates basic passive solar techniques to tame the harsh high-elevation climate. The large rock wall ties the house to the towering cliff. Made of lichen-covered fieldstone, it marks the transition between the meadow and the rocky precipice above.

The great wall also organizes traffic flow and divides the house into open and enclosed spaces. The living spaces and bedrooms are arranged along the south side to take advantage of the view, while enclosed spaces such as the kitchen, bathrooms, laundry, and storage areas are located on the north side, which is earth-sheltered for energy efficiency. Skylights spaced at regular intervals along the earthen berm allow daylight to suffuse the enclosed spaces. The wall is pierced at the very center, framing a view of the cliff from the dining-room table.

Views of the surrounding terrain are also captured through the glass walls of the "sun-

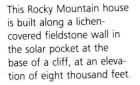

This Rocky Mountain house is built along a lichen-covered fieldstone wall in the solar pocket at the base of a cliff, at an elevation of eight thousand feet.

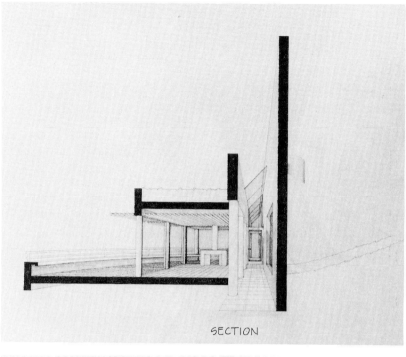

SECTION

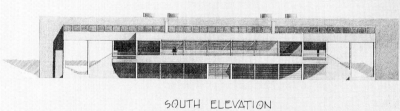

SOUTH ELEVATION

Above left: Inside, a sloped, south-facing skylight allows the sun to strike the wall along its entire length. The solar heat is stored in the rock and warms the rooms later in the day, when temperatures plummet. The fin-shaped solar collectors strung beneath the skylight provide hot water.

Left: On the north side, the wall is earth-sheltered for energy efficiency. Skylights suffuse the rooms below with natural light. The dining-room window, *center*, frames views of the towering cliff behind the house.

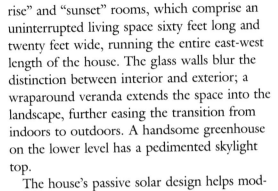

Left: A wraparound veranda extends the living rooms into the landscape, easing the transition from architecture to nature. At right is the greenhouse with its pedimented skylight top.

Below: The house is dramatic by night and fuel-efficient by day, making the most of the abundant Colorado sunshine.

rise" and "sunset" rooms, which comprise an uninterrupted living space sixty feet long and twenty feet wide, running the entire east-west length of the house. The glass walls blur the distinction between interior and exterior; a wraparound veranda extends the space into the landscape, further easing the transition from indoors to outdoors. A handsome greenhouse on the lower level has a pedimented skylight top.

The house's passive solar design helps moderate the broad temperature swings of the sub-alpine setting. The rock cliff affords natural protection from fierce north winds and provides a pleasant solar pocket in the meadow. A sloped, south-facing skylight, which extends beyond the living spaces to form covered entries on the east and west sides, allows the sun to strike the great wall along its entire length. The wall's mass collects the solar energy and reradiates it to the interior after dark, when temperatures plummet. Winter sun also streams through the south-facing glass walls; the solar heat is stored in the tile floors of the sunrise and sunset rooms. Two heat-circulating fireplaces in the great wall provide additional warmth. Warm air that collects where the wall meets the skylight is pulled through vents into the earth-sheltered north-facing spaces. Also under the skylight, a hot-water pipe and fin-shaped solar collectors are strung along the stone wall to provide hot water for domestic use. There's also a conventional electric heating system for supplemental warmth.

By harnessing the sun to moderate the climate, and by echoing the powerful rock cliff with a massive stone wall, the architects created a house uniquely suited to its Rocky Mountain site.   ■

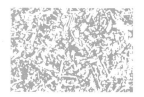

A BRIDGE HOUSE

Bainbridge Island, Washington

Architect:
James Cutler Architects

For this tiny waterfront lot, architect Jim Cutler convinced a like-minded developer to erect a model environmental dwelling before there was even a buyer. The site is a thickly wooded, south-facing lot bisected by a seasonal stream. In winter, the stream rushes noisily toward the harbor of Port Blakely, an old lumber town on the southern end of Bainbridge Island, in the Puget Sound, not far from Seattle. Permission had been granted by the local government to divert the stream into a culvert and fill the streambed to create a level building site, but Cutler, who has a growing reputation for designing handsome houses that, in his words, don't "devour the land," proposed instead "a double-width Shaker house on a bridge" to span the forty-two-foot-wide gulf.

Cutler collaborated with structural engineer Greg Hiatt on a cost-effective spanning system, consisting of four glue-laminated beams supported by steel-reinforced, broken-face black granite footings and wood knee braces on both stream banks. The two-story, three-bedroom, 2,100-square-foot dwelling is clad in cedar shingles. The shimmering effect of its reflective metal roof adds to the Northwest waterfront atmosphere.

The living and dining areas occupy the midspan of the bridge. The kitchen and master bedroom are on the extreme ends of the house, seemingly built into the stream banks, with two additional bedrooms and a study upstairs. A series of energy-conserving small windows on the north side of the house (the street side), admit daylight while ensuring privacy. On the south side, fir-wrapped windows open up a sixteen-by-eighteen-foot area for a spectacular view of the ravine, stream, and beach; flanking side windows provide an additional vista. In winter, when the leaves of the

While local officials were willing to let developers culvert and fill the streambed to create a level building site, Cutler proved that an environmental alternative could be not only achievable but also spectacular. The result is a house that gracefully spans the creek, with views down the stream corridor toward the harbor of Port Blakely. Photograph: Peter Aaron/ Esto.

Right: To preserve the seasonal stream that bisects this tiny lot on Bainbridge Island, Washington, architect Jim Cutler designed a double-width Shaker house on a bridge that spans the forty-two-foot-wide gulf. Photograph: Peter Aaron/ Esto.

Left: Not your average foundation: four glue-laminated beams, black granite footings, and wood knee braces comprise the cost-effective spanning system. Photograph: Peter Aaron/Esto.

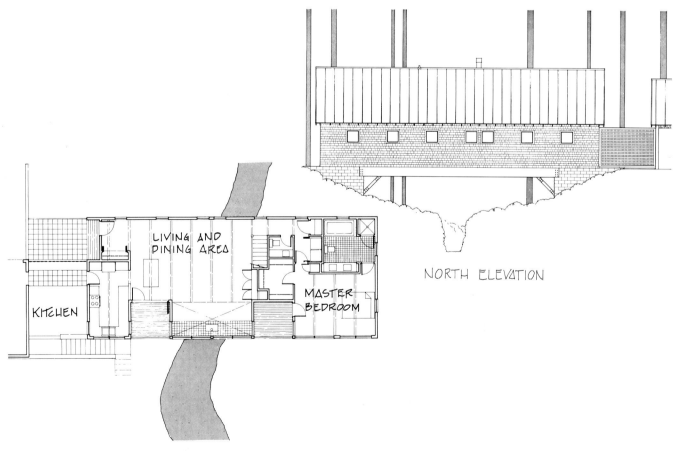

NORTH ELEVATION

FIRST FLOOR PLAN

KITCHEN

LIVING AND DINING AREA

MASTER BEDROOM

surrounding deciduous trees have fallen, sunlight penetrates the wall of glass and warms the house. Even the stream beneath the house can be viewed, through glass blocks inserted flush with the living room floor. The three-inch-thick glass blocks, which rest on a quarter-inch steel frame for support, double as the hearth for a wood-burning stove. For an experience of the bridge design that's more dramatic still, there are two covered balconies, one accessible from the master bedroom and the other from the dining area. The balconies have galvanized railings like those found on shipboard.

The design of the house kept damage to the stream and the surrounding vegetation to a minimum, and the materials used to build it were chosen with an eye toward minimizing pollution. Cutler avoided plywood for sheathing because it contains formaldehyde. The house was instead sheathed in the traditional way, by nailing boards diagonally. The interior is finished not with plasterboard but with wood, enhancing its connection with the heavily forested site. Douglas fir, a familiar conifer of the misty forests of the Pacific Northwest, was used for paneling, except in one bedroom, which was finished with pine; the stair railing leading to the second floor is likewise made of fir, with solid six-by-six-inch newel posts. Solid fir was also chosen for the kitchen cabinets. Nontoxic paints and stains were employed throughout the house.

This could have been just another beach house, eroding the coastline while calling attention to itself. Instead it sits back, enveloped by woods, gracefully spanning the creek with breathtaking views down the stream corridor toward the harbor. The detailing — the projected eaves and the balcony railings, for example — is exquisitely crafted but not fussy. The bridge house represents a bold idea executed with stylish simplicity, the epitome of natural elegance.   ■

The living and dining areas occupy the midspan of the bridge, while the kitchen and master bedroom are located on the extreme ends of the house, seemingly built into the streambanks. The dining room opens onto one of two covered balconies that offer a dramatic experience of the bridge design. Photograph: Peter Aaron/Esto.

AN EARTH-WALLED BUNGALOW

Napa, California

Architects:
Jeff Reed, Don Callahan, Henri Mannik
Builder:
David Easton, Rammed Earth Works

This California cottage with walls of earth is a late-twentieth-century take on the bungalow style that swept America at the turn of the century. Functional and elegant, the nouveau bungalow is proof that it's possible to live within one's means — and nature's means — with style and grace. Called the Compact House by its builder, David Easton, it has a practical design for comfortable living and living close to nature.

The structure is built out of earth, glass, and wood, materials that are constantly being renewed by nature. Earth has been the most essential of building materials since the dawn of the human race; it has been used in the Desert Southwest for a thousand years, first by the Pueblo Indians and later by the Spanish in their adobe, or mud-brick, structures. A house built of earth becomes a part of the landscape rather than an imposition upon it.

The Compact House's basic construction relies on a technique called rammed earth, a centuries-old technology that has taken an evolutionary leap forward with the incorporation of cement and power tools. David Easton has developed several rammed-earth techniques in which cement is added to clean mineral soil and a small amount of sand. Pneumatic tampers compact the mixture in removable plywood forms to create wall sections eighteen or more inches thick — a lot like adobe, but without individual bricks.

The Compact House, like other rammed-earth houses, uses relatively little wood for framing, thus conserving this increasingly scarce resource. Even the floors are made from a soil-cement mixture scored to look like tile and grouted when dry. The house is free of formaldehyde and other pollutants emitted by plywood and synthetic materials. The massive walls deaden noise, creating a hushed, soothing silence inside. Easton's various rammed-earth techniques are so stable — the walls of the Compact House, for example, are steel-reinforced — that they meet California's strict earthquake-driven building codes. Rammed-

The walls of this California bungalow are made of earth, cement, and sand. Pneumatic tampers compact the mixture between removable plywood forms. Photograph: Don Carson.

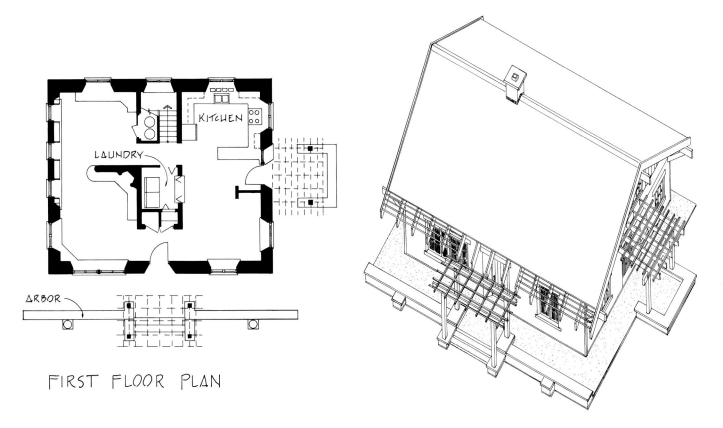

KITCHEN

LAUNDRY

ARBOR

FIRST FLOOR PLAN

earth structures are built to last for centuries, not decades, making them one of the ultimate forms of conservation architecture.

Earthen houses are especially suited to arid areas, where wood is often hard to come by and sunshine is, to put it mildly, abundant. The massive walls trap heat from the sun, keeping the house cool during the day; the stored solar heat is then reradiated into the house during the cool desert night. By morning, the walls have been drained of most of their heat and are ready to absorb another day's worth of intense sunshine. The energy savings start during construction: the earth doesn't need to be transported long distances, like lumber milled in British Columbia or insulation from the Carolinas.

Like other earthen structures, the Compact House relies on its mass and orientation to the sun for solar efficiency. The walls — which are eighteen inches thick, increasing to twenty-four inches on the cool north side — and the slab floor provide thermal mass. A radiant heating system was also installed in the floor slab when the mixture was poured, to provide backup heat. Cross-ventilation from windows

Left: Rammed earth is much like adobe, but without the individual bricks. The exterior walls have a warm earth tone and an exquisite texture.

Inside, the earth walls are sculpted and tinted. Even the floors are made from a soil-cement mixture that is scored to look like tile and grouted when dry. Photograph: Don Carson.

on opposite walls, deep roof overhangs, and vine-covered pergolas ensure natural cooling.

The Compact House, as its name implies, is distinguished by its economy of space. The two-bedroom, two-bath house comprises about 1,400 square feet. Like a turn-of-the-century bungalow, it features extra-wide built-in window seats, which economize on space and are easier to clean than upholstered chairs and sofas. The water heater was installed inside the wall, and the laundry room was tucked under the stairs leading to the loftlike bedrooms on the second floor.

By and large, the household fixtures in this earthen bungalow are recycled. Sinks, tubs, the gas stove, and the refrigerator were salvaged from junkyards and refurbished. Even the driveway was paved with granite from a slag pile at a nearby quarry before being landscaped with native, drought-resistant plants. ∎

The household fixtures in this earthen bungalow are recycled; the gas stove, for example, was salvaged from a junkyard and refurbished. Photograph: Don Carson.

Like other designs by architect Obie Bowman, this one is inspired by its setting rather than by an architectural trend of the present or the past. The setting is Sea Ranch, a development along a stretch of northern California coast that is often described as wild, lonely, brooding, and enchantingly beautiful. Above the coastal bluffs, a broad meadow is traversed by hedgerows of tall, wind-sculpted cypresses, which form a line of windbreaks from the ocean to an upland forest of pine and redwood, tanbark oak and madrone. Higher still is the spine of the mile-wide development, a wooded, six-hundred-foot-high ridge that plunges steeply down to the Gualala River. Deer and other wildlife roam freely throughout Sea Ranch, and whales can be seen migrating off the coast. In spring, the meadows are a brilliant carpet of wildflowers.

A soft, sloping sod roof blends the house, owned by the Brunsell family, into a sweep of meadow along the ocean's edge. The house is well camouflaged from the inhabitants of neighboring homes who must look beyond it for views of the ocean. The sod roof, planted with indigenous species, replaces the meadow displaced by the structure's footprint, minimizing disruption of plant and animal life as well as natural drainage patterns: runoff from the roof percolates back into the ground, as does much of the precipitation falling on the gravel driveway and parking court. Here and there, the roof is pierced with dramatic skylights, bathing the house in natural light.

The Brunsell house is attuned to nature in many other ways as well. The shape of the house, determined partly by setback requirements and partly by the Brunsells' request for two separate bedroom wings, is like that of a seagull in flight. The shape creates a wind foil, deflecting the cool northerly winds that blow throughout the spring and summer up and away from the sunken deck on the south side.

The house is heated by the sun and cooled

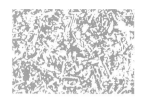

A SOD-ROOFED HOME FOR A COASTAL MEADOW

Sea Ranch, California

Architect:
Obie G. Bowman

The design of the Brunsell house was inspired by its magnificent setting on the northern California coast. The softly sloping sod roof, planted with indigenous species, blends the house into a sweep of oceanfront meadow and minimizes disruption of plant and animal life and natural drainage patterns.

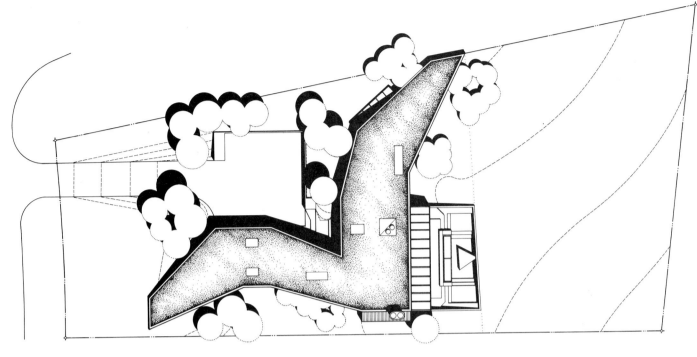

 SITE PLAN

FLOOR PLAN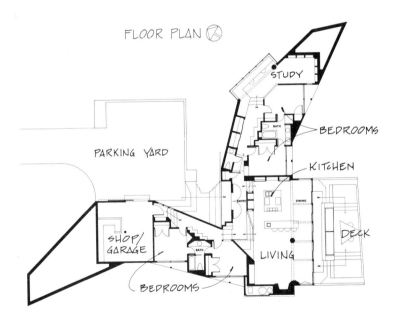

Skylights flood the sod-roofed house with natural light.

by natural ventilation. Sun shines on the south-facing solarium and is stored in the floor, which is brick over concrete slab for thermal mass. The stored solar heat is re-radiated into the living space later in the day, when the sun sets and temperatures drop. The walls have been insulated well beyond code to retain the heat. Discreet solar panels below the deck heat hot water for domestic use, and a

gas-fired radiant system in the slab floor provides supplementary heating. Cool air is drawn in through the louvers that flank the main entry on the north side; it moves through the house as the hot air that collects at the top of the solarium exits through vents in a wall on the leeward face.

The heart of the Brunsell house is the combined kitchen and living area, which separates

The kitchen is illuminated by a skylight and by the sunlight that streams into the solarium. The owners enjoy dramatic 180-degree views of the meadow and coast as they dine.

Left: A small eucalyptus column is one of the highlights of the study on the north side of the house, which is earth-bermed for energy efficiency.

The Brunsell house is cooled by natural ventilation. After being drawn in through the louvers that flank the main entry on the north side, cool air moves through the house as the hot air that collects at the top of the solarium exits through vents in the wall on the leeward face, shown here.

The heart of the Brunsell house is the combined kitchen and living area, which separates the guest and master bedrooms. This space is completely open to the south-facing solarium, an integral part of the passive solar heating and cooling system. The eucalyptus trunk helps support the sod roof.

Above right: A quirky fireplace designed by architect Obie Bowman is embellished with brick chunks salvaged from a pile of debris.

the guest and master bedroom wings. The large central living area is completely open to the solarium with its uninterrupted, 180-degree views of the meadow and the coast. The sunroom and adjoining deck project out into the meadow, linking the living area with the land.

Bowman's use of indigenous materials and his quirky detailing enhance the connection between natural and human habitats. The poured concrete retaining walls are finished on the outside with redwood tongue-and-groove walls, while the inside is Douglas fir; both woods are native to the Pacific maritime forest. One focal point of the central living area is a thick, weathered trunk taken from a stand of dead eucalyptus trees. The column, which seems to grow out of the floor, supports a massive ceiling beam that in turn holds up the weighty sod roof. The pièce de résistance of the living space, however, is a spectacular masonry fireplace, embellished with recycled brick chunks plucked from a pile of debris. ∎

PART THREE

DESIGNING AND REMODELING THE
Naturally Elegant Home

In the preceding sections, you've gotten a glimpse of how homeowners and professional designers across the country have created stylish houses and gardens that go easy on the planet. How can you do the same with your house? Before you get started, you may want to consider the following rules of thumb:

1. **If you can do all your renovations in one fell swoop, by all means do it.** Renovation — yes, even naturally elegant renovation — can make life miserable. It's no fun to trip over tools and inhale plaster dust for months or, worse, years. Chronic renovation is not just a hassle; it can be downright unhealthy. It's best to get it over with at once, especially if you've just bought a house and haven't moved in yet.

2. **If your budget is tight, think of your house as a work in progress.** Proceed step-by-step, starting with the improvements that make the most sense for your house and your wallet.

3. **Don't bite off more than you can chew.** Begin with the worst room in your house — let's say the kitchen. Confine the turmoil to this one area, or at least make sure there's one room you can escape to as a refuge from the noise, the chaos, and the dust. Make sure the work is complete in the kitchen before tackling the next space.

4. **Remember, many environmentally responsible home improvements cost little, but the payoffs can be big.** A low-flow showerhead or a ceiling fan, for example, is not a big-ticket item, but one will save a great deal of water and the other will save energy. By slashing utility bills, they will also save you money. If money is extremely tight, stick to these modest measures.

5. **Remember, too, that price tags can be misleading.** Some of the improvements described in the pages to come cost a lot up front but pay for themselves surprisingly quickly in lower heating and water bills.

6. **Salvage, salvage, salvage.** Don't go overboard with the remodeling. Example: instead of just trashing your existing kitchen cabinets, salvage them with a fresh coat of paint or a sealer that prevents formaldehyde fumes from being released from plywood or particle board in the doors or drawers. The idea is to make changes that look good and benefit both the environment and your own health — not to generate garbage.

7. **Let the style of your house be your guide.** There's no need to savage a bungalow or a quaint Cape Cod in the name of environmental improvement. Whether you're replacing windows, adding a sunspace, or remodeling your kitchen, choose the style or materials most suitable to the style of your house.

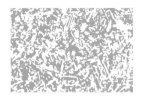

NATURAL CLIMATE CONTROL

When you arrive in the Desert Southwest, you buy a hat — a great big hat that shades your face, like the ten-gallon hat immortalized in Western movies. In Nova Scotia, you dig up a sweater. Different climates call for different clothing. Different climates also call for different dwellings: no matter where you live, your climate can provide clues on how to design a home that is comfortable and economical to heat and cool — and has a strong sense of place.

The Comfort Zone

The human body is comfortable in a surprisingly narrow range of temperatures and humidity levels. This comfort zone, as it's called, varies somewhat according to culture and individual physiology, but it usually falls between about sixty-five and seventy-five degrees Fahrenheit and 30 and 65 percent humidity. The higher the humidity, the lower the air temperature must be if you're to feel comfortable.

The comfort zone for most Americans has changed since the advent of central heating in the late nineteenth century. In 1900, anything between sixty-five and seventy-five degrees was considered comfortable. By 1960, we'd become rather more fussy, demanding temperatures of seventy-five to seventy-eight in winter and seventy-two in summer. We grew accustomed to being in shirt sleeves indoors, even when blizzards were lashing the outside of the house. Then came the OPEC oil embargo of 1973. One of the first reactions to oil shortages and soaring prices was a public campaign for a more energy-conserving notion of comfort — sixty-eight degrees in winter and seventy-eight in summer. America did begin to open the windows or reach for a sweater — but not without a lot of grumbling, and for good reason. Without the furnace or air-conditioner working at full tilt, our houses simply weren't comfortable. They weren't designed right.

Some Rudimentary Physics

Heat can be transferred in three ways: by radiation, convection, and conduction. Radiant heating is the direct transfer of energy via electromagnetic waves traveling in straight lines through air and fluids until they hit another object and are absorbed or reflected. Convection involves the movement of heated liquids or gases such as water or air; warm air is less dense and rises, and cool air is heavier and falls. Conduction is the direct transfer of heat when two objects touch.

Since the 1950s and '60s, the typical American house has been designed to provide comfort mostly by convection, by heating and cooling air by means of high-powered mechanical heating and cooling systems. However, human comfort is a result of a delicate balance of several factors — not only air temperature but also air movement and the temperature of surrounding surfaces such as floors and walls. When you're hot, you may be hot for three different reasons — hot air, hot walls, or not enough breeze — but your thermometer measures only one of these. When you're cold, you may be cold for one or all of three reasons — cold air, cold walls, or drafts — but again, your thermometer shows only air temperature.

The temperature of the walls, floor, and ceiling of a room is as important as the temperature of the air. For example, when summer sun shines on your house, it often heats up the exterior. In a few hours, some of that heat seeps through to the inside, and the inside walls warm up a few degrees. The warmer walls keep you from radiating your body heat at them, so it remains bottled up and you feel hot. In winter, on the other hand, the outside cold comes through the walls and windows. Heat jumps from your warm skin directly to those cooler walls and windows, and you feel chilly.

To make up for this radiant heating or cooling effect, you have to keep the air in the house extra warm or extra cool. That's why, in

Heating with Wood

In the 1970s, millions of Americans installed wood-burning stoves in their homes. The smoke from all those flues had the sweet smell of independence — from OPEC, from the oil companies, from local utilities. Burning wood also satisfied some primeval urge: fire has shaped the life of our species since it first appeared on earth. And what made wood even better was that unlike fossil fuels, it comes from a renewable resource — trees. Alas, we soon learned that the wood stoves were also blanketing the atmosphere with noxious pollutants. State and federal regulators stepped in and issued strict regulations, spurring the development of a new generation of stoves that burn cleanly and much more efficiently.

Some manufacturers met the new standards by adding a catalytic converter to their stoves. Others achieved a cleaner burn by employing sophisticated airflow designs. Still others have turned to a new form of wood fuel — pellets — that burns cleanly and with great efficiency in specially designed stoves. Another advantage of the pellet stove is that it makes use of waste wood that has been pulverized and then compressed.

U.S. Environmental Protection Agency regulations focus on particulates, tiny bits of unburned hydrocarbons that can lodge in the lungs and cause respiratory problems. In July 1990, the emission standard became 4.1 grams of particulates per hour of burning (g/hr) for catalytic stoves and 7.5 g/hr for noncatalytics. (Catalytics are more stringently regulated because the catalyst degrades over time.) By way of comparison, an older stove may pollute five to ten times as much.

By the 1990–91 burning season, the EPA had approved 281 stove models; sixty-six emit a minuscule 3 g/hr or less, and a dozen emit less than 1.5 g/hr.

A circa-1975 stove probably burned at an overall efficiency rate of less than 60 percent, meaning that less than 60 percent of the potential heat in the wood actually went into the room. When the state of Oregon tested 228 new models, the average efficiency was 72 percent; several stoves operated at efficiencies of 80 percent or more.

Emissions may be down, but prices are up. The

EPA estimates that its regulations have added $120 to $200 to the cost of a stove. When shopping for a wood stove, look for models with the best emissions ratings and those that burn most efficiently.

The Eurostyle Stove

An efficient and clean-burning wood-heat technology that has been used for centuries in Europe is now attracting an ever-larger following on this continent. Unlike traditional North American stoves, which are made of iron, these stoves are made of masonry; unlike iron stoves, masonry stoves (also known by the German word *kachelofen*) are heat-storage systems. Designs differ, but the operative principle remains the same: heat built up rapidly in the firebox travels through a long maze of built-in channels, or flues, is stored in the stove's masonry mass, and is released into the room over a period of hours. Consequently, masonry stoves require fuel only once or twice a day, making them eminently suitable for hectic modern life-styles.

The high temperatures in the firebox and the

Because masonry stoves, used for centuries in Europe, are designed to store heat and release it over a period of hours, they require wood only once or twice a day. They burn cleanly, don't get hot to the touch, come in a variety of styles, and can be faced with brick, stucco, or glazed tile.

Masonry stoves are a handsome architectural feature that will last as long as your house.

complex flue systems of masonry stoves also make for a clean burn. Two masonry heaters tested recently at the Virginia Polytechnic Institute (VPI) averaged emissions of 1.4 g/hr, with the cleaner of the two testing out at 0.99 g/hr. Tests in Finland, Sweden, and central Europe have shown that the efficiency of the masonry stove is in the neighborhood of 70 to 90 percent. Unlike iron stoves, masonry heaters don't get hot to the touch. *Kachelofen* come in a wide variety of styles and are faced with brick, stucco, or glazed tile, making them a handsome architectural feature in almost any home.

Not surprisingly, a stove that lasts for centuries, requires only two or three dozen pounds of wood to heat a house for an entire day, is as decorative as it is functional, and is typically cleaner than other wood-burning systems doesn't come cheap. But if you're putting in a new heating system or shopping around for a system for a new house, the cost may not be out of line.

Masonry stoves work best in well-insulated homes with open floor plans that allow the heat to radiate freely. You can choose between a small room heater or a massive hearth that includes a cooktop and bake oven. It will need a chimney and usually a foundation as well. Keep in mind, too, that masonry heaters can overheat a home during warm spells in spring and fall. It's a good idea to outfit your house with a small iron stove that can take the chill off a spring or autumn morning, then cool down quickly as the mercury climbs.

Efficient Fireplaces

In the standard fireplace, 90 percent of the heat escapes up the chimney. Such fireplaces are also dirty, with emissions of 45 g/hr, according to VPI tests. If you're renovating an old house, consider retrofitting the fireplace with an energy-efficient Rumford design. A Rumford design is also the most efficient choice for a new home if you can't live without the sparkle and crackle of a fireplace.

Rumfords are named after Count Rumford, who revolutionized fireplace design in the eighteenth century, making them smaller and shallower so they would radiate heat better. He also streamlined the throat to carry away the smoke with less air loss. Rumford fireplaces were common from 1796 to about 1850. Jefferson had several at Monticello, and Thoreau listed them among the modern amenities that everyone took for granted in his day.

To install a Rumford fireplace in your home, you or your mason must first build the firebox out of brick. Specially designed throats, cast-iron dampers, and smoke chambers can be mail-ordered from one of the handful of companies that still produce them (see Appendix A, page 221).

One final word about wood-burning stoves and fireplaces: be sure to use ductwork to bring in outside air for combustion. In energy-efficient homes, this is especially important to keep noxious combustion fumes from "backdrafting" into the house.

Further Information

For more information on certified wood stoves, including a list of models, their manufacturers, and their emissions ratings, write to Federal Programs Section (EN-341), U.S. E.P.A., 401 M Street, SW, Washington, D.C. 20460.

Two good sources of information on masonry heaters are David Lyle's *The Book of Masonry Stoves: Rediscovering an Old Way of Warming,* available from Heating Research Co., P.O. Box 300, Acworth, New Hampshire 03601, and Albert Barden's *Finnish Fireplaces: Heart of the Home,* available from Maine Wood Heat Co., RFD 1, Box 640, Norridgewock, Maine 04857.

For further information on masonry stoves, write or call the Masonry Heater Association, 11490 Commerce Park Drive, Suite 300, Reston, Virginia 22901; (703) 620-3171.

the 1970s, turning down the thermostat for the furnace and upping it for the air-conditioner felt so uncomfortable. Our homes weren't designed to effectively keep out winter cold and summer heat, nor to keep in heated or cooled air.

Improving a house's radiant environment — for example, adding insulation to minimize conduction — allows you to feel comfortable at lower air temperatures in winter and higher air temperatures in summer. So you conserve energy, and in winter your rooms are more invigorating, less stuffy. The same effect can be achieved with a radiant heating system such as a wood-burning stove or radiant floor heating. Radiant heating is 8 to 10 percent more efficient than convection heating. Less convection also means less floor-to-ceiling temperature stratification and less dust — an all-around healthier indoor environment.

You can also increase comfort and save energy by controlling the third variable governing comfort: air movement. Air movement should be prevented during winter because it increases heat loss from the body — and when the moving air is freezing-cold outside air entering through leaky windows and doors, the cooling effect is even more pronounced. Caulking, weather stripping, and other relatively simple measures can reduce air infiltration dramatically. Air movement must be encouraged during the warmer seasons, however, especially in humid climates. Here again our houses fail us. American homes are rarely sited to catch prevailing summer breezes or designed for cross-ventilation or to encourage the flow of hot air upward and out of the house. Installing a ceiling fan can increase air movement and make you feel cooler.

■ The Tools of Climate Control

The tools that determine whether a house works with the climate or against it need not be costly mechanical systems. They're all things that need to be considered anyway in designing a new house: the placement of windows, the location of trees, the way a house sits in relation to the sun and wind. Get these right, and your house will be both comfortable and energy-efficient. A good architect can help you choose the most aesthetically pleasing and energy-efficient combination of climate controls for your budget. If you're renovating an existing house, knowing what the ideal components are can help you compensate for bad design.

Siting

Almost anywhere you are in the United States, you want all the sun you can get. Sun makes your house warmer in winter and saves you money; it melts snow and ice off your driveway. This means that the ideal house will face south, or slightly east of south. A south-facing house will let the most sun in through the windows in winter, when you want it most.

Having plenty of sun in winter doesn't necessarily mean you'll fry in summer. Contrary to popular belief, southern exposures aren't extraordinarily hot in summer because the sun is so high in the sky. In fact, since the sun shines at your house out of the northern half of the sky for several hours of every summer day, northern exposures can be just as hot as any. In summer, the sun rises not in the east, as it does in winter, but in the northeast; it sets not in the west, but in the northwest. Because morning sun is more welcome after cool night temperatures, eastern exposures are better than western ones, in winter and summer. Houses that face west are worst: they get the most sunshine just when the air is hottest, in the late afternoon.

How much sun you get also depends on the slope of your land. Let's say you live in Pennsylvania, for example. If your lot is level, you'll receive an average amount of sunshine for your latitude. If you live on a lot that slopes moderately down toward the south, however, your house may be at the same angle to the sun as a house on level ground in South Caro-

Solar Electricity

Photovoltaic cells are the wave of the future, a truly elegant means of producing electricity on site. No more going to the ends of the earth for scarce fossil fuels. No more nuclear power plants. No more electric bills. The silicon-based cells simply make electricity out of sunlight.

Over the past twenty years, the price of photovoltaic (PV) panels — each panel comprises an array of cells — has dropped 100 percent. Today's panels are better constructed, and much of the auxiliary technology has improved greatly as well. PV systems are far from free — a new system big enough to free you from the power company (or get you "off the grid," in alternative-energy jargon) can cost anywhere from $5,000 to $50,000 — but with quality storage batteries, they can pay for themselves within a decade.

If the power lines are near your property, PV probably won't be cost-effective for you. However, solar electricity makes a lot of sense for a house in a remote area where the cost of hooking into the local grid is high. Solar electric panels are also commonly used on recreational vehicles and boats, to open and close security gates far from conventional power, and for outdoor lights.

It's important to keep in mind that PV cells produce 12-volt direct current (VDC), not the standard 110-volt alternating current (VAC). Most household appliances are available in VDC, but it's best to do without electrical resistance devices such as electric stoves and ovens (buy a propane version), toasters (use the stovetop's flame), electric charcoal lighters (go back to the old-fashioned match, newspaper, and kindling), electric coffee percolators (use manual drip filters), incandescent bulbs (switch to fluorescent or halogen bulbs), electric blankets (use a down comforter), and electric space heaters (design the house to be solar heated or use clean, efficient wood heaters). The biggest potential snarls, alas, are the hair-dryer — you'd be shocked at the cost of the PV array needed to run one — and the air-conditioner.

The main expense in PV systems is the number of panels required. With a few life-style changes, you can save enormous amounts of electricity and lower the cost of the system. A basic off-the-grid system should have at least four 48-watt PV panels, batteries to store the power for nights or rainy days, a charge controller to regulate the batteries, circuit breakers, some monitoring gauges, an inverter to convert the 12VDC power to 110VAC electricity if you want to keep some of your old appliances, and a backup generator. Such a system, according to Douglas Bath of Real Goods Trading Corporation, a national PV retailer, would cover the interior lighting, a television with a satellite receiver, a VCR, a low-powered microwave, a few kitchen appliances, a computer, a small vacuum cleaner, a sewing machine, a power drill, and about thirty minutes' worth of any other devices using 600 watts or less. The backup generator provides power during long overcast spells or when days are too short to build up much reserve electricity. More panels and extra battery storage reduce the need for the generator.

PV panels can be mounted flush with the roof line, provided that the house is oriented toward solar south and the angle of the roof is right (approximately your latitude plus or minus ten degrees); mounting the panels at a different angle will disturb the silhouette of the roof. Mounting panels on a tracking device will increase their efficiency by 20 to 40 percent, but these devices are large and awkward-looking and best cloistered out of view.

Photovoltaic cells play many less grandiose roles around the home. One common and very cost-effective PV device is the solar trickle battery charger for seldom-used cars, RVs, and boats. For large properties with an automatic gate at the driveway entry, a PV-powered gate controller may be cheaper than running 110VAC to the site.

The roof of the future will be covered with photovoltaic cells that make electricity out of sunlight. Solar electricity is already economical in remote areas where the cost of hooking into the local utility grid is high. Design: Solar Design Associates.

PV-powered outdoor lights have been a big disappointment. In many cases, they are more expensive than 12VDC fixtures with a transformer connected to 100VAC power and buried wiring. Many models have been plagued with problems. If conventional wiring isn't an option, be sure to find several people who own and are satisfied with the model you're considering.

Designing a PV System

There are three types of solar electric cells: crystalline, polycrystalline, and amorphous. Crystalline cells are made of slices from one large cultured silicon crystal; they are the most efficient and usually the most expensive. Polycrystalline cells are a "family" of cells. They're slightly less efficient than crystalline cells, which means that more panels are needed, but they're also cheaper per watt. Amorphous cells are noncrystalline; they're applied to a base in a process not unlike veneering or laminating and cost slightly less than crystalline cells. All three types are reliable and come with a five-, ten-, or twelve-year warranty.

If your house gets a daily average of four unobstructed hours of sunlight, preferably around noon, a PV system is probably a feasible option. To figure out how many panels you'll need, first add up the total number of watt-hours your home will require per day (this is simply the number of watts each appliance uses times the total average hours it will be used each day). Then divide the total watts you'll be consuming per day by the average number of hours of sunlight in your area (this information should be available from local PV suppliers) to get the total wattage needed. Next, choose the size panel you'd like to use, note its output in watts, and divide your total wattage figure by the panel's watt output to get the number of panels needed. To compensate for dust and bird droppings on the panels, inverter inefficiencies, and other variables, multiply the number of panels by 1.2 to get an adjusted total.

Another method of calculating how many panels you'll need involves using your current electrical usage as a basis for the PV system you plan to install. If you spend $100 per month for electricity that costs $.08 per kilowatt hour, you're using roughly 41,600 watt-hours per day. Assuming a good six hours of direct sunlight each day, you'll need to "collect" about 6,900 watts from the array of panels. This equals 115 panels each rated at 60 watts — or 138 after 115 is multiplied by 1.2 for an adjusted total. With an average cost of $400 per 60-watt panel, you'll spend $55,200 to match your current power needs — which is why you'll probably want to conserve energy and convert to more efficient appliances.

Batteries are the second-biggest expense in PV systems. Unfortunately, lead-based batteries are the only cost-effective option for most people. Some have a working life of five to seven years, while others will last ten to twelve years. Because lead is toxic, lead-based batteries must be properly disposed of. Nicad batteries last from thirty to forty years but are very expensive, and with their cadmium and nickel, they offer little advantage, as far as toxicity is concerned, over lead. To calculate the number of batteries you'll need, take the total amps generated by your PV system and multiply by 30 or 50 to get the size, in amphours. For example, if your panels generate a total of 15 amps, you'll need enough batteries to store between 450 and 750 amphours.

A tracking device costs $100 to $300 per panel but will greatly improve efficiency, enabling you to reduce the total number of panels needed by 20 to 40 percent.

Further Reading

Two good books on domestic photovoltaic systems are *The Solar Electric House: A Design Manual for Home-Scale Photovoltaic Power Systems* by Steven J. Strong with William G. Scheller (Emmaus, Pa.: Rodale, 1987) and *The New Solar Electric Home* by Joel Davidson (Ann Arbor: Aatec, 1987).

lina; at noon on a sunny day in March, it will feel like spring. But if your land slopes toward the north, your house may be at the same angle to the sun as northern Ontario, and March will still feel like winter. A south-facing slope in Pennsylvania won't have the same climate as South Carolina — noon-hour sunshine is only one of many elements involved — but spring will come sooner to your house, and many winter days will be less cold.

Windows

Window technology is improving so fast that the building industry is still trying to catch up with it (see "Sunspaces and Outdoor Rooms," pages 111–114). Today, for example, it's possible (for a price) to get super-energy-efficient windows for the north side of the house that will gain more heat than they lose in any American climate. It's also possible to find glazings with low "shading coefficients" — meaning that they let in light but deflect some of the sun's warming rays before they enter the house — to reduce the tremendous solar heat gains of west windows.

As always, you shouldn't be wary of south-facing windows. They permit the greatest solar heat gain during the heating season while allowing relatively little of the heat gain that leads to overheating in summer. There is one complicating factor in choosing glazing for south-facing windows: in order to admit the most solar heat in winter, the glass should have high shading coefficients, but the glazings with the best insulating values, or R-values, tend to be those with the *lowest* shading coefficients. This trade-off between more limited transmission of beneficial solar heat and greater resistance to heat loss should be balanced carefully.

Don't rush to replace existing windows without good reason. In recent years, the replacement window has been oversold as an energy-saving measure. If your house has single-paned windows, it makes sense to add storm windows in all but the mildest climates; single-pane glass has very little insulating value, losing as much as thirteen times more heat than an equal area of wall. True, storm windows aren't nearly as energy-efficient as some high-tech glazings now on the market, but they still dramatically increase a window's thermal efficiency. And when you look at the larger picture — more expensive replacement windows will take longer to pay for themselves, and your old windows will need to be disposed of somewhere — storm windows make better sense than replacement windows. (What's more, if you own an old house, removing the original windows can wreak havoc with its historic character.) To be effective, though, storm windows must be well made and carefully fitted and installed.

Walls and Roof

Different climates call for different walls and roofs. Today, high-tech materials and new techniques are producing walls and roofs that are both climate-specific and relatively inexpensive. In southern states, radiant barriers (usually reinforced aluminum foils) are incorporated into walls and roofs to reflect solar heat and prevent it from radiating into the house. In the Southeast, "vent-skin" construction helps expel the sun's heat from within the walls before it can get indoors (see page 100). In cold climates, double-stud construction and other techniques produce super-insulated walls that retain winter heat and keep out cold in even the most bone-chilling weather (see page 94). Designing walls and floors for thermal mass to collect and store solar heat can also help moderate climate.

Windbreaks

Wind control gives you a milder winter, an earlier spring, and a longer autumn. An evergreen windbreak makes a good buffer (see "Energy-Conserving Landscaping," pages 194–200), and an earth-bermed wall can serve the same function. Locating garages and porches on the north and west sides of the house also reduces the wind's effects. Storage areas, stairs, halls, and laundry and other rooms that don't

Shading Devices

In the days before air-conditioning, awnings and shutters were a common antidote to debilitating summer heat. These handsome tools for natural climate control come in a variety of styles and colors and should be used to shade any window exposed to direct sunlight.

Awnings

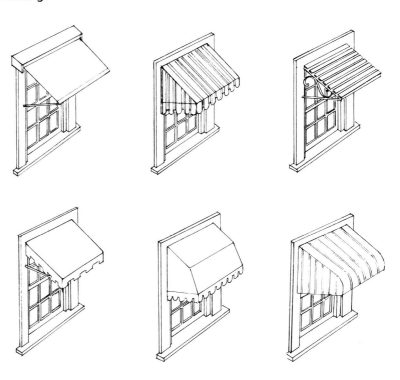

Exterior Blinds

Blinds are far more effective in blocking out hot summer sun when they are installed on the outside of windows, not the inside.

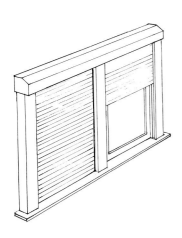

Shutters

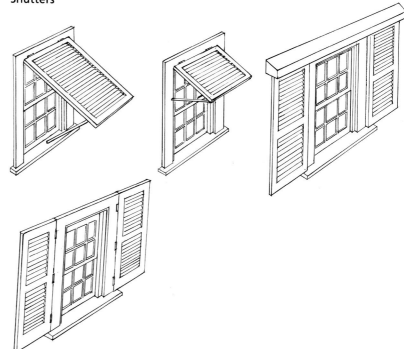

need to be heated to the same exacting standards as living areas may be placed on the windy side of the house to provide further protection.

Shading Devices

By shading a house's walls from the sun, pergolas and porches help keep the house cooler. Large shade trees also supply cooling shade; in cold and temperate climates, the trees should be deciduous so as not to block the warming winter sun. When placed on the east and west sides of the house in hot climates, closets, stairs, utility rooms, bathrooms, and garages make good buffer zones. Properly sized roof overhangs will shade windows in summer, when the sun is high, while still allowing the sun's warming rays to penetrate the house in winter. Exterior shades, awnings, or shutters can also provide shade for windows that are exposed to direct sunlight.

Ventilation

For comfort where summers are hot and humid, especially in the moist heat belt that extends from New York to New Orleans and Miami, a house must be sited to catch prevailing breezes and designed for ventilation — both cross-ventilation and upward ventilation, which allows warm air to flow up and out the top of the house while cooler night air flows in on the ground floor.

■ Climate-Sensitive Houses

Studies of housing design and climate distinguish among four major climate types: cool, temperate, hot and humid, and hot and arid. Climate does vary to some degree within each of these regions — indeed, California alone has been divided into seventeen climate zones by the California Energy Commission, which has recommended climate-specific building practices for each — but conditions are similar enough within each zone that it is possible to

A House for a Cool Climate

Maine architect John Silverio's Chimney House takes full advantage of the natural fuel available in thickly forested northern regions — wood. Living spaces wrap around a warming masonry core and are enclosed in a protective thermal shell. The house's small masonry heater burns hot, cleanly, and efficiently (see "Heating with Wood," pages 87–88), radiating heat slowly over a number of hours. The double walls and roof are stuffed with insulation to minimize the amount of wood that needs to be burned. A small gas furnace provides convenient backup heating.

In such a superinsulated house, air quality is an important concern. To keep indoor pollutants to a minimum, the Chimney House is made of natural materials, including pine boards for sheathing instead of plywood. Both the masonry heater and the

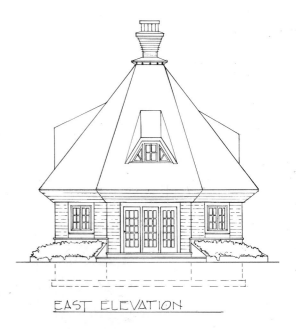

EAST ELEVATION

Unlike desert and prairie houses, which are low and sprawling, this house for the northern forests is tall and narrow. It is designed to be heated with wood.

gas furnace have their own sources of outside air to prevent fumes from backdrafting into the house. The open floor plan encourages good air circulation, and exhaust fans ventilate stale air and moisture from the bathroom and kitchen.

The house's tall, narrow design makes the most of rising warm air and the vertical character of the chimney. What's more, just as we pull our hats down over our ears and our collars up around our necks in cold weather, in this cool-climate house the roof is pulled down over the walls and the ground is pulled up around the base. The extended roof overhang and wide, sloping soffit protect the upper wall from the elements without blocking warming winter sun. The earthen berm forms an extra thermal seal around the foundation. Together the roof and bermed foundation protect nearly a third of the exterior wall from the howling winds and bitter cold of the house's northern clime.

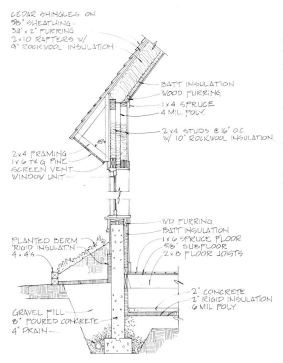

TYPICAL WALL SECTION

Double-stud construction makes the walls extremely energy-efficient. Two two-by-four studs and the space between them are packed with ten inches of mineral wool insulation, for a total R-value of 36. In the roof, two-by-ten rafters, rather than the more usual two-by-eights, accommodate extra insulation and are framed down to allow for still another layer of batt insulation, for a total R-value of 48.

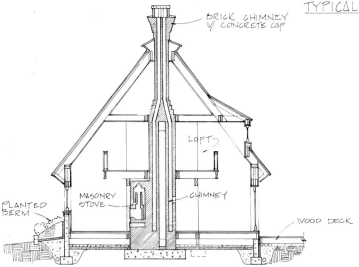

SECTION THROUGH CHIMNEY HOUSE

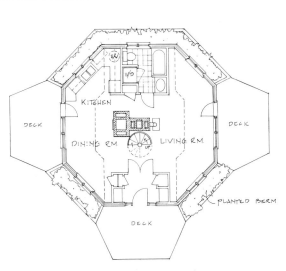

FIRST FLOOR PLAN

The house's design makes the most of rising warm air and the vertical character of the chimney.

Living spaces wrap around the central chimney and are enclosed by a superinsulated shell. The house is made of local woods: rough-cut spruce for framing, white cedar for shingles, and white pine for sheathing and interior finishes.

generalize somewhat about how to build a house well suited to its climate.

Houses for Cool Climates

Most of Canada falls in the cool climate zone. In the United States, this region stretches from Montana to Maine along the northern tier of states and includes most of the Rocky Mountain highlands. Not surprisingly, winter dominates throughout this zone, but in some areas, summers, though relatively short, are hot. Temperatures in cool climates can range from thirty degrees below zero to over a hundred degrees Fahrenheit. The amount of solar radiation generated — and hence the feasibility of solar technologies — varies greatly within the region.

The best homesites in cold areas are sheltered from winter winds and have maximum exposure to the warming sun. South-facing slopes provide the most solar radiation. Outdoor living areas on the south side of the house, with exterior walls and fences to create sun pockets and to block chilling winds, can extend the outdoor season by weeks or even months. If possible, the dwelling should be located on the leeward side of a hill or in any other area protected from cold northwest winter winds. In areas without such natural insulation, stands of trees should be saved or windbreaks planted on exposed sides. Earth-bermed north and west walls can also shelter the house from the wind.

If you can, steer clear of exposed ridges, hillcrests, north- or west-facing slopes, or any windy location or shallow cold pocket in the cool climate zone.

Well-insulated walls, ceilings, and floors and windows with high R-values are all extremely important in cool climates. (Windows and insulating materials are assigned "R-values," or resistance values, to indicate how well they resist conducting, and therefore losing, heat; the higher the R-value, the better.)

Make sure your house is designed and built so that air leakage is minimized around doors and windows, around switches and outlets, where the foundation meets the walls, and in other vulnerable areas. Entrance vestibules, or air locks, conserve energy.

In cold climates, new houses built to airtight, superinsulated standards, called superinsulated houses, are insulated to R-40 in the walls, R-60 in the ceiling, and R-30 in the basement. To prevent drafts, or air infiltration, plastic sheets are wrapped around the entire house, on the outside, underneath the siding.

In an energy-efficient house, ventilation is critical to ensure good indoor air quality. Most U.S. authorities recommend an air-exchange rate of 0.3, meaning that roughly one third of the home's air should be replaced by fresh outside air every hour. (Much research is being done in this area; this recommendation may change in the years to come.) Most houses rely on windows and air leaks in the building shell for ventilation, rather a hit-or-miss approach since the air-exchange rate — and therefore the indoor air quality — depends on such factors as wind velocity and the location of the leaks, factors that are out of your control. And leaky houses by definition are not energy-efficient. Superinsulated houses, in contrast, must have sophisticated ventilation systems to maintain high-quality indoor air — usually heat-recovery ventilators that exhaust stale, warm air from the house and transfer its heat to fresh, cold incoming air. As the Environmental Protection Agency moves to regulate indoor air quality in the 1990s, some form of controlled ventilation will probably be required or recommended for *all* houses. Whether your house is supertight or not, you should try to minimize indoor pollution by avoiding materials that release formaldehyde and other harmful fumes when you build, renovate, or redecorate (see the section on materials, pages 154–163).

When it comes to designing a house in those parts of the cool climate zone where summer is hot — the Minneapolis–St. Paul area, for example — it's important to pay some attention to moderating summer heat, but not as much as to moderating winter cold. One way to level off the climatic extremes is to put all or part of the house below ground. Save or plant deciduous trees to help shade the west side of the house, where most summer heat comes from. Casement windows, when thrown open in summer, can help scoop up a passing breeze.

For one architect's approach to design for a cool climate, see John Silverio's Chimney House, on pages 94–95.

Houses for Temperate Climates

The temperate zone spans the continent from southern New England and the Middle Atlantic to the Pacific coast of Canada. Although neither winter nor summer predominates, there's nonetheless a great deal of variation in the temperate belt. Year-round mild weather prevails in most of the Pacific Northwest, while in the southern Midwest, summer and winter are equally harsh, and southern New England is considered moderate. Winds in this climate zone tend to be from the northwest in winter and from the south in summer. Much of the temperate region has periods of high humidity and lots of precipitation. Mean daily solar radiation ranges from relatively low in southern New England and the Pacific Northwest to relatively high in northern California.

The best homesites in the temperate zone take maximum advantage of the winter sun and, in most areas, summer ventilation and shading. Gentle south-facing slopes are best for capturing the winter sun. The poorest sites are windy ridges, steep north- or west-facing slopes, and unventilated depressions.

The same techniques used in cool climates to shelter houses from wind and to keep warm air in and cold air out also apply to the temperate zone, though the levels of insulation generally don't have to be as high. Superinsulated houses are being built in the colder parts of the temperate zone, but the economic case for these houses isn't quite as strong as it is in cool climates — except, of course, where energy prices are unusually high.

In areas where summers get hot, it's impor-tant to provide for shading. Pay particular attention to the hot west wall and try to shade it with a deciduous tree, a hedge, a vine-covered trellis or pergola, or a porch. A garage on the west side of the house, with a breezeway connecting the two, is another excellent means of climate control.

In some temperate areas such as New York, Pennsylvania, and St. Louis, as in the Southeast, the old saw is only too true: it's not the heat that bothers you most, it's the humidity — in the form of warm, moist *air* imported from the tropics by southerly winds. Moist air is slow to pick up additional moisture from your skin, so you feel sticky and hot. In these areas especially, therefore, breeze is even more important than shade, so houses need lots of windows for cross-ventilation. And for those times when the breeze dies down, the house must be designed to take advantage of another principle of ventilation: hot air rises. Bedrooms should have not merely two windows but two windows at different levels, one way up high, just under the ceiling, and another down low, as close as possible to ground level. Warm air flows out the high window, and cooler air comes in the low one, even if there's no breeze at all. You can carry this principle even further by making your whole house a sort of chimney in which warm air rises and escapes from the top (see "Houses for Hot and Humid Climates," below). Remember, though, that a house in a temperate climate must be designed to close up and stop this upward flow of air in winter.

See pages 98–99 for architect Donald Watson's house for Rhode Island's temperate climate.

Houses for Hot and Humid Climates

The hot and humid climate region extends from the Carolinas to Florida to East Texas. High temperatures combined with high humidity levels can make the wrong house unlivable, not to mention expensive to cool. Wind direction tends to vary. Mean daily solar radiation is high, making this prime territory for solar hot water and other solar technologies.

A House for a Temperate Climate

On Block Island, as in other temperate areas, neither summer nor winter predominates. Winters can be bitter on this picturesque island off the Rhode Island coast, and high temperatures combined with humidity can make summers uncomfortable. Architect Donald Watson came up with a design that moderates both extremes and so in a sense is a house for all seasons.

Watson took cues from the local architecture and from the villas of Italian Renaissance architect Andrea Palladio, whose stylish designs are eminently suited to this specific climate and landscape. This house, for example, is built partially into a gentle south-facing slope to protect it from the winter storms that lash the island from the northeast and northwest. The upper-level belvedere traps solar heat in winter, floods the living room area with natural light, and provides 360-degree views of the surrounding terrain. Lots of south-facing windows and a sunroom also help warm the house in winter.

Summer is made more bearable by a shaded deck and a screened porch that captures southerly breezes. Because ventilation is crucial where summers are both hot and humid, the house takes advantage of another principle of physics, the fact that warm air rises. Even when there is no breeze, hot air flows up to the top of the belvedere and escapes, and as it does, cool air enters the windows on the lower levels.

SOUTH ELEVATION

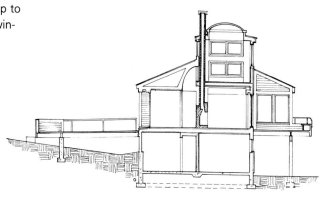

SECTION

Above right: The seaside house includes such Palladian touches as an upper-level belvedere, which traps solar heat in winter and helps vent away hot air in summer.

Right: To beat summer heat and humidity, the house is designed for upward ventilation. As hot air rises and escapes out the belvedere, cool replacement air enters the windows on the lower levels.

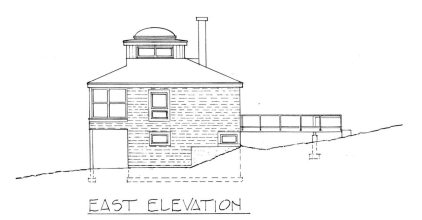

EAST ELEVATION

Left: This Block Island house, clad in cedar shingles bleached silvery gray by the sun and salt spray, moderates both winter cold and summer heat.

Opposite above: A south-facing sunroom provides passive solar heating during the cool season, while a screened porch on the southeast side catches summer breezes. Decks provide a further link between the house and the seascape.

In the hot and humid zone, you should by-pass sites without breezes or trees and those on hot, steep slopes. Instead, choose a spot in a mature woodland on any gentle slope, flat site, or breezy site. Your house should be oriented so that its long axis runs from east to west, leaving only its smallest sides exposed to the intense morning and afternoon sun.

Make the most of shading in your design, but don't be afraid of large south windows, even in this hot climate. Properly sized roof overhangs will shade them in summer but admit warming winter sun. Because there's so much diffuse solar radiation in the humid Southeast, large overhangs make sense for north, east, and west windows and walls as well. Where overhangs are impracticable, windows exposed to direct sun should have exterior shutters or awnings and glazing with low shading coefficients. Traditional wraparound verandas also keep the sun out of ground-floor rooms, and with overhangs or verandas, you can leave windows open during the frequent downpours in this climate zone.

Make sure there's plenty of vegetation to

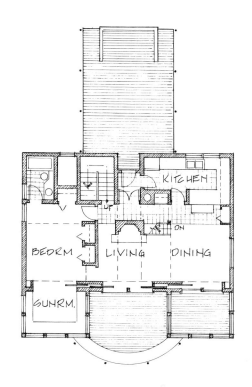

UPPER LEVEL PLAN

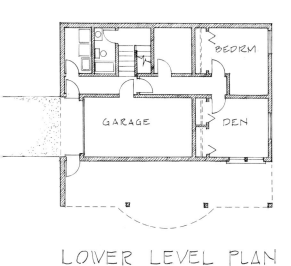

LOWER LEVEL PLAN

Left: The deep overhang of the large, sheltering roof shades this house in rural Arkansas. (For more on the house, see pages 57–59.)

The old Florida Cracker houses were topped by cupolas to vent away hot air. Warm air escapes through the many vents of the cupola-like upper story of this updated Cracker house. (For more on the house, see pages 54–56.)

shade the east and west sides of your house. Trees will shade the walls and portions of the roof, while lower vegetation that comes to within a few feet of the house will provide extra shade without obstructing air currents.

Most important, in a hot and humid climate you want to wash everything with air. Many southern plantation houses were comfortable because warm air rose to the top of their high-ceilinged rooms, while a multitude of tall windows encouraged ventilation. Even the attic was ventilated: hot air flowed up staircases and out of the attic and was replaced by cool air at the ground floor. Whether or not there was a breeze, there was always some air movement.

Make ventilation a high priority in your house, too. Build in cross-ventilation by placing operable windows on opposite walls. Better yet, open up living rooms to the breeze with folding or sliding outside walls that disappear entirely. You can keep the wall folded away much of the time, with only screens separating you from the great outdoors. High ceilings and operable clerestory windows (windows set way up high, where the walls meet the ceiling) together comprise a great system for expelling warm air. But be sure to put the clerestories on the leeward side of the house; if they face into the prevailing wind, the breeze will push the warm air back down into the house before it can escape. (Keep in mind, too, that high ceilings and clerestories can make your house more expensive to cool with air-conditioning. You may be able to divide your house into two or more separate zones — the living and dining areas, for example, can be naturally cooled, while the bedrooms can be tightly constructed and air-conditioned.) For maximum ventilation, you may even want to build your house on stilts, above the damp ground, like settlers in Florida and Louisiana did (see "An Updated Cracker House," pages 54–56, and "A House for a Hot and Humid Climate," at right.)

Remember the chic colors of TV's *Miami Vice*? In the tropics, pastel pinks and aquas are functional as well as fashionable. Your roof

A House for a Hot and Humid Climate

For his own house in Fort Myers, on Florida's hot, humid southwest Gulf coast, solar energy consultant Herb Beatty combined time-tested cooling techniques with state-of-the-art technology. Like Florida's early settlers, Beatty built his house on stilts for improved ventilation. The large screened porch on the southeast side of the second level is positioned to catch prevailing summer breezes, and an adjacent south-facing deck has two eight-foot sliding glass pocket doors, which provide a sixteen-foot opening for full ventilation of the living and dining rooms.

The house is also designed for upward ventilation. Hot air rises up through a central core area consisting of a utility room on the ground level and the kitchen on the second level, escaping through vents and operable windows in an upper-level loft. Cooler replacement air from the shaded area beneath the main floor is drawn in through adjustable louvers and awning windows.

A four-foot overhang protects the main living areas, which face south, from the intense summer sun, while allowing the lower winter sun to provide some solar heating. Because summer heat comes from the low morning and afternoon sun as well as the sun that beats down on the roof, Beatty used cutting-edge technology — radiant barriers and vent-skin construction in the roof and the east and west walls — to keep the house cool. The radiant barriers reflect most of the solar heat that strikes these surfaces away from the house, and the vent-skin construction exhausts hot air out of the wall and roof cavities.

Beatty's solar hot-water system makes the house even more energy-efficient. The hot-water storage tank is located in the utility room on the ground floor, where a photovoltaic-powered pump lifts the water to a solar collector atop the south loft roof.

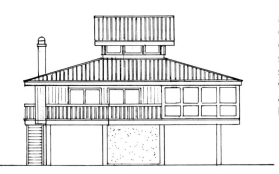

SOUTH ELEVATION

WEST ELEVATION

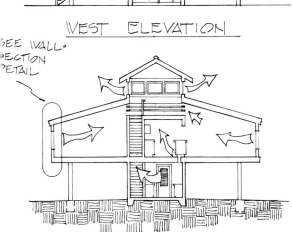

SECTION THROUGH HOUSE

Left: The four-foot roof overhang shades the large glass areas on the south side from the hot summer sun but allows the lower winter sun to penetrate and provide some solar heating.

Left: Because the low afternoon sun striking the west wall can overheat the house, there are few windows on that side.

Above right: The main living areas face south, while the large screened porch faces southeast to catch prevailing summer breezes. The sleeping areas are on the east and north, away from the late-afternoon sun.

Right: Even the walls and roof are ventilated, to expel solar heat from the building envelope before it can reach the interior of the house. Warm air rises through the vent spaces and exits through the space between the galvanized roofing and the flashing at the base of the loft wall. Cool replacement air enters through the screen at the foot of the vent-skin wall and through soffit vents. Reflective foil radiant barriers in the east and west walls and the roof reflect solar heat away from the house.

The house is designed for ventilation. The average wind velocity is measurably greater at the second-story living areas than at the ground floor. The raised living area also allows for enhanced upward ventilation, as hot air that rises up and out of the upper-level loft is replaced with cooler air from the shaded area at ground level.

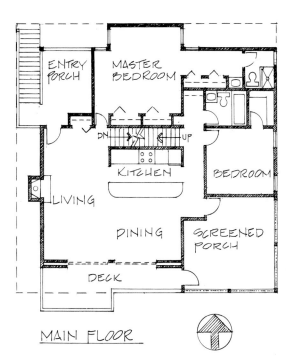

MAIN FLOOR

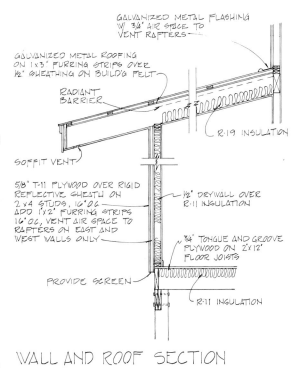

WALL AND ROOF SECTION

should be a light color — preferably white — and the exterior walls should also be light, as light colors throw much of the sun's heat back into the sky before it can get into your walls or roof and from there into your house.

Ventilating your walls and roof is almost as important as ventilating the inside of your house. Double-skinned, or vent-skin, construction expels the sun's heat from within the walls before it can reach the interior of the house. Warm air rises through the vent spaces and exits at the roof peak, while cooler replacement air enters through screens at the foot of the vent-skin walls and through soffit vents, at the bottom of the roof overhang. Vent-skin construction should also include insulation as well as radiant barriers on the east and west walls. Radiant barriers are particularly effective in roofs: according to research by the Florida Solar Energy Center, in areas where cooling is the overriding concern, a roof insulated to R-19 with a radiant barrier is more energy-conserving than a roof insulated to R-30 with no barrier.

Herb Beatty used radiant barriers, vent-skin construction, and other natural climate-control strategies in his South Florida house; see pages 100–101 for a closer view.

Houses for Hot and Arid Climates

The hot and arid climate zone extends from southern California through the heart of the Desert Southwest, through central Texas, and south throughout the Sonoran and Chihuahuan Desert areas of northern Mexico. This region is hot, like the Southeast, but also dry, like Arabia. In most areas, you can count on large temperature swings from day to night. The hot, arid zone gets more solar radiation than any other area in North America; solar technologies make a lot of sense here.

The best place for a house in this zone is either on flat land or on a shallow north- or southeast-facing slope. Try to stay away from sites that face southwest or northwest, those on steep north slopes, and those in hot valley bottoms.

A House for a Hot and Arid Climate

Adobe houses take advantage of the wide daily temperature swings in the Desert Southwest. The earthern walls are so thick that one day's worth of sun can't heat them through. After dark, the cold desert sky and air suck the heat right out again.

This economical house, designed by the Southwest Solaradobe School, incorporates modern passive solar techniques as well as traditional adobe construction. The walls are massive — ten inches thick on the south side, and fourteen inches thick on the north, east, and west, plus insulation and a protective outside layer of stucco. The house is oriented toward the south, which is the optimal passive solar design even for the desert. Because it was designed specifically for Albuquerque's relatively cool middle-elevation desert climate, the house includes a substantial amount of south-facing glazing for passive solar heat gain during the winter months. Backup heating is provided by the efficient Rumford fireplace in the bedroom (see "Heating with Wood," pages 87–88), while two flues between the living room and kitchen give the owners the option of adding wood-burning stoves to warm those areas. The transom windows — the small windows above the doors on the north, east, and west sides of the house — can be opened up on warm winter days to vent away excess passive solar heat.

A deep roof overhang shades the south windows in summer, when the sun is high in the sky, preventing the house from overheating. Photovoltaic-powered fans in the roof can be turned on when necessary to expel hot air, and an energy-efficient evaporative cooler provides additional relief during the hottest hours.

SOUTH ELEVATION

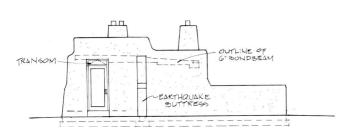

WEST ELEVATION

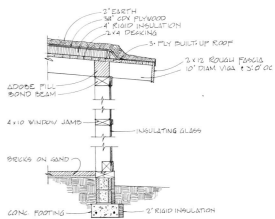

2" EARTH
3/4" CDX PLYWOOD
4" RIGID INSULATION
2 x 4 DECKING
3 PLY BUILT-UP ROOF
2 x 12 ROUGH FASCIA
10" DIAM VIGA @ 3'-0" OC
ADOBE FILL
BOND BEAM
4 x 10 WINDOW JAMB
INSULATING GLASS
BRICKS ON SAND
CONC. FOOTING
2" RIGID INSULATION

SOUTH WALL SECTION

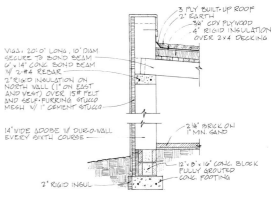

3 PLY BUILT-UP ROOF
2" EARTH
3/4" CDX PLYWOOD
4" RIGID INSULATION
OVER 2 x 4 DECKING
VIGA - 20'-0" LONG, 10" DIAM
SECURE TO BOND BEAM
6" x 14" CONC. BOND BEAM
W/ 2-#4 REBAR
2" RIGID INSULATION ON
NORTH WALL (1" ON EAST
AND WEST) OVER 15# FELT
AND SELF-FURRING STUCCO
MESH W/ 1" CEMENT STUCCO
14" WIDE ADOBE W/ DUR-O-WALL
EVERY SIXTH COURSE
2 1/4" BRICK ON
1" MIN. SAND
12" x 8" x 16" CONC. BLOCK
FULLY GROUTED
CONC. FOOTING
2" RIGID INSUL

NORTH WALL SECTION

Even in the desert, a house should face south. Designed for a relatively cool middle-elevation desert climate, this house has lots of south-facing glazing for passive solar heat gain in winter.

To limit heat gain from the hot, low afternoon sun, the west side of the house is narrow and has few windows.

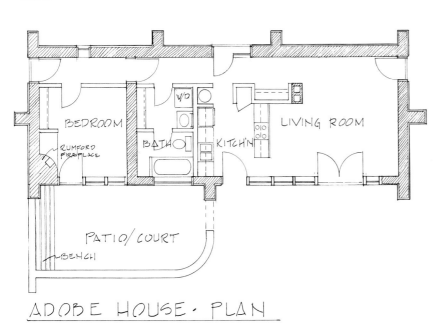

ADOBE HOUSE·PLAN

Left: The doors on the east and west sides of this compact one-bedroom home make it easy for the owners to add on at a later date. The curving garden wall gives the house character and creates a warm microclimate that extends the outdoor season.

Top: On the south side, the adobe wall is ten inches thick. Energy-efficient insulating glass is used in the south-facing windows, and low-E glass in the north-, east-, and west-facing ones. The deep roof overhang shades the south windows in summer, when the sun is high in the sky.

Above: The massive north wall consists of fourteen inches of adobe, two inches of rigid insulation, and a protective outside layer of stucco.

Earthen houses are especially suited to arid areas. The massive walls are energy-efficient and deaden noise, creating a hushed, soothing silence inside.

Throughout the hot and arid region, the sun comes up with a bang and shines hard all day, pouring down heat on your house. Unlike summer heat in the Southeast, which is primarily the result of warm, moist air, in the Desert Southwest heat comes directly from the sun. You don't need a lot of breeze, as you do in places with moist heat; sun control is everything.

How do you get sun and shade when and where you want them? The most important side of the house to shade is the west side. You can put a carport, garage, or deep porch on the west side to take the brunt of the sun. Use wing walls, which extend out beyond the living space, to shield south and north walls and windows from the slanting evening sun. Avoid windows on the west side. Period. If you can't live without them, make sure you have roll-down blinds, awnings, or shutters on the outside of the glass to keep the afternoon sun out. Keep bedrooms away from the west

side of the house, where they're subject to the most solar heat gain in the early evening — just before it's time to go to sleep. Plant trees and other vegetation to shade the east as well as the west wall. On the south side of the house, an overhanging roof will keep out the high summer sun and let in the low winter sun; a big overhang is best since it will need to shade your windows for more months of the year and more hours of the day than elsewhere. In fact, in the Desert Southwest, it makes sense to have a deep overhang all around.

In the desert, the ground is often bare and stony; when it's bombarded by the violent sunshine, it becomes extremely hot and sends out strong heat radiation of its own. Trees, shrubs, vines, and ground covers can keep the sun from bouncing off the ground and onto your house; tall garden walls or fences can likewise help reduce reradiation and ground glare.

The same clear, dry air that makes the days so hot also makes the nights cold. To take advantage of the wide daily temperature swings, inhabitants of the Desert Southwest once had a formula for a naturally elegant house. It had thick adobe walls so massive that the sun could shine on them all day long without appreciably heating them up. After dark, the cold night sky and cool desert air would drain most of the heat right out again.

This same principle can provide you with a comfortable house in the hot, arid region today. Adobe and rammed-earth houses that rely substantially on natural heating and cooling are still being built throughout the Desert Southwest. New Mexico has led the region in getting desert wall construction down to a science, rating the thermal performance of mass walls not just according to their thickness but also according to their orientation (whether the wall will face south, east, north, or west) and color. For example, in Tucson, Arizona, a light color such as a desert tan, which reflects heat, is the best choice for an exterior wall. In Taos, New Mexico, which is at a much higher elevation and gets substantially cooler, heat-absorbing darker colors such as reds and chocolates are optimal. New Mexico calls its rating system the effective U-factor (the U-factor is an indication of a material's ability to conduct heat).

Modern adobe designers have begun incorporating passive solar techniques in their designs, producing houses that are extremely energy-efficient. The amount of south-facing glass needed for solar heat gain varies widely depending on whether the house is at a low elevation (low desert), a middle elevation (middle desert), or a high elevation (high desert). In Taos, for instance, an area of glazing equal to about 24 percent of the total floor area is optimal. In Phoenix, you'd bake in a house with that much glass; in this low-desert location, about 4 percent is plenty.

Roof radiant barriers make good sense in the Desert Southwest, as they do in the Southeast. But reflective foils manufactured in a honeycomb configuration are a better choice for hot and arid climates.

For a look at a solaradobe house for Albuquerque's middle-desert climate, see pages 102–103.

How to Fix Your House's Climate

Okay, you already have a house, and natural climate control wasn't one of the builder's highest priorities. In all the climate regions it is possible to retrofit to get the ideal building, but in most cases it is probably neither practical nor cost-effective — unless, that is, you're doing extensive renovation anyway. But by taking some commonsense — and relatively inexpensive — measures, you can doctor your climate to save energy and ease your impact on the planet. The following checklists for the four climate regions suggest places to start.

A Retrofitter's Checklist for Cool Climates

In cool climates, the lion's share of your retrofitting dollar should go toward buttoning up for winter comfort. Most of your house's heat is lost through either conduction or air infiltration, so that's where you should focus your attention.

■ Plant an evergreen windbreak or windbreaks to buffer the house from prevailing cold winter winds.

■ Plug any air leaks. Drafts can account for 30 to 50 percent of the load on a heating system, even in a well-insulated house. A host of readily available publications will tell you how and where to caulk and weather-strip your house, so there's no need to address the subject in detail here. Be sure to make as great an effort to reduce sources of pollution in your home as you do to tighten up (see the section on materials, pages 154–163, for tips on which building products to use and which ones to avoid). Consider installing fans in bathrooms, a vented range hood in the kitchen, or even air-to-air heat exchangers for proper ventilation.

■ Add an airtight entryway, or air lock. It can double as a place to store muddy boots and wet slickers.

■ Add insulation. See the map on page 225 for minimum acceptable insulation levels in your area. Before you install insulation, however, consult a specialist to find out whether you have any moisture problems, what kind of vapor barrier you should put in, and how to provide for adequate ventilation.

■ Upgrade your windows. If your home has single-paned windows, add storm windows. If your windows have seriously deteriorated, don't operate easily, or can't be made to fit tightly in their frames, replace them with window units with the highest possible R-values.

■ If you're adding supplemental heating to a summer cottage or replacing the heating system in a year-round house, consider some form of radiant heating.

■ If you live in an area where summer is short but hot, see the checklists below for hot and humid and hot and arid climates for ideas on how to shade your house and provide natural ventilation.

A Naturally Elegant Renovation

Mary Otis Stevens of the Boston architectural firm Design Guild would be the first to say that you need not start from scratch to have a home that's both energy-efficient and beautiful. Indeed, Stevens has made environmental redesign a specialty. Recently she was asked to transform a quaint summer cottage in Rockport, Massachusetts, into a year-round dwelling. The Browns, whose family has owned the property since the 1920s, wanted to add a ground-floor bedroom and bath. Energy conservation was a high priority, as was preserving the house's historic Arts and Crafts character.

The site is a bluff overlooking the Atlantic on two sides, with a view of two lighthouses to the south and another to the northeast. Fog horns wail intermittently, warning mariners of the rocky Cape Ann headlands. Lobster buoys bob up and down with the swells, and an occasional lobster boat knifes through the water. Rugosa rose, orange daylilies, and other denizens of turn-of-the-century cottage gardens mark the point where the bluff falls sharply away to the sea.

The original cottage faced east, toward the ocean. To take advantage of the sun, Design Guild developed a new, east-west axis. On the east side, a new sunspace offers spectacular water views and a place to bask in the winter sunlight. Banks of windows were added to the existing living area, which projects out from the elongated south elevation and affords dramatic water views of its own. The new bedroom and bath wing is tucked behind and to the west of this space, providing a restful area sheltered from the full fury of the ocean.

The large glass areas on the south side admit warming winter sun; the windows are tight-fitting casements with energy-efficient low-emissivity glass. Ceramic tiles over concrete slabs in the added east and west wings store the solar heat and reradiate the warmth when the sun sets and temperatures dip.

The house's highly insulated walls and roof keep in the heat: the entire roof was reframed so that batt insulation and special energy-efficient sheathing could be added. New exterior walls were framed with two-by-sixes instead of two-by-fours to

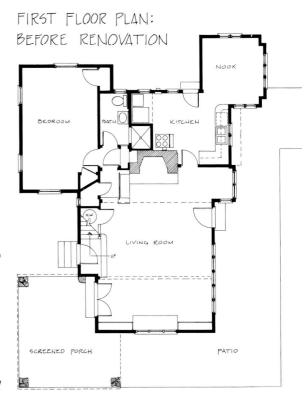

FIRST FLOOR PLAN:
BEFORE RENOVATION

make room for extra insulation. The small portions of existing wall that remain exposed were stripped back to the studs and packed with insulation. It was important to prevent unwanted breezes in both new and old construction by properly caulking around electrical boxes, pipes, grilles, and other openings. Both the walls and the roof were wrapped with Tyvek, which keeps out the wind but allows moisture through. All joints were taped to further minimize drafts.

The original summer house sat on brick and granite piers. Stones on site were used to fill gaps and create a continuous foundation that is thermally sealed and watertight. Crawl spaces were also insulated. Thanks to the high levels of insulation and the passive solar heat gain, two energy-efficient radiant fireplaces are all that is needed to heat the house in spring and fall (for a more detailed discussion of energy-efficient fireplace design, see "Heating with Wood," pages 87–88). An energy-conserving low-temperature, warm-water baseboard system provides supplemental heat in winter. An air-to-air heat exchanger ensures healthy indoor air

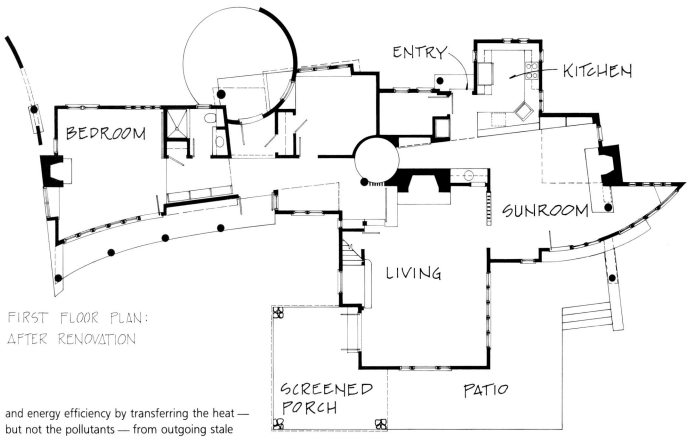

ENTRY

KITCHEN

BEDROOM

SUNROOM

LIVING

FIRST FLOOR PLAN:
AFTER RENOVATION

SCREENED
PORCH

PATIO

and energy efficiency by transferring the heat — but not the pollutants — from outgoing stale air to incoming fresh air.

Design Guild incorporated trellises and windscreens in the redesign to help moderate the climate on this exposed site and to give the Browns a choice of outdoor living spaces. A sliver of east gable wall was retained to provide a solar pocket and shelter a south-facing balcony off the bedroom on the second floor from northeast winds. On the other side of the gable wall is another balcony that faces east — the perfect place from which to watch the sun rise. The sunroom below opens onto a terrace that wraps around the east and south sides of the living room. Doors on the west side of the living area lead to the screened porch, positioned to catch summer breezes. A deep overhang curves around the south side of the ground-floor bedroom like the leech of a sail to keep out sun; a trellis that connects the columns of the adjoining brick terrace supplies additional shade.

Windows of various shapes and sizes on different levels do double duty, framing vistas and flooding every room with natural light. On the cold north side, glazing has been kept to a minimum; a number of small round and square windows impart visual interest as they let in soft daylight. The windows are also designed for optimal cross-ventilation in summer's heat.

When renovating older structures, Mary Otis Stevens and her colleagues strive to pick up elements of the vocabulary of the existing house without being enslaved by them. In the Brown house, they've preserved the intimate scale of the original turn-of-the-century cottage while adding what seems to be a series of nooks and crannies. At the same time, they've created a light and airy contemporary interior. The curvilinear forms in the new east and west wings contrast whimsically with the rectilinear geometry of the original house, and lend a nautical flavor quite fitting for an oceanfront site.

If your house has no roof overhang to shade windows from the high summer sun, you can grow one, using annual vines on a trellis.

■ In cold but sunny climates, consider solar hot-water heating.

A Retrofitter's Checklist for Temperate Climates

Because temperate climates have summers and winters that are either equally harsh or equally mild, you should divide your retrofitting dollars accordingly.

■ Plant an evergreen windbreak to shelter your house from prevailing winter winds.

■ Use deciduous trees and creepers to shade east and west walls and prevent overheating in summer.

■ Plug air leaks (see the checklist for cool climates above). Be sure to pay just as much attention to eliminating sources of pollution in your home and improving ventilation.

■ Add an airtight double entry, or air lock, to your most frequently used doorway.

■ Add insulation. See the map on page 225 for the minimum recommended R-values in your area. Consult an expert about how to provide adequate ventilation and prevent possible moisture problems.

■ Upgrade windows (see the checklist for cool climates above).

■ Consider installing an efficient radiant heating system if you're winterizing a summer cottage or replacing the heating system in your house.

■ If you live in the huge swath of the temperate belt where humidity is the main comfort problem in the summer months, see the checklist for hot and humid climates below, for ideas on how to shade your house and provide natural ventilation.

■ Consider installing a solar hot-water system.

A Retrofitter's Checklist for Hot and Humid Climates

If you live in the Southeast, ventilation and shading are your paramount concerns.

■ If you don't have adequate roof overhangs, make a "deciduous overhang" — a trellis with a thickly growing vine that loses its leaves in winter. It will shade south-facing windows from the summer sun and still let in warming winter sun.

■ Shade the hot east and west walls of your house with trees, trellises, trellised vines, or covered porches. Shade any window exposed to direct sun with awnings or shutters. (In the days before air-conditioning, awnings and shutters were an important antidote to debilitating summer heat — along with pitchers of cool lemonade. It's time for a revival.)

■ Take good care of tall trees around the house — they'll keep you cool by shading the roof. If there are no trees, plant some.

■ Repair or replace poorly designed windows. Caulk old windows and add storm windows if you live in an area where they will make a difference. It may make sense to replace some permanently closed windows with operable ones. Consider replacing jalousies and sliding windows with units that seal better. For north, east, and west windows, look for glazing with the lowest possible shading coefficients; in areas with colder winters, windows should have high R-values.

■ Allow for cross-ventilation by installing operable windows opposite each other on north and south walls. A whole-house fan installed in the attic can ventilate and cool a home in a location where there isn't enough wind to provide natural ventilation through windows alone; such fans are also effective in densely developed neighborhoods and in town houses. They work by pulling air in through windows and exhausting it through the ceiling and out the attic.

■ Use ceiling and oscillating fans to extend the natural ventilation season. Even when the air-conditioning is on, fans enable you to save energy and money by setting the thermostat two to six degrees higher, with no reduction in comfort. Avoid box fans, which eat up more energy.

■ Paint your house a pastel color, and be sure your roof is light, preferably white.

■ If you're reshingling your roof, add ridge vents at the peak and soffit vents at the eaves to cut heat flow into the house by up to 35 percent. A good rule of thumb is to provide two to three square feet of vent for every three hundred square feet of roof area.

■ Insulate your roof and add a radiant barrier. For minimum insulation levels in your area, see the map on page 225.

■ The infiltration of hot, humid air into your house through cracks and other openings is responsible for a major portion of your air-conditioning load. Caulk or seal as necessary. Consider installing an air lock for the entry you use most. As in any climate, remove sources of pollution in the home and improve ventilation as you tighten up.

■ Install exhaust fans to get rid of heat in the kitchen, bathroom, and laundry room. Put the hot-water tank and clothes washer and dryer in a space that isn't air-conditioned.

■ Do as much cooking as possible outdoors.

■ Investigate a solar hot-water system.

A Retrofitter's Checklist for Hot and Arid Climates

In the Desert Southwest, proper shading is everything.

In hot and humid areas, where ventilation is a paramount concern, ceiling fans are excellent climate-control tools. They extend the natural ventilation season and, when the air-conditioner is on, allow you to set the thermostat higher with no reduction in comfort, saving energy and money.

■ Use trees, shrubs, and creeping and climbing plants to reduce ground glare and shade east and west walls. Use them, too, to shade doorways and outdoor living areas to make the transition from inside to outside easier on your eyes.

■ Shade your west windows! They're vulnerable to tremendous solar heat gains year-round. Exterior roll-down blinds, awnings, or shutters are most effective.

■ Add wing walls on the west side of your house to shade north and south windows and walls from the low afternoon sun.

■ Shade your east windows from the summer sun with trees and tall shrubs.

■ Shade any south-facing windows that are exposed to direct summer sun with "deciduous overhangs" (see the checklist for hot and humid climates above) or canvas roof overhangs.

■ If you live in the high desert, add storm windows. If your windows don't fit well, replace them with units with high R-values to conserve heat. On east and west windows throughout the Desert Southwest, glazing with the lowest possible shading coefficients is best.

■ Infiltration of hot, humid air through cracks and into the house is responsible for a major portion of your air-conditioning load. Caulk or seal as necessary. Be sure to remove sources of pollution in the home and improve ventilation as you tighten up.

■ Insulate your roof and add a radiant barrier. For minimum insulation levels in your area, see the map on page 225.

■ In low desert areas, make sure that your walls and roof are light enough in color that they don't absorb solar heat. Avoid white, which is too harsh and reflective in a desert environment. Softer hues such as desert tans minimize heat gain and blend soothingly with the surrounding terrain. In high desert areas, chocolates and reddish browns, which absorb some heat, are recommended.

■ Add a fountain or other water feature that uses water sparingly. It will provide a psychological respite from the extreme desert climate as well as a bit of evaporative cooling, and will help ease the abrupt transition from the desert to the house.

■ Your region receives more solar radiation than any other in North America. Use a solar water heater. Photovoltaics may make sense as well.

■ Further Information

For more information on natural climate control, contact:

American Solar Energy Society, 2400 Central Avenue, Unit B-1, Boulder, Colorado 80301; (303) 443-3130. The ASES has publications on every aspect of solar energy, including active, passive, cooling, daylighting, and photovoltaics.

Conservation and Renewable Energy Inquiry and Referral Service, Box 8900, Silver Spring, Maryland 20907; (800) 523-2929. A good source of information on active and passive solar, energy conservation, and wood heating.

Earthbuilders' Encyclopedia, available from Southwest Solaradobe School, Sabinal Research Station, P.O. Box 153, Bosque, New Mexico 87006. The ultimate reference on adobe and rammed-earth houses, this is must reading for anyone contemplating building a house in the Desert Southwest. The Southwest Solaradobe School also offers classes for do-it-yourselfers.

Energy-Efficient Building Association, Technology Center, University of Southern Maine, Gorham, Maine 04038; (207) 780-5143. This is the best place to go for information on super-insulated houses.

Florida Solar Energy Center, Public Information Office, 300 State Road 401, Cape Canaveral, Florida 32920-4099; (407) 783-0300. The FSEC is by far the best source of information on passive cooling in hot and humid climates.

Massachusetts Audubon Society, Educational Resources Department, South Great Road, Lincoln, Massachusetts 01733; (617) 259-9500, ext. 7250. Several well-researched and useful booklets on weather stripping and insulating homes and apartments are available.

National Appropriate Technology Assistance Service, Butte, Montana; (800) 428-2525. NATAS is an indispensable source of information on climate-sensitive building. It even has a toll-free hotline.   ■

You don't have to live in a Frank Lloyd Wright house to enjoy an intimate relationship with the natural world. Any home in any climate can be linked more closely with nature by means of a sunspace or outdoor room — or even a carefully designed bank of windows that bathes a sitting room in sunlight and affords year-round views of the bird feeder and the garden.

■Windows

In the 1970s, we spent millions of dollars to seal up our houses and stuff our attics and walls with insulation. In the 1980s, we opened our houses to the daylight. Bay and bow windows were all the rage in remodelings. The Palladian window, a tall window with an arched top and long rectangular windows on either side, was de rigueur in remodelings as well as in new construction. The transom window returned. Bedroom skylights revealed constellations in the nighttime sky.

Not long ago, such fascination with windows would have sent heating bills through the roof. Twenty to 30 percent of an average home's heat is lost through its windows: it has been estimated that the amount of energy flowing out of America's windows is equivalent to the amount of oil flowing through the Alaska pipeline — 1.8 million barrels a day. But this astonishing waste of fuel is being slashed by a new generation of energy-saving windows that represent a quantum leap in glazing technology. We're fast approaching the day when windows are as good as walls — or better, because they enable us to open our cocoonlike shelters to the sunlight.

Window Shopping

Nowadays, sorting through window catalogs from more manufacturers with more materials, colors, sizes, shapes, glazings, and performance claims than ever is guaranteed to make your head spin. The most important thing is to choose a style that's appropriate for your house. Advertisers give do-it-yourselfers the impression that bays and greenhouses can be added anywhere — and the more the better. The results quite often are disastrous. Unbroken expanses of glass destroy the period charm of a New England Colonial, while small-paned, double-hung windows look silly in a Prairie house. The arrangement of windows is one of the most difficult aspects of house design; when in doubt, consult an architect.

Next, turn your attention to energy efficiency. The following are some things to look for.

Glazing Glazing, or the panes of glass and the way they're sandwiched together in the window sash, is more important than any other factor in determining a window's thermal efficiency. The standard of comparison is the old-fashioned single pane of glass, which is rated 1 on the R-value scale. (The R-value, whether in insulation or in windows, is the measure of a material's ability to keep heat from flowing into or out of a room.) Stock windows are available single-glazed or double-glazed; triple glazing may even be an option.

The term *double glazing* usually refers to insulating glass, which consists of two panes of

Metal window frames should have "thermal breaks" to reduce the amount of heat they conduct and therefore lose in winter and gain in summer. When equipped with thermal breaks, they rival the wood frame in energy efficiency.

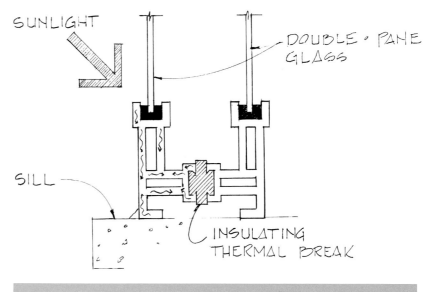

glass with a hermetically sealed airspace in between. Insulating glass achieves an R-2 rating by trapping the layer of air between the panes.

In the early 1980s, Southwall Technologies of Palo Alto, California, introduced the first "low-E," or low-emissivity, coating. Called Heat Mirror, it is a thin plastic film that is stretched inside the airspace between double panes of glass. With this innovation, glazing technology has taken off. Virtually every major manufacturer now offers a low-E window, either with coated glass or with a coated plastic film such as Heat Mirror suspended between two panes of glass. The beauty of a low-E coating, an atoms-thin layer of metal, is that it reflects heat but lets through almost all incoming light, with the exception of the ultraviolet rays that damage fabrics. Most low-E glass looks virtually clear, though some types do show a faint blue tint or iridescence.

Low-E windows make sense not only in cold climates but also in warm ones. In cold areas, heat trying to escape is reflected back into the house, increasing the window's energy efficiency to approximately R-3. The low-E coating is best applied to the outside of the inside pane, where it will also reduce heat gain through the window in summer.

In hot regions, a window's R-value is often less of a concern than its "shading coefficient," the measure of its ability to transmit solar heat. Low-E windows have the lowest possible shading coefficients because the coating deflects the sun's warming rays before they can enter the house. In this case the low-E coating is best applied to the *inside* of the *outside* pane. In warm climates, low-E makes the most sense in windows facing east and west, as those are the ones that transmit the most solar heat in summer; most south-facing windows transmit less solar heat in summer because the sun is so high in the sky. Except in the hottest climates, there isn't much point in spending more money for the lower shading coefficients of low-E for north-facing windows, either.

Some low-E windows use argon gas instead of air in the space between the panes, boosting the window's energy rating to R-4 or more. Argon conducts heat less readily than air. It is an environmentally safe, cheap, and widely available gas that comprises about 1 percent of the earth's atmosphere. European manufacturers have been filling their windows with argon for years. In the United States, however, there has been some concern that the gas will leak out of the window and eventually be replaced with plain air, leaving the window only as good as regular low-E glazing. Many window manufacturers fill their units with argon at no extra cost, while others offer a twenty-year guarantee against leakage.

Improvements in glazing technology continue at a breathtaking pace. So-called superwindows with R-ratings as high as 8 or 10 are already available. One version, produced by Alpen, Inc., in Boulder, Colorado, and rated R-10, comprises two layers of Heat Mirror suspended between two panes of glass, one with a low-E coating, with krypton gas between the panes. (Krypton, another environmentally safe gas, conducts even less heat than argon.) The window looks like ordinary double glazing but is more than five times more energy-efficient. According to the Lawrence Berkeley Laboratory in California, in virtually any American climate, an R-7 or better window will gain more winter heat than it loses, even facing north.

Frame and Sash   Both frame and sash play a substantial role in a window's thermal efficiency. The sash consists of the vertical and horizontal pieces of wood, metal, or plastic into which the glass is set. The sash fits into the frame, which comprises the jambs and sill that surround the window opening. Wood is the traditional material for both sash and frame, and it's by far the most energy-efficient as well — about 70 percent better than vinyl, the next-best alternative, and many times better than aluminum.

Of course, wood is also vulnerable to weather, and must be coated with a potentially toxic stain or paint every few years. Windows made of weather-resistant species such as mahogany don't have to be painted or stained as often, but they're expensive and may be made of trees from threatened rain forests or temperate forests. Some metal frames have "thermal breaks" to reduce the amount of heat they conduct and therefore lose; these rival wood frames for thermal efficiency.

How a sash works — that is, whether it slides or swings — also affects its thermal performance. The least energy-efficient windows are sliding ones such as the double-hung variety, the most popular window in America: because they must be free to slide, these sashes can't make an airtight seal with the window frame. Swinging windows such as casements and awnings are more energy-efficient because the weather stripping is fully compressed on all four sides when the window is closed.

Fixed windows are even more airtight than swinging ones, but they provide no ventilation. A combination of fixed and ventilating windows generally is the best way to go, and most window manufacturers offer a variety of options. Different-shaped windows — from trapezoids to octagons to ellipses — are available to pair with the conventional rectangle, or they can be used alone to add charm to an undistinguished space or frame a view.

Evaluating Claims Manufacturers tend to tout the R-value of the glazing alone when they talk about the energy efficiency of their windows. Yet for all the reasons described above, the R-value of the glass may be quite different from the R-value of the window as a whole (which includes not only the glass but also the frame, the sash, and other components). Be sure to ask about the overall R-value of the window assembly.

Comparing manufacturers' claims about the thermal performance of their windows can be confusing because there is no national standard for testing and evaluation. Uniform testing standards are currently in the works; it is hoped that in addition to making it easier to

During the day the sun streams through the greenhouselike south facade of this solar house, providing heat. The energy-efficient glass is double-glazed, with a thin layer of plastic and argon gas between the panes to keep in the heat when night falls and temperatures plummet. (For more on the house, see pages 67–69.)

compare product claims, they may also lead to an energy-performance label like the ones on refrigerators and other home appliances. But it will be several years before the system is in place.

For now, look for tests performed by independent laboratories using the test standard specified by the American Architectural Manufacturers Association (AAMA 1503.1-1988). The 1988 test specifies standard sizes, wind speeds, and wind directions, so the results can be compared. If the windows you're considering were tested before 1988, the earlier AAMA test standards are still better than nothing.

Purchase Price vs. Lifetime Cost　Don't just look at the ticket price when you're shopping for windows; be sure to factor in the future energy savings that the various kinds of insulating windows will offer. For example, low-E windows typically cost 10 to 15 percent more than ordinary double glazing, but the savings on heating and cooling costs can quickly justify the higher initial cost. It has been estimated, for instance, that over their lifetime, low-E windows installed in an average-sized home in Chicago would save $3,480 in energy costs over conventional double-pane windows. On a house in the Sunbelt, low-E windows could cut the cost of air-conditioning by $100 a year. The lifetime cost of new windows will differ somewhat according to the climate and the cost of energy in your area.

On a national scale, the new glazing technology could produce impressive savings in energy and heating and cooling bills. According to the Lawrence Berkeley Laboratory, if low-E windows were installed in all new homes and additions in the United States, the resultant energy savings would exceed $225 million a year.

■ Sunspaces

Installing a sunspace or glass addition is a particularly effective way of extending your house into the landscape. In recent years, sunspaces have become increasingly popular as rooms for living, exercising, soaking in hot tubs, and entertaining guests by candlelight under a moonlit sky. These solariums differ from the greenhouses of the 1970s in one important respect: they're designed primarily for people, not for plants or solar-energy collection. The emphasis is on comfort, outdoor views, and (especially for Northerners) the sun itself.

In northern climes, winters seem endless. The land wakes up slowly in spring and has a short, frantic burst of growth in summer before retreating again with a blaze of foliage in fall. In frigid climates, a sunspace bathes a part of the home in sunlight when it's needed most. A sunroom can give you a new outlook on winter, both literally and figuratively.

Everyone wants a sunspace that will heat his or her home *and* overflow with beautiful and fragrant plants *and* be the most spectacular room in the house. However, we've learned a lot of lessons about sunspaces since the 1970s — often the hard way.

Lesson number one is that greenhouses designed solely to collect solar heat rarely work. In the 1970s and early 1980s, many passive solar houses included an attached greenhouse. The theory was that sunlight would warm the space, be stored in the structure's mass, and then be circulated via convection to the rest of the house. Vents high on the wall of the greenhouse would filter warm air into the house, and the cooler air from the house would flow through lower vents and be reheated. The attached greenhouse was also supposed to enhance summer cooling by venting hot air to the outside and drawing cooler air in through the house from its shady north side. That was the theory, at least. In practice, attached greenhouses in cold climates often

ily for people. The key to designing a successful glass addition is to decide what you want most and then try to fit any other functions around that. If you decide that living space is what you want, for example, you can always squeeze in some houseplants, grow seedlings for the garden on a windowsill, and vent some hot air to the house on sunny days.

Another thing to consider is the sunspace's effect on the exterior of your home. Ideally, a sunspace should form a transitional space, with the solid mass of the house giving way to the transparent glass structure, then perhaps to a pergola or deck leading to a designed kitchen garden or garden room, and finally to the natural landscape. The different degrees of enclosure ease the transition from nature to architecture and offer a variety of areas for use at different times of the year. Extending the same flooring — whether flagstone, tile, or another material — out of the sunspace and into the garden enhances the sense of connection.

As with windows, let your home's style guide your choice of sunspaces. We've come a long way since the homely plywood and polyethylene solar greenhouses of the 1970s. Off-the-shelf greenhouse units are generally cheaper than custom designs and come in a variety of styles, from glorified bay windows three feet deep and eight feet long, which can enlarge an existing room, to two-story solariums big enough to fit a swimming pool inside. The Victorian conservatory, with its tiny panes and slender glazing bars that lend crystalline charm and cast intricate patterns of light, is still the best choice for many late-nineteenth-century houses, but these extravaganzas in glass are as expensive today as they were a century ago. A more modest design that alludes to the exquisitely detailed nineteenth-century conservatory — say, one with a pointed or ogee arch roof — might do almost as well.

Greenhouse units with wooden frames, when stained, can make handsome, natural-

If your goal is simply a bright, cheerful room, you may be better off with a conventionally framed addition than with a greenhouse. This kind of sunroom can have a pleasing array of insulating windows and a ceiling pierced with skylights. Design: South Mountain Company.

dragged their houses along on an inevitable daily thermal roller-coaster ride, as nighttime temperatures took a forty-degree nosedive. Even in milder climates, air circulation was frequently inadequate, resulting in cool spots in the house. And in climates with humid winters, such as coastal northern California, Oregon, and Washington, the extra humidity from the greenhouse plants increased the growth of molds and fungi, a nuisance and potential health risk, and sometimes even rotted the wall between the greenhouse and the house, necessitating costly repairs.

Lesson number two is that a sunspace designed primarily for plants differs in some very important respects from one designed primar-

Sunspaces are a staple of the naturally elegant home — even modest versions such as this mobile home. Architect: J. Carson Bowler.

looking extensions, particularly for more contemporary house designs. Keep in mind, though, that the wooden frames are often made from redwood and cedar cut from disappearing old-growth forests in the Pacific Northwest and British Columbia (see "Materials," pages 154–163). If you must use such a species, try to find a source of recycled lumber, or at least make sure that the structure is designed, constructed, and maintained so that it will last as long as it would take to grow another tree. Most manufacturers offer models with slim aluminum skeletons with dark bronze or white baked-enamel finishes; these are almost maintenance-free, and the white finish is the best match for many house styles, including Georgian and Colonial Revival.

Not only are the new sunspaces more elegant than their 1970s counterparts, they're also more comfortable and economical, utilizing everything we've learned about energy-efficient construction and high-tech glazing. The best units are virtually sealed against air or water leaks, and the metal-framed versions have thermal breaks to minimize heat loss. In addition, most sunspace manufacturers now offer glazing options to suit nearly any climate and budget, including single-glazed, insulating glass, low-E glazings, and even bronze-coated glass, which provides shade. The high-tech glazing options conserve energy in heated sunspaces used as living space, an important consideration, but all of them restrict solar transmission to some degree, making them less ideal for a greenhouse intended for plants (see "The Sunspace as Greenhouse," pages 118–119). And their low shading coefficients mean that the sunspace will be less effective as a passive solar heating device for your home. Rigid plastics are another option, but for optimum transparency, nothing beats glass.

The ideal exposure for most sunspaces is south, for maximum winter sun. However, a sunspace intended only for living, and not inhabited by sun-cravers from northern climes, need not face south; in fact, in a glass addition facing north or east, the quality of light will be less harsh, and glare will be less of a problem.

The Sunspace as Living Space

If your goal is simply a bright, cheerful room, you may be better off with a conventionally framed room addition with a pleasing array of insulating windows. This kind of sunroom will probably lose more energy than it gains and limit what you can grow to the typical low-light ficus or philodendron, but it will be cheaper to build.

If you decide on a true glass addition, the first requirement is an exterior-grade wall and door to separate it from the rest of the house. This means that your sunspace will be more than a porch but less than a living room. However, it will also be a lot more energy-efficient: on a sunny winter day, you can open the door and bask in the balmy heat, and at night, when the temperature in the greenhouse drops forty degrees, you can close the door and stay snug. As a compromise, you could install French doors or, even better, sliding pocket doors, which would be totally invisible and out of the way when opened. You could also increase the number of windows in the wall separating the two spaces or put a wall of insulating glass between them.

In most parts of the country, a walled-off solarium will be either self-sufficient or use no more than a little backup heat. It may even slightly lower your home heating costs by reducing heat loss through the wall to which it is attached.

The second major consideration for a glass addition used primarily as living space is whether or not to have overhead glazing. Roof glazing admits a lot more sunlight and thus makes the sunspace more hospitable to plants, but it also makes it hotter in summer and colder in winter and therefore less comfortable for people. Some solarium units omit overhead glass entirely, while others minimize its use by piercing a solid roof with skylights.

You should also make provisions for shading. In most areas, greenhouses overheat in summer, and even on a sunny winter day when outdoor temperatures fall well below freezing, a sunspace can be uncomfortably bright. A canopy of vines (preferably deciduous perennials or annuals, which grow in summer but die back in fall) can help beat summer heat and cast delightful dappled light. Adjustable blinds or canvas shades can help cut down on glare, but in order to cut down on heat as well, they must be installed outside the glass, not inside.

Ventilation is critical in any kind of sunspace. If possible, place doors and windows where they can capture prevailing summer breezes. Old-fashioned horticultural greenhouses made the most of natural airflow with rows of awning windows located low on the side walls and rows of glass panels along the ridge of the roof, all of which could be opened by means of cranks. The low vents admitted cool, fresh air, and the roof vents let hot air out. This is still the best way to ventilate a greenhouse. More sophisticated systems, such as louvered vents that work in conjunction with electric fans automatically activated by a thermostat and/or humidistat, are also available.

Sunroom flooring should be durable, moisture-proof, and easy to clean. Ceramic tiles are handsome, tough, and simple to main-

Banks of windows and a skylight flood this Martha's Vineyard kitchen with natural light and link it to the outdoors. Ceramic tiles on a concrete slab floor store solar heat and radiate it when night falls. Design: South Mountain Company.

tain, and they can be extended into the garden to link indoors with outdoors. What's more, ceramic tiles on a concrete slab add to the passive solar potential of your sunspace: during the day, they absorb heat, which helps keep the sunroom warm when temperatures begin to taper off at night.

If you want to beef up your sunspace's passive solar potential, there are several measures you can take to encourage a natural convection cycle between the house and the sunspace. Closable vents high on the old exterior wall will allow warm air to flow into the house, and additional vents near the floor will let cool air from the house flow into the sunspace. A thermostatically controlled fan in an upper vent can speed up the process. On cold or cloudy days or nights, a reversible fan can be used to force warm air from the house into the sunroom to keep it comfortable.

The Sunspace as Greenhouse

A sunspace can provide the kind of environments in which many plants thrive. Suddenly you will be able to grow expensive plants that were once available only from the florist — fragrant freesia and jasmine, for instance, or citrus trees and bulbs forced for midwinter bloom. If the greenhouse is kept warm enough, you can grow orchids and other spectacular tropical plants or enough fresh herbs and vegetables to feed your family all winter long. In sunny climates, even tomatoes are possible in the depths of winter.

Before you plunge headlong into greenhouse gardening, however, ask yourself how many plants you really want to grow. Be brutally honest. Tending a greenhouse can easily become a dreaded chore: there's always a plant that needs to be pinched back or repotted, or pests wreaking some kind of havoc. If your plant collection is small and you want to keep it that way, a greenhouse window is a far less expensive and demanding alternative to a full-sized greenhouse.

A greenhouse that is to be used primarily for growing must be designed with the needs of plants — not human needs or maximum heat collection — foremost in mind. The first big difference between a sunspace used mainly as living space and one used mainly for plants is that with the latter, you can't just shut the door when temperatures plummet. Wild temperature swings put a lot of stress on most plants; ideally, the day and night temperatures shouldn't be more than fifteen or twenty degrees apart. That means that in most climates, backup heat is necessary, while in hot, dry climates, an evaporative cooling unit or humidifier may be needed.

The first thing you should do when planning a greenhouse is compile a wish-list of the plants you've always longed to grow, grouped according to their preferences for heat and light. The typical greenhouse has one dominant growing climate, and you should be sure to tailor yours to the optimal conditions for the majority of your plants.

Camellias, cyclamen, and hardy bulbs, for example, prefer a relatively cool environment, while almost all edible plants require either bright sunlight and warmth (tomatoes, cucumbers, melons) or moderate light and cooler temperatures (broccoli, spinach, lettuce). A serious edible landscaper can grow an astonishing variety of plants indoors by designing a greenhouse that includes as many microclimates as possible (see "The Sunspace as Bioshelter" below), but even the average greenhouse can accommodate a considerable range of plants if they are placed in different positions. It's warmer against the back wall, for example, than it is close to the glass, and higher levels tend to be warmer than lower ones.

Because the amount of light the greenhouse receives is such an important factor, its placement is critical. Ideally, you should locate the greenhouse in a spot that gets the maximum number of hours of winter sun without any shading from buildings or trees. (Even a tree with bare branches can reduce the available light by as much as 50 percent.) For best exposure to the sun's rays, the greenhouse should face within 25 degrees east or west of solar south. (Just as sailors must know the difference between true north and magnetic north, greenhouse gardeners must know the difference between solar south and magnetic south, which is the south that's indicated on a compass. Check declination charts at your local library.)

Because different glazing materials transmit differing amounts of light, glazing is another critical consideration in a horticultural greenhouse. While energy-efficient double glazing makes economic sense in all but the mildest climates, low-E and other high-tech glazings should not be used because they block too much of the available light. Single glazing transmits approximately 89 percent of available light, and double glazing about 80 percent; glazing that reduces light transmission below 80 percent does not let in enough light for most flowering plants.

Because light transmission is more important in a greenhouse than visual clarity, rigid plastic glazings are becoming increasingly popular. They're lightweight, don't break easily, and cast a diffuse light. However, some plastics degrade when exposed to ultraviolet rays, becoming brittle and less transparent over time. Acrylics are one exception, but they're expensive. Be sure to study the advantages and disadvantages of the various plastic glazings carefully before making your choice.

To provide maximum light, most horticultural greenhouses should have glazing overhead as well as in the side walls, to admit sunlight from the east and west during the early morning and late afternoon.

To moderate the wild temperature swings that will accompany all this glazing, try to design in as much thermal mass as possible — put down tile floors on a concrete slab, for example, and build masonry growing beds. The thermal mass will absorb the daytime solar heat and release it slowly, reducing the need for supplemental nighttime heat. If backup heat is needed, the simplest way to provide it is with an electric heater, while the most reli-able way is to extend your home's existing heating system into the greenhouse.

The cheapest way to ventilate your greenhouse is to take advantage of the natural convection provided by ridge vents combined with awning vents located low in the greenhouse's side walls. Automatic vent openers set off by a thermostat can be a vital safety valve when no one's at home. Exhaust fans can quickly replace hot, stale air with fresh outside air. Because the vents will be closed in cold weather to conserve energy, in areas with humid winters, fans are essential to promote constant air circulation and prevent damping off and other plant problems.

Shading may be required on sunny summer days to prevent harsh rays from incinerating tender foliage. Some gardeners apply white-wash or shade cloths to their glass greenhouses in summer, but both reduce light regardless of the weather and must be removed every fall. Blinds are more useful because they can be rolled up on cloudy days.

The best finishes for these utilitarian sunspaces are those that readily reflect light, are easy to clean and maintain, and are resistant to rot. Finally, don't forget to design in a door to the garden — tramping through the house with dirty pots and dripping watering cans soon becomes a nuisance.

The Sunspace as Bioshelter

Over the past twenty years, the New Alchemy Institute and the Great Work company, both on Cape Cod, Massachusetts, have been pioneers in the development of sunspaces called bioshelters. A miniature ecosystem that includes people, animals, and plants, a bioshelter enables a family to produce a significant amount of food year-round. In cold climates, bioshelters can be an important part of the larger edible landscape.

Bioshelters can be small or large, elaborate or relatively simple. Like conventional greenhouses, they can be added to the south side of a house. The major difference between a bioshelter and an ordinary greenhouse is that the former is both biologically diverse and ecologically balanced.

A case in point is the bioshelter of Earle Barnhart and Hilde Maingay of the Great Work company. Attached to their Cape Cod–style house, it provides the indoor living spaces with passive solar heat gain and supplies fresh, pesticide-free food through the winter months. Inside the bioshelter are not only vegetables and fruits but also fish, which live in water-filled translucent tanks about three feet in diameter. The fish subsist on the algae that forms in the solar tanks and fertilize the lettuce and watercress growing rafted on the surface. Outside the bioshelter, a variety of plants offer shade, flowers, food, or fragrance in the warmer months.

One of the most important design determinants of a bioshelter is thermal mass. Different kinds of thermal storage add to the structure's energy efficiency and provide for the many microclimates that nurture the bioshelter's diverse animals and plants; a high masonry north wall, for instance, creates a vertical warm zone for climbing and espaliered plants such as grapes and figs. Raised masonry beds on different levels add to the thermal mass; the stepped levels create more microclimates and add visual interest.

Water in ponds and fish tanks is another source of thermal mass. Experience has shown that above-ground transparent ponds are more efficient than in-ground ponds because they absorb more low-angle winter sunlight; they're also handier for indoor aquaculture.

The soil itself is still another means of thermal storage. Rather than being planted in pots, plants in a bioshelter are typically set in soil that is separated from the earth outside by insulated walls that extend below the frost line. This not only provides passive thermal mass but also enhances the biological diversity of the mini-ecosystem, making it more hospitable to earthworms and a variety of soil organisms. What's more, it allows fruit trees or other large trees with sizable root systems to be included in the bioshelter. These large plantings ensure

summer shade, alleviating heat buildup somewhat and reducing the load on the ventilation system.

Heating, cooling, and ventilation are particularly important in a bioshelter. Air currents that encourage pollination and the exchange of water vapor and carbon dioxide across leaf surfaces can be enhanced by means of mechanically triggered fans and vents. Depending upon the size and complexity of the bioshelter, as well as the climate, one or more thermostats may also be needed to regulate heating and cooling — or the bioshelter may be hooked into the home's heating and cooling system.

◼ Cooling Arbors

Anyone who follows the latest home-decorating trends knows that the porch, an outdoor room that first appeared in mid-nineteenth-century America, is making a comeback. If home magazines are any indication, the porch — ignored for decades and now lavished with well-worn wicker furniture, plump pillows covered in linen and chintz, and vases of fresh flowers — is one of our favorite rooms. Now it's time to revive another venerable outdoor room: the arbor.

An arbor is to a warm area what a sunspace is to a colder clime. While sunspaces enable Northerners to bask in sunlight in the depths of winter and commune with nature through transparent walls, arbors allow Southerners to enjoy soft breezes protected from the sun's scorching heat by a leafy canopy. Cooling arbors have in fact proven so versatile that they've been adopted by inhabitants of temperate climates as well.

An arbor, quite simply, is a bower formed by trees, shrubs, or vines supported by latticework, columns, or other minimal structural elements. A pergola is an arbor comprising a double row of posts or pillars with joists above, curtained with the obligatory climbing plants. An arcade is an arbor with a rounded, or arched, top. A pavilion is an arbor with a

The Sunspace as Bioshelter

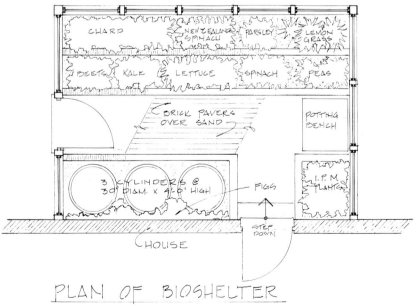

PLAN OF BIOSHELTER

A bioshelter is a miniature ecosystem that can produce a significant amount of food year-round. A high masonry north wall creates a vertical warm zone for espaliered grapes or figs. Raised masonry beds on different levels provide thermal mass for heat storage. Water in large cylindrical tanks is another source of thermal mass. The tanks can also be used for indoor aquaculture, and edible plants can be rafted on the surface. Instead of being planted in pots, plants in a bioshelter are placed in soil that is sepa-rated from the earth outside by insulated walls that extend below the frost line, making it more hospitable to a variety of soil organisms. The I.P.M. (integrated pest management) plants harbor beneficial insects that prey on pests.

The bioshelter in the photograph above is at the Burnham house in New Marlborough, Massachusetts. (For more on the house, see pages 51–53.)

This Texas ranch house is surrounded by an arbor topped by a leafy canopy of grapes for cooling shade. (For more on the house, see pages 60–62.)

sunlight and ever-shifting shadows can quite poetically ease the passage from darkness to light. In bungalows and other post-Victorian homes, they often run along one side of the house or wrap around two or more sides, like a leafy bower of a porch. They can also make a graceful transition from kitchen garden to natural landscape or from house to garage or gazebo. They can help define the boundaries of a garden room or coax strollers toward a breathtaking view.

Arbors are far from being mere aesthetic conceits, however; they're practical, too. They can shade the house from the blistering rays of the sun, and what's more, they provide a cool, inviting space for reading, dining, entertaining, or quiet contemplation.

An arbor can be an inexpensive wooden framework — whitewashed to complement a Colonial Revival home, stained for a contemporary look, or made of rustic poles with the bark left on for an informal country house or a wooded site — or a more substantial structure with stone, brick, or adobe columns and heavy timber crosspieces, with built-in seats and a rough floor. As to the best materials to use, the advice *The Craftsman* offered its readers some eighty years ago still rings true: "The resources of the immediate locality should be drawn upon in preference to all others. Stone piers built of cobble will be most suitable to one neighborhood, while split stone is better in another, and in some places it would be possible to have them of whole fieldstone. Pillars of rough brick are decoratively valuable at times, terra cotta at others, cement at still others. They can be placed singly, in pairs or in groups to harmonize with the surrounding type of garden and house."

Rugged tables, chairs, or benches able to withstand the weather are the most suitable furnishings for arbors. Plants are the draperies in these outdoor rooms; fragrant species add incentive to linger. In the seventeenth century, Shakespeare described an arbor "Quite overcanopied with lush woodbine/With sweet musk roses, and with eglantine." Roses and

roof — a convenience in wet climates, as an arbor whose only ceiling is its tangle of fragrant and flowering plants can drip for hours after rain has stopped.

An arbor of any style is an enchanting leafy shelter where you can be enveloped by nature, experiencing the heady fragrance wafting from flowers overhead and the sound and sight of leaves rustling in the wind and casting moving patterns on the floor. It is a picturesque support for climbing plants, with roses, honeysuckle, and wisteria being the traditional favorites. But an arbor is more than just a prop for plants: in winter the bare bones of the structure are revealed in all their splendor.

Pergolas, arcades, pavilions, and simpler arbors also function as truly transitional spaces between the solid enclosure of the house and the airy spaces of the garden. Their dappled

Cooling Arbors

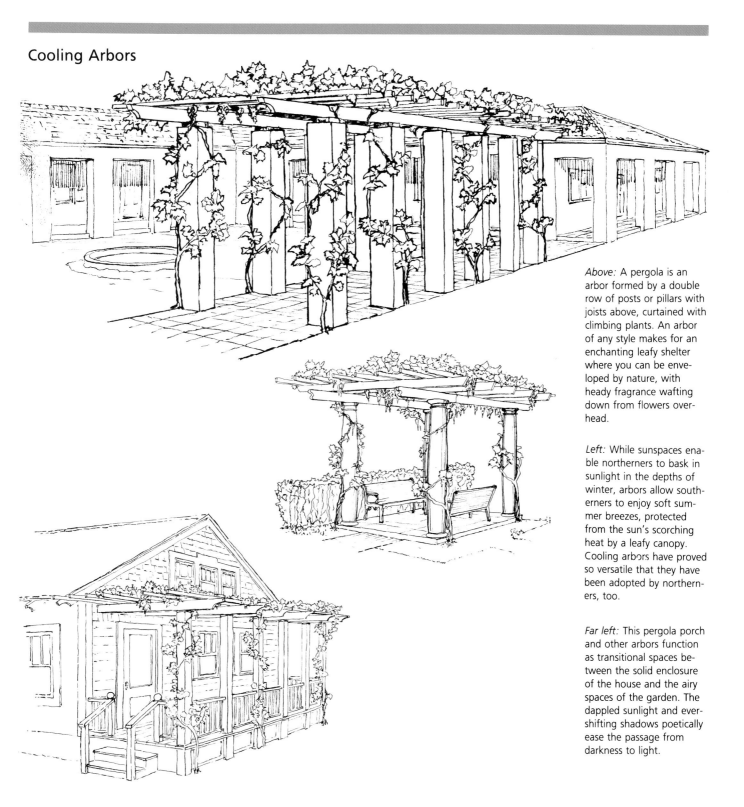

Above: A pergola is an arbor formed by a double row of posts or pillars with joists above, curtained with climbing plants. An arbor of any style makes for an enchanting leafy shelter where you can be enveloped by nature, with heady fragrance wafting down from flowers overhead.

Left: While sunspaces enable northerners to bask in sunlight in the depths of winter, arbors allow southerners to enjoy soft summer breezes, protected from the sun's scorching heat by a leafy canopy. Cooling arbors have proved so versatile that they have been adopted by northerners, too.

Far left: This pergola porch and other arbors function as transitional spaces between the solid enclosure of the house and the airy spaces of the garden. The dappled sunlight and ever-shifting shadows poetically ease the passage from darkness to light.

An Integral Landscape Plan

In this naturally elegant home, a sunspace and garden rooms ease the transition from architecture to nature, and a pergola links the house with the garage.

Close by the kitchen on the south side is a formal edible garden. To the east and north, meadow blends freely into natural woodland.

1. BEDROOM
2. FRONT PORCH
3. LIVING ROOM
4. DINING AREA
5. KITCHEN
6. SUNROOM
7. TERRACE
8. PERGOLA
9. GARDEN WORKSHOP
10. GARAGE
11. KITCHEN GARDEN W/ TRELLIS
12. GAZEBO
13. NATURAL LANDSCAPE · MEADOW
14. NATURAL LANDSCAPE · FOREST

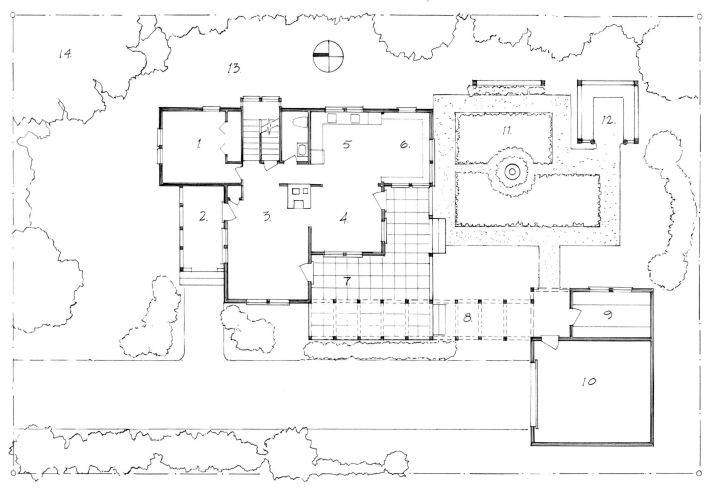

honeysuckle (or woodbine) are the tried and true favorites for clambering over an arbor on both sides of the Atlantic. But be sure to seek out roses that are disease-resistant, hardy in your area, and fragrant; many modern hybrids produce large, blowsy flowers at the expense of scent. Two intensely fragrant climbers recommended by Stephen Scanniello, the rosarian at the Brooklyn Botanic Garden, are 'Don Juan', which has five-inch, velvety, dark-crimson flowers, and 'Sombreuil', which has large, flat, creamy-white flowers with a hint of blush in the centers. If you live in the Middle Atlantic states, beware of the bewitchingly sweet scent of the Japanese honeysuckle (*Lonicera japonica*), which can spread like a weed through the woodlands.

Countless other fragrant climbers are equally suitable for an arbor. The well-loved wisterias have elegant, pendulous flower clusters in shades of purple and white, with an intoxicating scent. *Actinidia kolomikta,* a relative of the kiwi fruit, is a sought-after ornamental grown for its lush green leaves tipped with white and bright pink and its deliciously fragrant flowers. The jasmines are legendary for their fragrance, but many are suitable only for the subtropical climes of the far South (zone 9 or higher on the USDA plant hardiness map). However, with summer heat and some winter protection, poet's jasmine (*Jasminum officinale*), and a pink-flowered hybrid, *J.* x *stephanese,* will grow in zone 7.

Fast-growing annuals are also an option. The moonflower vine, *Ipomoea alba,* lights up the evening with its large white saucerlike blossoms. And in cool-summer areas, nothing surpasses the sweet pea, *Lathyrus odoratus,* not only for luscious scent but also for range of colors and profligacy of bloom.

Some species are so spectacular that they more than make up for their lack of fragrance. Laburnum makes magical flowering tunnels with its golden tassels. *Laburnum* x *watereri* 'Vossii', for example, with its long, elegant racemes of deep-yellow pealike flowers, technically isn't a climber, but it can be trained to grow on an arbor. Many clematis species and hybrids are also beautiful, and some are fragrant.

Edible arbors are another possibility. For centuries grape vines have tumbled over arbors in Italy. The scarlet runner bean, *Phaseolus coccineus,* is a handsome vine that produces bright scarlet flowers up to an inch long and large beans that are quite meaty and delicious. Scores of other kinds of beans, peas, and squash are additional candidates for the edible arbor.

By practicing the ancient art of pleaching, or training the branches of trees and some shrubs along taut wires, you can even have a living arbor. Suitable plants must be pliable enough to have their lateral branches woven together. Linden, hornbeam, yew, box, holly, hawthorn, privet, willow, crabapple, apple, and pear are the best choices for this treatment. You'll need a wire frame at first, but once the branches knit together, the artificial framework can be dismantled (see "Living Garden Furniture," pages 170–171).

■Further Reading

Two of the best books on designing greenhouses are *Greenhouses and Sun Spaces* by Andrew M. Shapiro (Emmaus, Pa.: Rodale Press, 1985) and *Sun Spaces: New Vistas for Living and Growing* by Peter Clegg and Derry Watkins (Pownal, Vt.: Garden Way, 1987). Miranda Smith's *Greenhouse Gardening* (Emmaus, Pa.: Rodale Press, 1985) is a good introduction to growing plants organically in a sunspace or greenhouse.

For more on bioshelters, contact the New Alchemy Institute, 237 Hatchville Road, East Falmouth, Massachusetts 02536.

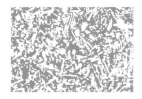

THE KITCHEN

Kitchen remodeling is one of the great American pastimes. The National Kitchen and Bath Association estimates that we spent $24 billion on our kitchens in 1990 — 80 to 85 percent on remodeling and the rest on new construction. But there's no need to spend a fortune to turn your existing kitchen into one that's handsome, healthy, and environmentally sound. There are a number of relatively inexpensive measures that even renters can take, all of which will make an enormous difference. Where's the best place to begin?

■ The Kitchen Sink

This important work center is where fruits and vegetables get washed and plates and pots get scrubbed. It's also our main source of pure water for drinking and cooking. In the modern kitchen, the "kitchen sink" is likely to include not just the traditional basin but two or three of them, not to mention a dishwasher. Opportunities for water conservation abound.

David Goldbeck, author of *The Smart Kitchen* (1990), recommends that every kitchen have at least two sinks: one for food preparation and one for cleanup. This may seem extravagant, says Goldbeck, but because it makes food preparation so much easier — and thus encourages the use of healthy, fresh foods — and because these days households are likely to include more than one cook, it's a worthwhile indulgence. If your food-preparation sink is in a separate area, it need not have more than one basin, unless you make a habit of cooking for an army. However, the dishwashing or utility sink should have at least two basins. If there's room in the kitchen for only one sink, a triple-basin model is a good idea. Sinks are available with one, two, or three basins in a variety of dimensions. The sink that is used primarily for washing vegetables or for final dish rinsing can be hooked up to a graywater system that will carry the relatively clean used water to irrigate the garden (see "Water-Conserving Landscaping," pages 201–210).

Flow Restrictors and Faucet Aerators

Okay, you're stuck with your present kitchen sink. The simplest and cheapest environmental measure you can take is to get an add-on flow restrictor at your local home center or hardware store; it can reduce water usage by 50 to 75 percent. Even better, consider installing a faucet aerator. This gadget neither increases nor restricts the flow of water, but by adding air bubbles, it makes the flow *seem* greater than it actually is. As a result, you can cut your water usage by 50 to 75 percent. Aerators are inexpensive, easy to install, and will pay for themselves in a year or less through reduced pumping and hot-water heating and correspondingly lower electric bills. Because you'll be filling pots and pans, you'll need a higher flow than you would in, say, the bathroom sink, but 2.0 to 2.5 gallons per minute is generally sufficient. Faucet aerators are widely available in hardware and plumbing-supply stores, where there's usually a display to help you find the right size for your faucet.

New Faucets

If your existing faucet is old and drippy, consider replacing it. Some faucets conserve more water than others: single-lever faucets, for instance, make it easy to turn the water on and off at a predetermined mixture of hot and cold, so you don't waste gallons getting the temperature just right. These days, most good faucets come with aerators.

Carbonated-Water Taps

Many faucet manufacturers also make soda-water dispensers that can be installed in the kitchen sink. Not only are they a low-calorie convenience; they also eliminate the need to lug soda bottles home from the supermarket, and fewer bottles have to be recycled.

Water Filters

Water quality is a big concern, particularly at the kitchen sink, the primary supplier of drinking water for most of us. Many municipal water authorities test water for free; if yours

An Integral Kitchen

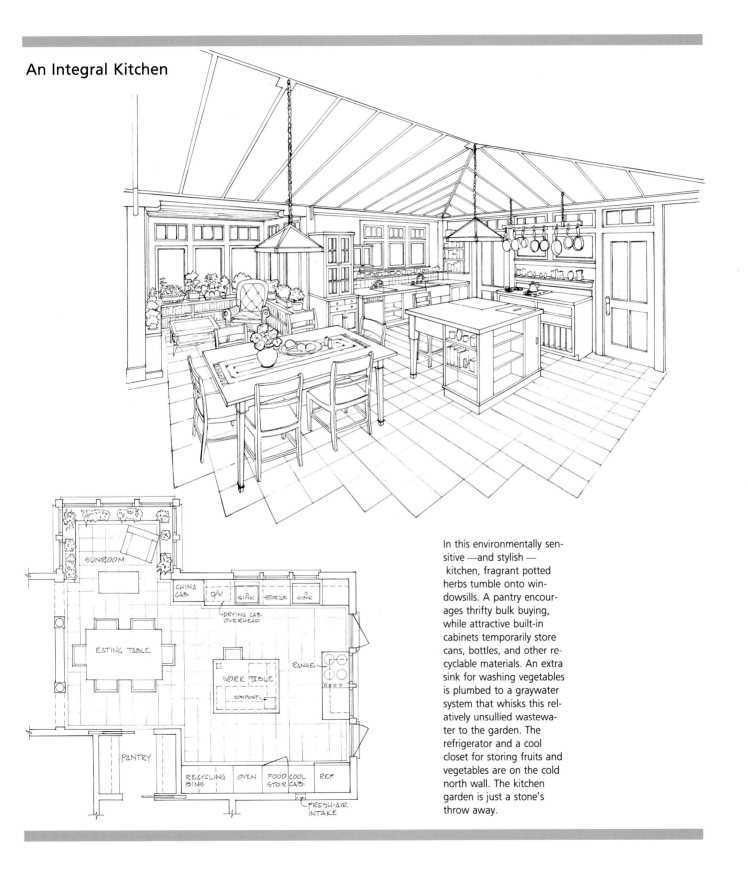

In this environmentally sensitive —and stylish — kitchen, fragrant potted herbs tumble onto windowsills. A pantry encourages thrifty bulk buying, while attractive built-in cabinets temporarily store cans, bottles, and other recyclable materials. An extra sink for washing vegetables is plumbed to a graywater system that whisks this relatively unsullied wastewater to the garden. The refrigerator and a cool closet for storing fruits and vegetables are on the cold north wall. The kitchen garden is just a stone's throw away.

A Finnish drying cabinet located above the dishwasher and near the sink is designed to let dishes washed in the dishwasher or by hand air-dry in a dust-free locale. Using the dishwasher without the heated drying cycle saves an estimated 15 percent on electricity.

doesn't, look in the yellow pages for private labs that do water testing. If it turns out that you have a contamination problem, you can buy one of the many water-filtering systems on the market that can be installed right at the kitchen sink. (Serious water-contamination problems may call for entire-household systems.) Most domestic filtering units use either activated carbon to filter out contaminants or a process called reverse osmosis. *Consumer Reports* has evaluated a number of these products.

The Dishwasher

Now for the best part: dishwashers need not be banned from the naturally elegant kitchen. According to a 1988 study at Ohio State University, the average dishwasher uses 9.9 gallons of water to wash the average load of dirty dishes; washing the same dishes by hand takes 15.7 gallons, or almost *60 percent more*. And there's no question that having a dishwasher to clean up the mess will make you more inclined to cook and less inclined to zap a TV dinner in the microwave and toss out the container.

This defense of the dishwasher does come with a few caveats: Don't waste water rinsing dishes before you put them in the dishwasher, unless you've discovered through trial and error that it's absolutely necessary. If you're in the market for a dishwasher, buy only the most energy-efficient model, with low-energy wash cycles, cold-water rinses, an internal hot-water heater, and air-dry or no-dry options. To conserve water and energy, use the dishwasher only when it's full. And whenever possible, let your dishes dry naturally.

The dishwasher should be located next to the sink to facilitate both loading and plumbing. Above the sink and close by the dishwasher, a Finnish drying cabinet is an attractive option. Designed to let dishes air-dry in a dust-free locale, drying cabinets have been used in Finland for more than sixty years; similar wall-mounted dish racks were also popular in colonial America. If antiques stores and fashionable boutiques are any gauge of popu-

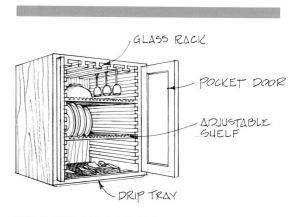

GLASS RACK

POCKET DOOR

ADJUSTABLE SHELF

DRIP TRAY

lar trends, such racks may be poised for a comeback. The Finnish drying cabinet is basically a kitchen cabinet with dish racks instead of shelves; a drip pan can be installed on the bottom if you can't put the cabinet directly above the sink.

■ Getting Rid of Fumes

Good ventilation is one of the most important — and most overlooked — aspects of kitchen design. According to the Home Ventilating Institute, the average kitchen generates two hundred pounds of grease a year, plus odors, moisture, and a variety of health-threatening pollutants. Two of the worst offenders are the gas stove and the gas oven. Although most knowledgeable cooks prefer gas stoves, gas generates significant indoor pollution, most particularly nitrogen dioxide (NO_2) and carbon monoxide (CO), linked to respiratory and cardiovascular problems, respectively. The formaldehyde employed in the fabrication of particleboard and plywood, both of which are used extensively in kitchen cabinets, is another significant source of air pollution in the kitchen. Formaldehyde is a probable human carcinogen and can cause a variety of other problems, from eye, nose, and throat irritation to asthmalike symptoms. The plastic laminates used for kitchen counters are frequently made with formaldehyde-based glue, constituting yet another source of emissions (see "Materials," pages 154–163).

If you're doing extensive remodeling or building a kitchen from scratch, consider installing cabinets of solid wood. A less expensive option is to look for cabinets constructed of plywood made with phenol formaldehyde rather than urea formaldehyde, which is a greater health hazard. Stone, stainless steel, and *solid* plastic are the best choices for counters. If you're stuck with existing cabinets, seal the joints with one of the low-toxicity products now on the market to prevent "outgassing." Good ventilation will also mitigate the formaldehyde problem.

Good ventilation is absolutely essential to rid the kitchen not only of formaldehyde but also of noxious combustion fumes. The standard approaches to kitchen ventilation are the recirculating range hood and the exhaust fan. From an environmental point of view, neither is perfect.

The typical nonvented or recirculating range hood won't do you much good at all. The best models may remove grease and smoke by forcing cooktop air through a filter before sending it back in the room, but they certainly won't remove combustion gases.

The most effective way to get rid of combustion pollutants is through a vented exhaust system. It can be either a wall or ceiling fan or a range-hood type; over-the-stove versions work best. Determining the correct size for an exhaust fan is critical. You want a fan powerful enough to replace all the air in the room with fresh air in five minutes or less. For a wall or ceiling system, divide the cubic footage of the kitchen by five to calculate what the fan's capacity should be. (In other words, a kitchen ten feet long by ten feet wide with a ten-foot ceiling will require at a minimum a 200-cfm fan — that is, one that can vent 200 cubic feet per minute.) For range-hood fans, multiply the length of the cooktop in feet by 40 if the hood is mounted against the wall and by 50 if it's mounted above an island or peninsula. (For example, a wall-mounted model over a three-

Ventilation is one of the most critical and most often overlooked aspects of kitchen design. Over-the-stove vented exhaust systems are best at getting rid of noxious combustion fumes. Design: Rammed Earth Works.

foot cooktop should vent 120 cfm; an overhead model over the same cooktop, 150 cfm.)

Until recently, no one thought much about the fact that standard exhaust systems waste enormous amounts of energy because heated or cooled air is swept outdoors along with the pollutants, forcing the furnace or air-conditioner to work harder. Air-to-air heat exchangers (also called heat-recovery ventilators) can now replace indoor air in such a way that the heat in the exhausted air is transferred to the incoming air. Air-to-air heat exchangers are designed mainly for new, superinsulated homes, but a few HRVs are made just for the kitchen.

■ Reducing Noise

The kitchen is a noisy place — indeed, according to the U.S. Environmental Protection Agency, it's the noisiest room in the house. The loud hums, rattles, and vibrations from the refrigerator, dishwasher, exhaust fan, blender, and assorted other gizmos disrupt normal conversation and make concentration or relaxation impossible.

The most effective noise-reduction strategies are simple commonsense measures: Buy only the quietest equipment and be sure to install it properly. Locate the kitchen as far as possible from bedrooms and studies, and if possible, soundproof the entire space. Building or re-modeling using lots of insulation and other acoustic materials is the best way to eliminate noise, but if that's out of the question, you can at least install doors in all kitchen entries — not just any doors, but *solid* doors fitted with soft gaskets all around to dampen noise. In-stalling an acoustical ceiling will also help.

You can minimize the noise made by large appliances by wrapping them with acoustical material or insulation where possible, putting them on rubber pads with a hard plate on top to distribute the weight evenly, making sure they're at least two inches away from the wall, and installing strip-type gaskets or rubber spacers between the appliance and the cabinet, if any, that encloses it. To minimize the noise made by blenders, food processors, and other small appliances, place them on a soft rubber pad when operating them.

■ Growing Food Indoors

Nothing beats healthy homegrown food. Ideally, of course, such food is grown out-doors, but many city-dwellers and renters — and, during the off-season, those who live in cold climates — have no alternative but to grow it indoors. If space and money are no object, an attached greenhouse can provide you with bushels of organically grown food that's ripened to perfection. But for the rest of us, there are less elaborate alternatives that work almost as well.

Sprout Shelves

In recent years, many people have discov-ered that any kitchen, of any size, can be used to grow unlimited quantities of sprouts. Sprouts are produced from seeds or beans moistened just long enough to germinate into tender, succulent — and tasty — "seedlings." To make sprouts, all you have to do is flush the seeds or beans daily in their own tray or jar.

You can produce sprouts in an ordinary kitchen jar or bottle. Over the years food writer David Goldbeck has found that tray sprouting produces better yields and enables you to sprout several different kinds of seeds at once. Goldbeck invented a way to make this easy task even more convenient by installing a small sliding shelf directly below his vegetable-preparation sink to hold the tray — an ideal location, as sprouts need a dark place to ger-minate and grow, and the position of the shelf under the sink facilitates daily rinsing.

Salads under Lights

Even in a sunless city tenement where the only view is of an airshaft, foods can be grown under lights. You can mount full-spectrum or grow lights under kitchen cabinets for counter-top herb gardens; installed in handsome éta-gères or Welsh cupboards, they can even make the living or dining room your lettuce patch.

Of course you won't be able to grow real sun-lovers such as plump eggplants or beef-steak tomatoes, but some lettuces are emi-nently suited to growing under lights, among them the delicate and beautiful bibb, oak leaf, and buttercrunch. Choice greens such as mache and arugula will thrive indoors as well. Mache, also called lamb's lettuce or corn salad, has a delicate nutty flavor and a distinctive tex-ture that enhance any winter salad. Arugula, a tangy member of the mustard family, when grown indoors not only thrives but produces a milder leaf than its outdoor counterpart, which is a bit too robust for some tastes. Some herbs will likewise do well under lights, including

basil (for year-round pesto) and parsley and chives (for *omelettes aux fines herbes*).

These plants aren't difficult to grow indoors. When seeds are germinating, be sure to keep the flats close to the lights, almost touching the fluorescent tubes; if the flats are too far from the lights, the seedlings will become leggy and weak. Keep the flats moist with a mister. As the seedlings acquire true leaves, gradually increase the distance between them and the grow lights; just how far and how fast you should move them is a matter of trial and error.

Windowsill Gardens

If you can grow that much under lights, imagine the variety possible with several sunny windowsills. With a sunny south or west window, you can grow fragrant Mediterranean herbs such as sage, rosemary, oregano, and bay. Avoid saturating the roots of these herbs with water. (Rosemary is an exception to this rule — when grown indoors, it should be kept constantly moist, or the aromatic, needlelike leaves will turn brown and drop off.) Watercress, a good candidate for a cool room, should be doused with water at least every

In these fast-food times, when food preparation and mealtimes are all but bereft of sensual pleasure, there is great satisfaction to be had in growing fragrant herbs and fresh vegetables in attached greenhouses and on sunny windowsills, as well as outdoors. Architect: Solsearch.

other day. A bright windowsill behind the sink is the perfect spot for this plant, whose small, oval, mildly pungent leaves are rich in vitamins and minerals, especially iron, and add zest to salads, soups, and other dishes.

Bay- and Greenhouse-Window Gardens

In recent years, bay windows in various styles and sizes have become popular in kitchen and other remodelings. These windows range from small box bays with six-inch projections scaled to fit into standard window openings to enormous bays incorporating window sections eight feet high and four feet wide, extending several feet out from the house wall. Almost any bay window can give a feeling of added space to a cramped area, flood a kitchen with natural light, and provide plenty of room for hanging plants — not to mention a deep sill on which to grow herbs and salads.

Installing a miniature greenhouse window in a reasonably sunny spot can be an intriguing way to make your kitchen productive. The typical greenhouse window hangs on the outside of the house, has a slanted glass "roof" with a slope of about 30 degrees, and features two or three shelves as well as a "floor" — all of which can be packed with greens and tasty herbs whose fragrance will waft through the kitchen. The same companies that manufacture bay windows and skylights are a good source of greenhouse windows.

Skylight Gardens

A skylight, too, can provide sun for winter herbs and salads or a place to start seedlings in early spring for transplanting outdoors.

In his kitchen, David Goldbeck capitalized on a three-by-four-foot skylight located in the eaves of his roof to grow food. The skylight reaches the kitchen via a four-and-a-half-foot-long light shaft, making it possible to install shelves for plants along one shaft wall. To allow maximum light to pass through, Goldbeck used Plexiglas for the shelving. The skylight garden is reached through a small door

conveniently situated in a second-floor bathroom.

Don't forget to consider access when designing your skylight garden — can you use a ladder, or will you need a trap door? An alternative is to hang one or more wire baskets on a small pulley beneath the skylight; by loosening the pulley cord, you can easily lower a pot of frequently used herbs or greens for harvesting or watering (don't forget to put drip pans under the pots). Whichever method you choose, remember that heat will build up behind the skylight on warm sunny days, so venting will be necessary. And finally, a skylight for growing herbs or greens cannot be made of tinted glass.

■ Appliances and Energy

A modest little booklet entitled *The Most Energy-Efficient Appliances* is a bible for home-energy-conservation aficionados; it should be a bible for kitchen remodelers as well. If you're considering a kitchen overhaul, or even if you just intend to replace a noisy old refrigerator, you should get your hands on a copy (see the bibliography at the end of this section).

Updated yearly by its publisher, the Washington, D.C.–based nonprofit group American Council for an Energy-Efficient Economy (or ACE³), *The Most Energy-Efficient Appliances* is packed with both buying tips (including comparisons of name brands and models) and telling statistics. If you pore through ACE³'s charts and tables, you'll soon realize that in its appetite for energy, the American kitchen is surpassed only by that other great guzzler, the American car. Largely because of poorly designed appliances, kitchens in the United States use about one quarter of all household energy. Nationwide, refrigerators alone consume the output of twenty-five large power plants; if every household in America were retrofitted with the most efficient model currently available, the savings in electricity would eliminate the need for twelve of these plants. The other worst kitchen offenders are gas ranges with energy-wasting pilot lights and inefficient dishwashers that use an inordinate amount of energy for heating water and for dish drying.

We're making some headway. The National Appliance Energy Conservation Act of 1987 established minimum efficiency standards for major kitchen appliances as well as for home heating and cooling equipment. The standards for dishwashers, for instance, took effect on January 1, 1988, requiring a cold-water-rinse option on new models. The standards for refrigerators took effect in 1990. These new regulations will make appliances 10 to 30 percent more efficient, reducing the peak electricity demand by the equivalent of twenty-five large power plants, according to ACE[3].

Although the new standards will eliminate the worst energy wasters in appliance showrooms, refrigerators, dishwashers, and other appliances will still be available in a wide range of energy efficiencies, so it will still pay to shop carefully. Some highly efficient appliances may cost more initially but will yield savings in the long term. When you buy a refrigerator, for example, not only do you pay the sales price, you also commit yourself to paying the costs of running it over its lifetime. This can add up: running a refrigerator for fifteen to twenty years typically costs about three times what it costs to buy it in the first place. Buying an energy-efficient model will save you money over time, often a substantial amount. (The true cost of purchasing and running an appliance is called its life-cycle cost, a key piece of information that the "Energyguide" labels in showrooms lack. *The Most Energy-Efficient Appliances* tells you how to calculate life-cycle figures so you can compare the true costs of various models.)

Refrigerators

Most refrigerators remain noisy hulks, but they're getting more energy-efficient. Manufacturers have increased insulation levels and improved compressors, motors, and door seals,

among other components. However, there's still a long way to go.

Most people are amazed when they learn how expensive it is to run a refrigerator every year. An eighteen-cubic-foot, frost-free model consumes between 1,000 and 1,300 kilowatt hours of electricity a year, costing anywhere from $125 to more than $250, depending on the model and the cost of electricity in your area. Theoretically, refrigerators could use as little as 200 kilowatt hours per year, resulting in astonishing savings: at an average cost of twelve and a half cents per kilowatt hour, the cost of running such an efficient fridge would plummet to twenty-five dollars a year.

In fact, the Japanese, Germans, and Danes already mass-produce superefficient refrigerators, and in the United States, Larry Schlussler, founder of the Sun Frost company in Arcata, California, manufactures and sells some of the world's most energy-efficient models. Sun Frost refrigerators use 60 to 90 percent less energy than standard models, thanks to a variety of design innovations. For example, the condensers and compressors (two of each) on a Sun Frost are at the top of the refrigerator, so that their heat dissipates into the air; in the typical unit, they're behind or beneath the food box, warming the interior and cutting cooling efficiency. In the typical refrigerator, the thirty-eight-degree fresh-food section is cooled by the same below-zero evaporator that serves the freezer; in the Sun Frost, the freezer and fresh-food compartments are cooled by independent systems, boosting efficiency. Schlussler also increased insulation and eliminated fans, which use electricity and produce heat. One new-model Sun Frost even has a heat pipe that allows the unit to use cold outdoor temperatures to cool the fresh-food section — without electricity. Sun Frost makes units that can run on conventional 110-volt alternating current or on 12- or 24-volt direct current for hookup to photovoltaic systems. The refrigerators are also mercifully quiet, with no nerve-rattling hums or rattles when the compressor

kicks on. Sound too good to be true? Sun
Frost refrigerators do have one drawback:
they're expensive. The sixteen-cubic-foot model
for standard alternating current costs $2,350.
But if your house is powered by solar electric
cells, if you can live with waiting for a long-
term return on your investment, or if you
want to be the first on your block to have this
handsome, superefficient refrigerator, then the
Sun Frost is for you.

For those who must settle for a more mun-
dane model, here are some features to look
for:

■ **Design.** Side-by-side refrigerator-freezers
typically use more than one third more energy
than models with the freezer on top, so they
cost more to run. They also cost more to
begin with.

■ **Method of defrosting.** Manual-defrost
models typically use about half the electricity
of automatic defrost units. Of course, they
need to be defrosted regularly to work properly and efficiently. Freezer walls covered with
frost thick enough to be hacked out with an
ice pick not only make you look like a slouch;
according to manufacturers, they also mean
that the motor must run longer to maintain
cool temperatures. Those who consider refrigerator defrosting a throwback to the Dark
Ages will be grateful to hear that there a few
energy-efficient automatic-defrost models out
there. Shop around.

■ **Size.** This is a consideration that is as important as it is obvious. Too large a refrigerator will cost more and result in wasted energy,
while too small a model will mean extra trips
to the store. Here's how to determine how big
a fridge you need: figure on eight to ten cubic
feet in the fresh-food section for a family of
two, plus one cubic foot for each additional
person; add two more cubic feet if you're an
inveterate entertainer. As for the freezer, two
cubic feet per person is plenty. (Note that
these figures will vary somewhat according to
life-style; obviously, if your weekly food intake
is heavy on takeout, you can make do with a
much smaller unit.)

■ **Power-saver switches.** Contradictory as it
may sound, many refrigerators have small heaters built into the walls to prevent moisture
from collecting on the outside. If you're in the
market for a refrigerator, look for one with a
switch that enables you to shut off these heaters. Leave the switch in the position labeled
"Energy-saving" unless moisture begins to
build up.

■ **Location.** If possible, keep your refrigerator
away from the stove and the dishwasher and
out of the sun, where heat will force it to
work harder. Ideally, you should place it near
a cool north or east exterior wall.

If you're not in the market for a new refrigerator, you can still take some measures to
make your old model more efficient (renters
take note). Door seals can deteriorate; if they
leak cold air or seal poorly, have them replaced. Also, check the temperature inside
your refrigerator and freezer with a thermometer. The refrigerator compartment should be
between thirty-eight and forty-two degrees;
the freezer, zero to five degrees. According to
ACE[3], if the refrigerator and freezer are kept
ten degrees colder than recommended, energy
consumption can increase by as much as 25
percent.

Cool Cabinets

It wasn't long ago that people had root
cellars to take advantage of the natural cooling
provided by the earth. A regional variation on
this theme is the California "cool cabinet."
Cool air from a crawl space or basement is
drawn through the cabinet and out a top
chimney-type vent. The floor of the cabinet is
made of strong wire mesh and the shelves are
made of wooden slats to facilitate the flow of
air; the vent is usually a six-inch duct. Cool air
flows from under the house to the warmer
roof vent. A tightly fitting door prevents
drafts, and the chimney vent is screened to
keep out animals.

Most homes have a corner, crawl space, cellar, or cabinet that stays cooler than the rest of
the house, and any of these would make a

Cool Cabinets

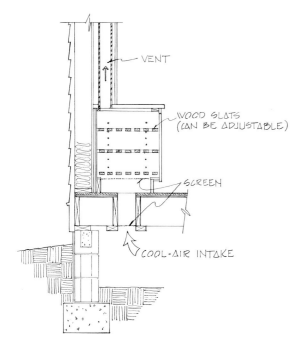

Many fruits and vegetables can be stored in cool closets. Cool air from a crawl space or basement (see left) or from outdoors (see below) is drawn through the closet and out a chimney-top vent. The floor of the cabinet is made of strong wire mesh and the shelves of wooden slats to facilitate the flow of air.

VENT

WOOD SLATS (CAN BE ADJUSTABLE)

SCREEN

COOL·AIR INTAKE

VENTED FROM BASEMENT OR CRAWL SPACE

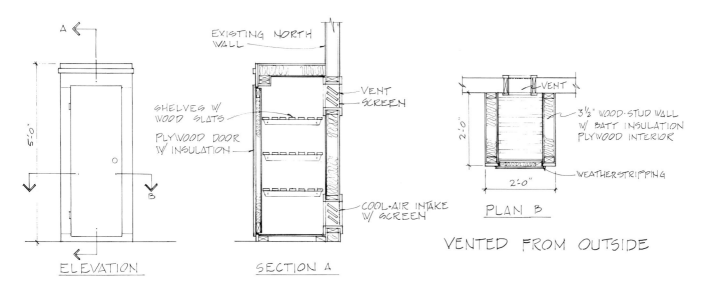

A

EXISTING NORTH WALL

VENT SCREEN

SHELVES W/ WOOD SLATS

PLYWOOD DOOR W/ INSULATION

3½" WOOD·STUD WALL W/ BATT INSULATION PLYWOOD INTERIOR

WEATHERSTRIPPING

COOL·AIR INTAKE W/ SCREEN

5'-0"

2'-0"

2'-0"

B

ELEVATION

SECTION A

PLAN B

VENTED FROM OUTSIDE

According to a study at Ohio State University, hand washing consumes 60 percent more water than the average dishwasher. Specially designed models, such as this one by Bosch, use even less water.

great place for a cool-spot pantry. Be aware, though, that humidity and temperature are both important considerations; you'll need a thermometer and a hygrometer to check the conditions in your chosen spot. Keep in mind, too, that certain fruits and vegetables require a cooler or more humid atmosphere than others: apples, grapes, and cabbages, for example, need a temperature of thirty-two to forty degrees and humidity of 80 to 90 percent, whereas winter squash or tomatoes will fare well in a warmer and drier environment — fifty to sixty degrees, and 60 to 70 percent humidity.

Dishwashers

About 80 percent of the energy used to run a dishwasher is actually used to heat the water, according to the Association of Home Appliance Manufacturers. When shopping for a new dishwasher, look for a built-in hot-water heater and a range of cycle selections. For a dishwasher to work properly, the water needs to be heated to 140 degrees. One way to ensure that is to set your home water heater that high — an uneconomical option because water doesn't need to be so hot for other household uses. Many dishwashers come with internal hot-water heaters to boost the temperature of domestic hot water (which is usually set at 120 degrees), cutting your hot-water bills up to 10 percent. A choice of short or long, light-wash or pot-wash cycles can save as much as one third in electricity. All dishwashers made after January 1, 1988, must have an option to dry without heat; this feature saves an estimated 15 percent in electricity costs.

Cookers

The question of fuel efficiency for stoves and ovens isn't as critical as it might seem, as none of them consume or waste huge amounts of energy. However, there are some considerations. Gas stoves should have automatic pilot lights. Different oven technologies vary in energy efficiency. Convection ovens, for example, are more efficient than standard models; by incorporating a fan that circulates air evenly throughout, such ovens eliminate hot and cold spots, lowering cooking temperatures and shortening cooking times. Microwaves consume only one third to one half as much electricity as conventional ovens. The microwave is one of the most phenomenally popular appliances of this century, but there's still the worrisome matter of potential exposure to radiation to consider: although independent tests indicate that potential leakages are within government standards, there's no consensus on what constitutes a "safe" level of microwave radiation. There's also the problem of toxic compounds leaching from microwave packaging into food. It's up to you to weigh the risks.

The pressure cooker is one time-saving alternative to the microwave that has withstood the test of time. Large, built-in pressure-cooker ovens, known as pressure steamers in the restaurant business, are another possibility. They're finding growing acceptance among gourmet cooks and others willing to pay for professional-quality equipment. Groen, of Elk Grove, Illinois, makes a combination convection/steamer oven that's ideal for home use. Called the Convection Combo, it can roast a twenty-pound turkey in ninety minutes, bake flaky croissants or crusty breads, steam fish and vegetables, and reheat foods without drying them. What's more, it has an attractive, all-stainless exterior. However, it does require 220-volt power, plus plumbing for a water and drain connection.

◼ Space for Trash

Making room for recycling in the kitchen is a hot new design frontier. Recycling cans, bottles, newspapers, and other materials is hardly an onerous activity, but some reluctant recyclers have nightmarish visions of their kitchens' suddenly being littered with dog-eared cardboard boxes full of bottles and clanking piles of aluminum cans. In fact, there's no reason recycling can't satisfy both the fervent environmentalist and the effete aesthete in all of us.

Architect Jonathan Poore of Gloucester, Massachusetts, was one of the first kitchen designers to grapple with this subject in print, in the September/October 1989 issue of *Garbage*. He offers a set of rules to smooth recycling's integration into daily life. These include:

■ **Make it really obvious what goes where.**

■ **Build in enough room for each type of recyclable.** This will vary according to what's being collected for recycling in your community. Bottles, cans, corrugated cardboard, and newsprint are the most commonly collected materials. If you're building a kitchen from scratch, though, it's smart to make room for additional items such as plastics and compostables or "wet wastes"; if they're not already being collected in your area, it's just a matter of time before they will be.

■ **Locate the holding bin near the use site.** Is it too obvious to emphasize that the compost bucket should be near the vegetable cutting board, and the bottle storage near the refrigerator?

■ **Bins or drawers must be easy to empty and easy to clean.**

■ **Design for recycling should meet basic tests of aesthetic acceptability.** A painted-pine bin uplifts, while an oily brown bag offends one's sense of taste (literally).

Designing for Recyclables

Recycling is revolutionizing the kitchen in ways that go far beyond matters of aesthetics. Since the turn of the century, kitchen design has been based on a notion of efficiency commonly known as the "work triangle" — defined as the well-traveled area between the refrigerator, the sink, and the stove. The idea, of course, is to streamline this area. With the arrival of the age of recycling, the work triangle is more like a parallelogram, with an extra "leg" between the refrigerator or the sink and

This freestanding cabinet can organize recycling in a compact kitchen. The tilt-out door provides easy access to several removable receptacles. Newspapers are easily stored on the shelf at the top.

In writer David Goldbeck's kitchen, a rolling cart stowed in a specially designed cabinet is used to store bottles, cans, and other recyclables.

Cabinet Design for Recycling

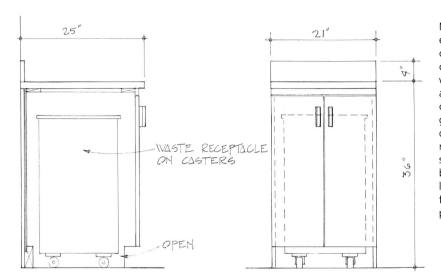

New stock cabinets or your existing kitchen cabinets can be customized for recycling. You can fit them with roll-out receptacles to allow easy transfer of recyclable materials to the garage or to containers outdoors (see left), with removable containers on slide-out drawers (see below), or with tilt-out bins like the flour bins in old-fashioned kitchens (see opposite page).

25"

WASTE RECEPTACLE ON CASTERS

OPEN

21"

4"

36"

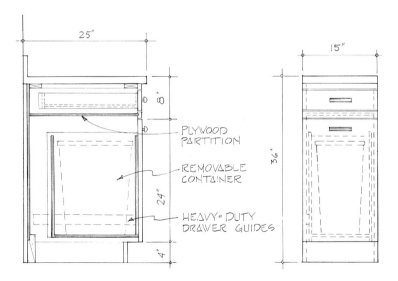

25"

8"

PLYWOOD PARTITION

REMOVABLE CONTAINER

24"

HEAVY-DUTY DRAWER GUIDES

4"

15"

36"

a recycling "zone" where rinsed-out bottles, jars, and cans are temporarily stored. In any case, the point is still to streamline, streamline, streamline.

One way to simplify recycling is to store all the materials in one place (with the exception of compostables and possibly newspapers). If you have to hunt all over the kitchen for the right container for your empty balsamic vine-gar bottle, it's likely to get thrown in the unsorted trash instead.

If space isn't a limiting factor, it's best to have two home recycling zones: one area either in the kitchen or as close to it as possible, with moderate-sized receptacles for the sorted materials, and another area, preferably in the garage or outdoors, to store larger volumes of recyclables. If you're lucky enough to

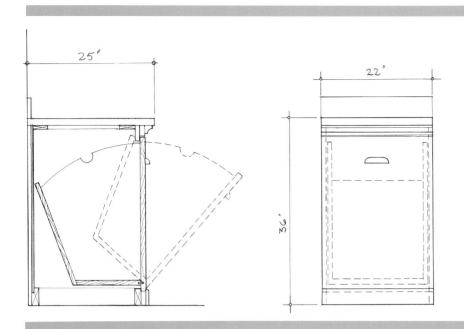

live in a town that has curbside pickup, this secondary area can simply be the special bin or bins designated for recyclable materials. If you have to drive to the local recycling center, you may need a more formal storage area in the garage, shed, or basement.

For those with cramped kitchens, the primary recycling area can be located in the laundry room, a storage room, the garage, the porch, the basement, or the living or family room (a handy place for old newspapers is a handsome bin, but for most other recyclables — yeech). The convenience of any of these areas increases in direct proportion to its proximity to the kitchen; the advantage of these areas — except for the living room or den — is that containers can be of the most functional design.

This does not hold true for the kitchen, however, where the recycling area should be as attractive as it is convenient. Mainstream houseware manufacturers now offer recycling receptacles in a variety of colors, shapes, and sizes. Another simple solution is a rolling cart with stacked wire bins for the various recyclables. If you prefer not to let it all hang out, new stock cabinets or your existing kitchen cabinets may

be customized for recycling. You can customize to suit your needs by dividing a cabinet with shelves, racks, and/or drawers fitted with removable or tilt-out bins, much like the flour bins found in period kitchens. Individual drawers, cabinets, or bins should be clearly labeled. One ingenious setup calls for a row of movable bins that slide conveniently under the kitchen counter when you open the cabinet door, topped by false drawer openings that tilt out, making small deposits convenient. This handy recycling center looks just like the rest of the kitchen cabinetry. A small closet, pantry, or kitchen island can also be outfitted for recycling.

Old houses are full of ideas for recyclers. Unlike the contemporary kitchen, which is designed for quick consumption of disposable goods, traditional kitchens included not only tilt-out flour bins but other thrifty features such as pantries for bulk storage and dumbwaiters for smooth transfer of materials (usually food) from one area to another. Elsewhere in the home were built-in hampers and clothes chutes.

These old-fashioned ideas can be adapted for the contemporary home. For example, in a two-story home with the kitchen and living room on the upper floor, a dumbwaiter can provide for effortless transfer of recyclables from the kitchen downstairs and outdoors. Old-house chute systems can likewise be adapted for recycling. If you're adventurous, or if you're doing major renovation anyway, consider building in simple chutes (one for each kind of recyclable) from the kitchen to containers in the garage or outdoors. (Consult your local building code or a knowledgeable professional first; in some areas, chute systems and dumbwaiters must be "fire-rated," or specially designed to discourage the spread of fire.)

A more futuristic home recycling system has been sketched out by Bill Stumpf, a Minneapolis-based industrial designer. Part of a scheme for what he calls the metabolic house, it includes chutes in the kitchen that carry presorted materials to the basement, where recyclables are "techno-mulched" into an effluent, paper is mixed with fuel to heat the house, and the rest is stored for removal to a regional processing center.

Designing for Compostables

Collecting organic wastes for composting presents its own set of design challenges. The major constraint, of course, is that eggshells, carrot peels, coffee grounds, and the like tend to be sloppy and smelly.

One conventional means of dealing with organic wastes — the garbage disposal — is not an environmentally sound idea. After being ground up, the organic material goes into the sewage system, where it must be treated at often overloaded sewage-treatment plants.

A convenient place to store kitchen scraps destined for the compost pile or municipal

Cabinet Design for Compost

The kitchen counter can be customized for temporary storage of vegetable peels, eggshells, and other compostable materials. A hinged lid near the cutting board opens to reveal a stainless steel container with its own tight-fitting lid. The container is easily removed through a cabinet door for emptying onto the compost pile and cleaning.

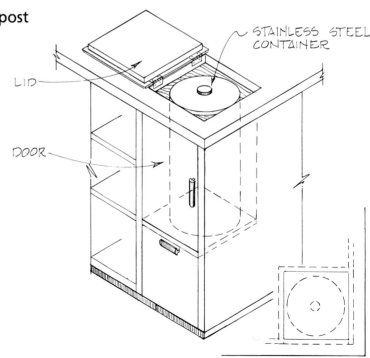

pickup is in a covered, stainless-steel container somewhere in the kitchen — preferably close to the sink or cutting board. The key words here are *stainless-steel* (plastic tends to absorb odors and become stained) and *covered* (a tight-fitting lid will keep odors in and flies out). Small, pedal-operated garbage cans (still another idea borrowed from period kitchens) with enameled lift-out buckets are also great for compostables. Trash cans designed specifically for this purpose are now available as well. The can is mounted under the sink; when you open the door, the can swings out and its lid opens automatically.

■ Further Reading

By far the most comprehensive reference on naturally elegant kitchen design is David Goldbeck's *The Smart Kitchen: How to Design a Comfortable, Safe, Energy-Efficient and Environment-Friendly Workspace.* The book was pub-lished in 1990 and is available from Ceres Press, P.O. Box 87, Woodstock, N.Y. 12498.

If you're in the market for a new kitchen appliance, be sure to get a copy of the American Council for an Energy-Efficient Economy's indispensable booklet *The Most Energy-Efficient Appliances,* which is updated every year. Write to ACE[3], 1001 Connecticut Avenue NW, Suite 535, Washington, D.C. 20036.

The first work devoted exclusively to kitchen design for recycling, which includes lots of imaginative suggestions as well as detailed architect's renderings of cabinet designs, was compiled by architect Nicolee Bradbury of Spokane, Washington. The plastic binder–bound booklet, entitled *Architectural Design Handbook for Household Recycling Centers,* is available from the Spokane Regional Solid Waste Disposal Project Office, at West 808 Spokane Falls Boulevard, Spokane, Washington 99201. The telephone number is (509) 456-7403.

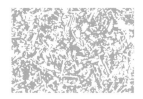

THE BATHROOM

Every year, the average American family of four uses anywhere from 72,000 to 93,000 gallons of pure drinking water indoors. The easiest way to start saving water in the bathroom is to reevaluate your habits and adjust accordingly. Some examples: Take short showers just to get clean. Those with military-like discipline can even turn on the shower to get wet, shut off the water to scrub and shampoo, and then turn it on again to rinse. Baths are certainly cheaper than therapy, but unless your tub is designed to filter and recycle the water, use it sparingly; a shower uses much less water. And do you really need the dulcifying sound of running water as you brush your teeth? If you're really bold, ask yourself if it's essential to flush the toilet after every use (having ultra-low-flush toilets is no excuse for wasting water).

■ Conserving Water in the Bathroom

Before you go out and buy new water-conserving hardware, check for, and repair, leaks. Some leaks aren't obvious. You can't hear a leaky conventional toilet, one with a tank ball valve or flapper valve, unless the flow is a relative torrent of more than 250 gallons per day. A 1990 study by the city of Pasadena,

California, found that 19 percent of the homes examined had leaks in their toilets, and 17 percent had leaky faucets wasting an average of 268 gallons per month. One way to check for leaks in your toilet is to add some food coloring to the water in the tank. If the color shows up in the bowl, you've got a problem.

Also check the house's entire plumbing system for unsuspected leaks. A pinhole leak may look insignificant but can waste up to 170 gallons per day. Turn off all water spigots and faucets, then write down the numbers on your water meter dial. Check the meter again a couple of hours later. If the dials or numbers have changed, you've got a leak. (No meter? You're out of luck here. Consider putting one in to better track your family's water consumption.) If you can't find the leak yourself, look in the yellow pages under "pipe and leak locating" and choose a service that uses electronic equipment to listen for leaking water. Repairing leaks can save you plenty of money in the long run.

To save water in the toilet, you can put plastic one-quart bottles or a plastic displacement bag full of water in the tank, or you can bend the metal rod that attaches to the float ball to shut the refill off sooner. A "toilet dam" can also be added to conventional toilet tanks to displace some of the flush water. These devices

The sink in a naturally elegant bathroom is outfitted with a low-flow aerator to conserve water.

can save two to three gallons per flush, but they still don't match the savings of the ultra-low 1.6-gallon-per-flush toilets (or ULFs). Toilet dams fit only certain-size tanks and have a tendency to leak over time.

Other big water savings are also possible when you build or remodel to create an environmentally sound bathroom.

No-Flush Toilets

The biggest water-guzzler in the bathroom is the toilet. Enthusiastic converts to the "environmental cause" often champion the waterless, or composting, toilet as the "wave of the future." But the no-flush-toilet option must be carefully considered. Perhaps nowhere else in the naturally elegant home can an ill designed or poorly crafted device cause such trouble and despair.

With a composting privy, you can't just flush and forget about the rest. Even assuming that the waterless toilet works as well as advertised, here are some things that must still be considered:

■ The only reliable waterless toilets are the commercially made models. Owner-built models usually end up infested with rodents or flies.

■ Commercial waterless toilets cost from $1,300 to $6,000 apiece. There is also the added cost of the exhaust vent and fan.

■ A reliable, quiet fan is essential to exhaust fumes from the holding chamber. Turning on the fan before lifting the lid will help eliminate fumes generated by the composting pile. Don't count on a solar-powered 12VDC fan unless a battery is included for nighttime use.

■ All decent-looking waterless toilets require considerable space below the bathroom floor to house the chamber. You will need a basement or other special construction, which will add significantly to the expense. The space required can range from 32 to 43 square feet and must be between 5 and 7½ feet high, with a door or stairs for easy access and convenient removal of the finished compost.

■ You must cover the waste to keep away flies and make life pleasant for subsequent users. This requires a regular, dry source of carbonaceous material — chopped straw, shredded leaves, sawdust, or wood shavings — to add to the privy after each use. The carbonaceous material absorbs some of the urine and is required for composting to balance the high nitrogen content of the waste.

■ While urine is a good source of nitrogen and other nutrients, it usually puddles in the bottom of the privy, forming a malodorous, anaerobic mess. Well-designed commercially available waterless toilets collect the urine in a separate chamber below the mass, but you still must periodically pump the urine either back onto the pile of composting feces or out into the landscape (making sure to dispose of the liquid below ground to prevent any possible disease problems).

■ You must have a landscape big enough to bury the finished material at least twelve inches beneath the soil surface. You must be sure to use a set of gardening tools reserved exclusively for this task, carefully clean them when you're done, and separate them from your other tools.

Waterless toilets are best suited to building sites with such poor percolation that no type of septic system will work, or sites in areas where water is so severely limited that even a 1.6-gallon ultra-low-flush toilet is out of the question.

Low-Flush Toilets

Water-conserving toilets are a much more realistic option for most people than no-flush models. The latest low-flush commodes work better than earlier designs — and look better, too.

In the 1970s, when low-flush toilets were first promoted, the only one available was an odd-shaped Swedish model. The large oval-shaped tank looked strange, but more impractical was the fact that there was no flat tank

In the 1970s, low-flush toilets had an odd shape, with no flat tank top on which to put tissues or jewelry. Today's ultra-low-flush toilet looks no different from a conventional model but uses a miserly 1.6 gallons of water per flush. Design: Rammed Earth Works.

top on which to rest magazines, tissues, or jewelry.

More to the point, some early models used only one gallon or even one-half gallon to flush, which resulted in a lot of so-called double flushing. Today, most ULF toilets use 1.6 gallons per flush (or gpf). Toilets that use less than that are not recommended because they clog more easily and require more double flushing.

The water seal in the bowl of those earlier, lower-volume models had a very small surface area and a shallow depth, which led to odor problems. And because the water seal was so small, the older ULF toilets were more susceptible to "skidmarks," or brown streaks on the bowl's porcelain walls, which required the use of a toilet brush after most uses.

All this has changed with the new generation of ULF toilets.

Choosing a ULF Toilet

A toilet can last the lifetime of a house. Consequently, it's a good idea to spend some time evaluating which model is best for you and your family. Just as you do when you buy a car, you should do your homework, visit the showroom, shop around, and take a "test drive." There are more than two dozen reliable and effective ultra-low-flush toilets currently on the market. Here are some things to keep in mind:

■ **Assess the costs and figure the payback.** ULF toilets offer a savings of 18,000 to 26,400 gallons per year for an average household. Use these general figures and your existing water and sewer rates to calculate the length of your payback — or, alternatively, determine how many gallons your current toilet uses and calculate its total water consumption, figuring on an average of three to five flushes per person per day.

There have been enough ULF toilets installed to develop some ballpark figures on savings. According to a National Wildlife Federation fact sheet on the National Plumbing Products Efficiency Act of 1989, "savings from more efficient toilets vary with local water and sewer rates, but savings . . . range from $25 to $50 per year." The Massachusetts Water Resources Authority estimates that retrofitting a 1.6-gpf toilet will save a Boston homeowner $74 per year in 1989 dollars. This means an average payback on investment in only three years, or a return on investment of 39 percent — making the toilet a better investment than a savings account or most stocks!

When a homeowner is considering a septic leach field, the savings accrued due to a reduced drain field can, according to the Rocky Mountain Institute, an environmental think tank, "easily exceed the added cost of efficient fixtures [such as a ULF toilet and low-flow faucet aerators and showerheads]."

■ **Don't go for the absolute lowest gpf, unless water in your area is very scarce.** Most toilets that use less than one gallon per flush are mechanical models that depend upon pumps, compressors, and other mechanisms. Such toilets don't work for long when the power fails, and any extra hardware you add is just another potential headache and could require costly repairs. Also, as mentioned above, any toilet with less than a 1.6-gallon flush is more prone to skidmarks and odor problems.

■ **Pick a toilet with a good-sized water seal.** Pay careful attention to the column listing the size and depth of the water seal in the chart on page 145. The deeper and wider the water seal, the more likely it is that skidmarks and odors will be kept to a minimum.

■ **Don't choose the newest model.** Those

A Sampling of Ultra-Low-Flush Toilets

Name	Manufacturer	Gallons per Flush (gpf)	Flush Mechanism	White	Color(s)	Suggested Retail Price Regular/Elongated (White)/(Color)	Regular Bowl Water Seal	
							Surface Size	Depth
Allegro	Mansfield Plumbing Products 150 First Street Perrysville, Ohio 44864 (419) 938-5211	1.6	Gravity-fed	Yes	Yes	$125/$165	5″ × 7″	2″
Aqualine	U.S. Brass 901 Tenth Street P.O. Box 37 Plano, Texas 75074 (800) 872-7277	1.5	Flush valve sleeve, open slotted rim	Yes	Yes	$150/$200	4″ × 5″	2½″
Atlas	Universal-Rundle 303 North Street Newcastle, Pennsylvania 16103 (800) 521-6793	1.6	Gravity-fed	Yes	Yes	$140/$170	7¼″ × 4¾″	2⅝″
Crane-Miser	Crane Plumbing 1235 Hartrey Street Evanston, Illinois 60202 (708) 864-9777	1.6	Gravity-fed	Yes	Yes	$250/$300	9″ × 8⅝″	3″
Cascade	Mansfield Plumbing Products 150 First Street Perrysville, Ohio 44864 (419) 938-5211	1.6	Flush valve sleeve, gravity-fed, water divider tube, open rim slot	Yes	Yes	$203/$268	5″ × 7″	2″
LF 16	Microphor, Inc. P.O. Box 1460 Willits, California 95490-1460 (800) 358-8280	1.6	Gravity-fed	Yes	Yes (bone gray only)	$139/$159	8″ × 7½″	2″
Ultra-One/G	Eljer Plumbingware 901 Tenth Street, P.O. Box 37 Plano, Texas 75074 (214) 881-7177	1.4	Siphon jet, gravity-fed	Yes	Yes	$208/$258	12″ × 11″	2½″
Wellworth Lite	Kohler Company Kohler, Wisconsin 53044 (800) 456-4537	1.5	Gravity-fed	Yes	Yes	$152/$161	8″ × 9″	2½″
Véneto	Porcher, Inc. 13-160 Merchandise Mart Chicago, Illinois 60654 (800) 338-1756 in U.S. (312) 923-0995 in Illinois	1.5	Gravity-fed	Yes	Yes	$595	5″ × 5½″	2¾″

who test-fire new toilets are venturing into uncharted waters. Pick a model that's been carried by a local supplier for a while. Be sure to ask the supplier about the availability and cost of parts and service.

■ **Get a listing of installations and visit some working models.** Ask your local supplier to give you a list of references. Many showrooms and companies have installed ULF models in their own restrooms; try one out.

■ **Study product reviews.** In the July 1990 issue of *Consumer Reports,* for example, ten ULF toilets are reviewed. But it's still a good idea to confirm that the reviews jibe with the experience of others.

■ **Ask friends about their experience with ULFs.** Ultra-low-flush toilets are not the most common topic at cocktail parties, but they are becoming more prevalent, so chances are someone in your neighborhood already has one. Get his or her opinion.

■ **Have someone with experience install the toilet.** If you've never put in a toilet before, save yourself the hassle and call in a professional.

Low-Flow Showerheads and Sink Aerators

Before you go out and buy a showerhead and aerators, check to see if you can get them free from your local gas company or water department. (In the arid West it's less expensive for water districts to give away water-saving devices than to develop new sources of water.) If there are no freebies, do a little homework. Compare the literature on the various showerhead models available at your local plumbing-supply store, from your water district conservation office, and in mail-order catalogs. The July 1990 issue of *Consumer Reports* included an excellent article comparing thirty-four low-flow showerheads tested by "sixteen soggy souls [who] took roughly 350 showers over the course of several months" in a special laboratory.

Still, a shower is a very personal experience. If possible, test some low-flow showerheads before buying. Most showerheads conserve water in part by reducing the diameter of the spray. Some are narrower than others, while some make a ring of water that leaves the center dry. More important to your family's well-being, some low-flow showerheads are prone to cause scalding if your water pressure is low, if the pipe to the bathroom is less than ¾ inch, or if you don't have an antiscald valve plumbed into the shower. If your existing shower gets uncomfortably hot when someone flushes the toilet, then a low-flush showerhead may well exaggerate the problem. But this is easily solved by having a plumber install an antiscald valve.

Water-conserving showerheads range in price from $3 to $75. There are a number of low-flow showerheads under $10; see the chart on page 147. You needn't give up your hand-held showerhead to conserve water; there are ten low-flow models in the price range of $11 to $95.

Choosing a low-flow aerator for the bathroom sink isn't complicated. Because performance doesn't vary much, go with the lowest-flow model, 1.5 gph or less, at the cheapest price.

Installing Your Showerhead and Aerator

Installing your new showerheads and aerators is simple enough to do at halftime during a football game or when a brief summer shower keeps you from gardening outdoors. A lockjaw wrench works fine, but a pipe wrench or wide-mouthed adjustable pliers will also do the job. Cover the chrome-plated pipe fittings with a cloth rag to keep from marring the finish. Wrap any threads several times around with pipe-thread tape to prevent leaks. The threads on bathroom fixtures are much finer than regular pipe threads; be careful not to cross-thread the fixtures.

Graywater Systems

Graywater systems can be perfectly safe and convenient. Using graywater means that

A Sampling of Low-Flow Showerheads

Fixed-Position Models	Price	Flow Rate in Use[a] @ 20psi	@ 80psi	Settings[b]	Shutoff Valve	Finish[c]	Comments
Sears Energy-Saving Showerhead 20170	$6	2.1	2.6	F	No	M, C	Highly rated in *Consumer Reports* survey/test (July 1991)
Thermo-Saver Dynajet CFO1	$6	1.1	2.3	M	Yes	M	Highly rated in *Consumer Reports* survey
Resources Conservation: The Incredible Head ES-181	$7	1.0	1.9	M	Yes	M	Doesn't function as well at low pressure (20psi)
Zin-Plas Water Pincher 14-9550	$10	1.2	2.4	F	No	M	Functions well at low pressure (20psi)
Chatham Solid Brass Showerhead 44-35	$39	1.8	2.7	F, C	No	M	Side-mounted adjustment lever
Vanderburgh Lovo Maximizer ME 4003	$25	1.7	2.4	F	Yes	M	Uses nonaerating design to reduce misting and reduce hot-water use
Hand-Held Models							
Sears Personal Hand Shower 20173	$23	1.5	3.1	F, P1	No	M, C	Highly rated in *Consumer Reports* survey/test
Teledyne Water Pik Shower Massage 5 SM-34	$43	1.2[d]	2.3	F, P2	No	M, P	Highly rated in *Consumer Reports* survey/test; can mix spray with pulse
Pollenex Dial Massage DM209	$24	1.8	2.5	F, C, P2	No	M, P	Works well at low pressure (20psi)

[a] in gallons per minute
[b] F = fine, M = mist, C = coarse, P1 = pulse one, P2 = two-pulse settings
[c] M = metal, P = plastic, C = chrome over plastic
[d] Tested at 20psi with flow restrictor reversed

you are the treatment facility; if you misuse the system, you may get sick, but that's a long shot. Do bear in mind, however, that gray-water use is illegal in all but a handful of drought-ridden communities in the West. The rewards are water conservation, money saved on your water bill, and a landscape that flourishes even during drought.

The safest sources of graywater are the washing machine, the tub, the shower, and the bathroom sink — everything but the kitchen sink, the toilets, and the automatic dishwasher. Even in a vegetarian household, the kitchen sink, especially if it has a disposal, has too much oil and too many food particles for practical filtering. (The exception is a double-basin sink with one side plumbed to the sewer and the other connected to the graywater system — but *everybody* must remember to use the graywater side only for washing vegetables and collecting clear water while waiting for hot water and when rinsing dishes.)

The most important guidelines for the healthy use of graywater — for both you and your landscape — are as follows:

■ **Water in, water out.** Never store gray-

An Integral Plumbing System

Drinking-quality water comes into the house from the local waterworks. Blackwater from the toilets and the kitchen sink goes to the septic tank or municipal sewage treatment plant. Relatively clean graywater from the tub, shower, sink, vegetable-washing sink, and washing machine is diverted to the garden to make the landscape flourish even during drought.

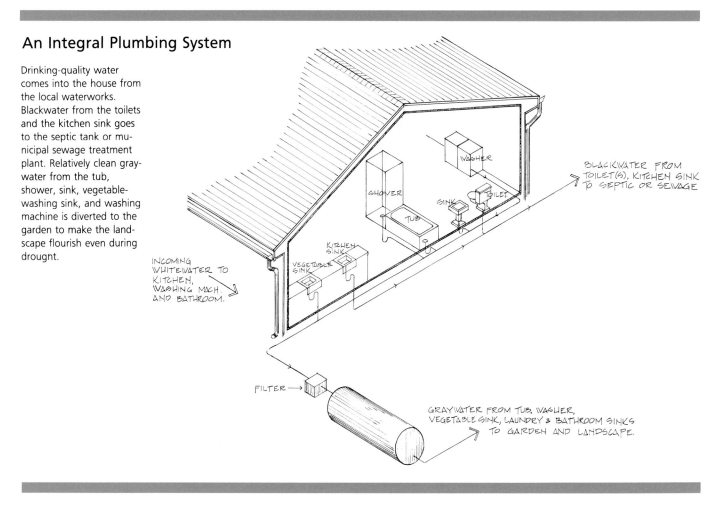

WASHER

SHOWER

TUB

SINK   TOILET

BLACKWATER FROM TOILET(S), KITCHEN SINK TO SEPTIC OR SEWAGE

KITCHEN SINK

INCOMING WHITEWATER TO KITCHEN, WASHING MACH. AND BATHROOM.

VEGETABLE SINK

FILTER

GRAYWATER FROM TUB, WASHER, VEGETABLE SINK, LAUNDRY & BATHROOM SINKS TO GARDEN AND LANDSCAPE.

water, not even for a day. The drums you see in properly designed graywater systems are called "surge" or "buffer" tanks. Their purpose is to collect graywater being generated by several sources at the same time and to hold it temporarily until a hose or pump can distribute it to the plants. On warm summer days, stored graywater quickly becomes a bacterial, septic soup, which smells bad and is more likely to breed disease.

■ **The surge tank should have an overflow port in case the system can't distribute the water fast enough during peak loading.** If possible, this overflow line should rely upon gravity flow and connect to the blackwater line (the larger three- or four-inch pipe to the sewer) with a minimum quarter-inch drop for every ten feet. Be sure to add a one-way swing

check-valve between the sewer line and the surge tank; this will allow graywater to drain into the sewer but will prevent a stopped-up sewer — heaven forbid! — from filling the surge tank. (Be sure to heed the positioning arrow embossed on the swing check-valve.)

■ **Never apply graywater with a sprinkler or onto a lawn.** Graywater should never puddle up or lie on the surface. The idea is to prevent, for example, the neighbor's kids from wandering over to play under the lawn's sprinklers on a hot day while your shower water is being sprayed. Graywater should be distributed under a thick mulch with drip-irrigation hose or into shallow gravel pockets, or leach fields, below the soil surface.

■ **Always plumb your graywater system with a set of two ball valves or a single** three-way valve to allow for convenient switching back to the sewer when it rains or if someone comes down with a serious communicable disease. This switching can be done with a remote-controlled electric solenoid three-way valve: one flip of the switch and the water is diverted to either the graywater system or the sewer.

■ Distribute the graywater to different sections of the landscape every couple of days. Never apply all graywater to the same spot. The soil will puddle and become anaerobic; the roots of plants will die in waterlogged soil; the standing water will attract animals and insects; and the soil's structure may even be destroyed. A set of simple manual valves in the landscape will allow you to rotate the graywater to a different section every couple of days, depending upon how well your soil drains and how much graywater you generate. After a week or two, depending upon the type of plants you have, you'll be back watering the same spot.

■ Avoid using graywater on the most acid-loving plants, as soaps and detergents will make it slightly alkaline. Most shade-loving woodland plants prefer an acid soil. (For a list of acid-loving species, see "Water-Conserving Landscaping," page 209.)

■ Be cautious about what soaps, detergents, and cleansers you use in the laundry and bathroom. As a rule, stick to old-fashioned, simple soaps and cleansers. Avoid products with boron, such as Borateam and Boraxo. Limit your use of bleach as much as possible, or even better, eliminate bleaches entirely. If you have hard water, add ⅛ to ¼ cup hexametaphosphate for each five gallons of laundry water in place of the bleach, and then use half the amount of soap you normally use. Clean with simple scouring powders such as Bon Ami.

You don't have to use detergents low in phosphate, since a well-tended graywater system won't leach into any other water sources. In fact, the phosphate will serve as a mild fertilizer for your plants. Always buy a liquid laundry detergent; the fillers in powdered detergents are mostly salt-based compounds that are hard on soil and plants.

In areas that get less than fifteen inches of rainfall annually, graywater systems work best in homes without sodium-based water softeners. Water softeners are best suited to protecting electric water heaters and solar hot-water systems from scale, ensuring a clean, stain-free laundry and making water taste better. If possible, plumb or replumb your system so that the water softener is used only for these purposes, and use unsoftened water for other tasks. In any case, switch to potassium pellets for the softener unit; they'll be slightly less harmful to the soil.

Water conservation in the bathroom needn't be a financially painful sacrifice just "for the good of the environment." The payback can be as quick as two months with a new sink faucet, six months with a low-flow showerhead, and no more than three years for a ULF toilet. And the savings keep growing. By switching to water-conserving showerheads and toilets, according to *Consumer Reports,* the average American family using city water could save $50 to $75 per year on water and sewage bills and $20 to $50 on utility bills through reduced hot-water use in the shower. No matter how you figure it, you'll save money as well as precious resources.

■ Conserving Energy in the Bathroom

More hot water is used in the bathroom than anywhere else in the home. A solar water heater is the environmental first choice, but where there isn't enough sun for solar, on-demand water heaters are an energy-efficient alternative to conventional water heaters.

Solar Hot-Water Heaters
The solar hot-water heating industry went through a boom period in the 1970s and then went bust in the early 1980s. Poorly designed

Naturally Elegant Septic Systems

Many environmental homes are far from the maddening crowd — and urban services. Living in the country often means being your own sewage company; when you build a new home in a relatively pristine area, you have an added responsibility to do it right.

Typically, the rural homeowner has some version of a septic tank with a leach-field, or drain-field, system. The septic tank, a buried container made of concrete, fiberglass, or plastic, receives the household's waste. Solids settle to the bottom of the tank and are broken down to some degree by bacteria. The cleaner wastewater from the septic tank flows into a series of perforated pipes sunk in gravel-filled trenches, and then it percolates, or drains, into the surrounding soil, where it is further purified by bacteria.

There's nothing particularly elegant about a septic system. Its only beauty lies in its being below ground, unseen, and, if all works well, odorless. In many instances, however, septic systems don't work well. One difficulty is "poor perc" — soils that can't percolate fast enough to keep the wastewater from backing up and creating a potential health hazard. In areas where the soil is extremely sandy, the problem is the exact opposite: soils percolate all too well, and the wastewater reaches precious underground water supplies before the pollutants have been adequately broken down.

Constructed wetlands and evapo-transpiration beds, or elevated drain fields, are solving these problems in counties with forward-thinking planning departments.

Evapo-Transpiration Beds

Evapo-transpiration beds are the less experimental alternative. Large quantities of sand, gravel, and topsoil are trucked to the site, and a drain field is constructed on the surface. A thick layer of sand, often at least two feet deep, is laid down first; next comes a layer of gravel in trenches in a loamy or sandy topsoil. Typical perforated drainpipe is then laid in the gravel trenches, as in an ordinary drain field. The mound is capped with a thick layer of

good loamy topsoil, usually at least three feet thick.

The bad news about evapo-transpiration beds is that they look like elevated mini–football fields, and their cost runs in the tens of thousands of dollars. The good news is that because they must be covered with grasses to help transpire some of the water, the mounds are a perfect spot for a patch of prairie or meadow.

Be sure to work with a specialist to properly size your mound.

Treatment Marshes

Constructed wetlands are the most novel, and certainly the most colorful, alternative septic technology. They treat the wastewater from a septic tank and at the same time beautify the yard. Also called microbial rock/plant filters, they are living beds of colorful flowers, rushes, cattails, and other marsh plants. The wastewater is purified as it flows through the attractive artificial bog, eventually getting clean enough to be released into creeks, streams, or lakes.

These naturally elegant home sewage-treatment plants were invented by Dr. Bill Wolverton, the en-

A colorful bed of canna lilies doubles as the sewage treatment plant for a group of mobile homes in Pearlington, Mississippi.

vironmental scientist who began developing larger-scale systems for NASA in the early 1970s.

Dozens of home marshes are now treating sewage in private yards in Louisiana, Mississippi, Alabama, and other southern states. Larger-scale systems are already operating in colder climates — in Monterey, Virginia, for example, where the temperature has dipped to twenty-five degrees below zero without any adverse effects. City-scale wetlands are used seasonally in South Dakota and a handful of other northern climes. The future for home-scale systems in the North looks equally bright.

The mini-marshes don't take up much yard space. Experience with twenty home marshes in Louisiana indicates that the average two-bedroom house requires only 210 square feet of rock marsh, typically a 3 × 70-foot trench or a 20½ × 10¼-foot shallow sump.

Construction is not terribly complicated. First a trench is dug, eighteen inches deep and large enough to retain the effluent for forty-eight to seventy-two hours as it flows naturally to the far, and slightly downhill, end. The entire excavation is lined with a PVC swimming-pool liner or an even sturdier membrane called EDPM, which almost never tears or punctures, doesn't get brittle and crack in cold winters, and is nontoxic to fish and aquatic plants. The lined trench is filled twelve inches deep with 1- to 1½-inch round river rock or gravel and capped with 6 inches of pea gravel to cover the water, eliminate odors, and even allow for foot traffic. Plants are transplanted into the pea-gravel layer with their roots reaching into the river-rock zone. Pollutants in the wastewater are broken down by microorganisms and become food for the plants. If necessary, a sump pump can be built into the end of the trench to lift the treated water to the landscape or a nearby stream.

Canna lilies, calla lilies, iris, ginger lily, elephant ears, and other ornamental plants have all been used successfully in home treatment marshes. Cattails, bulrushes, and other wetland plants are also used. An even more ecological approach is to re-create an entire native wetland plant community to treat your waste.

Maintenance of your personal wastewater marsh is relatively simple: you just cut away the dead leaves on the bog plants and weed out any non-aquatic grasses that sneak into the gravel bed.

What does a personal wetland system cost? The price is fairly competitive with that of a conventional septic system. In Louisiana, for example, they cost between $1,800 and $1,950 (if a pump is required to get water from the septic tank to the trench), compared to $1,300 to $1,400 for a traditional septic tank with drain field.

If your home is already hooked up to the sewer, forget about putting in any kind of alternative system; you wouldn't be able to get the permits needed even if you wanted to. But if your house in the country has a malfunctioning septic system, or if you're planning a new country home, you may be able to build in another element of environmental responsiveness and perhaps save some money at the same time.

Be sure to start working with your landscape architect and civil engineer early on to coordinate all aspects of the design. And be nice to the people in your local planning and health departments. They will pass judgment on everything you present, and they tend not to take kindly to experimental systems.

Further Reading

Peter Warshall's *Septic Tank Practices: A Guide to the Conservation and Reuse of Household Wastewater* (New York: Doubleday/Anchor, 1979) is the classic handbook and still the best work on septic tanks and drain fields. Alternative systems are also discussed.

A new generation of water-conserving shower-heads emit only half as much water as conventional models — and you'd never know the difference. Nor do you need to give up your hand-held shower-head to save water: a number of low-flow versions are available.

hardware, badly trained installers, and con artists stole a bit of the glow from solar hot water, but the biggest factor contributing to the bust was the loss of state and federal tax credits.

Solar-heated water is nevertheless still a cost-effective option for much of the United States. And today's solar water heaters are much better looking, better built, and more reliable. Gone are the days when the water heater resembled a wayward space probe that had crashed into the roof. The new, slim solar water heaters lie supine at the same angle as the roof, and an increasing number of units are actually being built *into* the roof, so that all you see is the sleek, silver-blue glint of the glazing, with the hardware tucked discreetly out of view.

The plethora of solar heaters available in the 1970s has been distilled down to two basic types: drain-down and drain-back. Both are active systems that use pumps to move the water around. The solar collector for either type can be an unobtrusive panel of copper sheet metal and tubing encased in an insulated and glass-covered array on the roof; the insulated hot-water storage tank can be located anywhere in the house. Both designs avoid the Achilles' heels of many early solar water heaters: winter freeze damage to the pipes and tanks, and nighttime heat loss, which resulted in tepid water at best by morning.

In drain-down systems, water is pumped through the collector on sunny days, and any water in the panel's tubing automatically drains down when the circulating pump shuts off on cloudy days and at night. This prevents the hassle of frozen pipes. Drain-down systems are more efficient than drain-back types, but they also cost about twice as much to operate and fix.

Drain-back systems also automatically drain the water every time the circulating pump shuts off, but they employ a special, non-potable fluid in a loop between the collector panel and the heat exchanger in the hot-water storage tank. In other words, the water you

shower with never comes in contact with the copper collector panel. These systems are about 10 percent less efficient than drain-down systems, but maintenance and repair costs are generally cut in half.

Other than the type of technology, there are three primary concerns to bear in mind when planning a solar hot-water system: the size of the panel(s) and storage tank, the angle and orientation of the panels, and the panels' exposure to sunlight. The square footage of the panels is directly linked to your hot-water consumption. If you have a low-flow showerhead and faucet aerators, you'll require a smaller — and less expensive — array. The size of the panels also varies greatly from region to region and even within different microclimates in the same region.

For example, in parts of northern California where conditions are relatively favorable for solar water heating, the typical family of four needs approximately sixty-four square feet of collector. The storage tank should hold one half gallon to two gallons of water for every square foot of glazed panel. Thus, in northern California, a typical sixty-four-square-foot system has an eighty-gallon storage tank. The angle of placement, any partial shade, morning fog, and prevailing winds can easily increase this figure. Always consult a local solar technician about what size panel and storage tank would best suit your climate and household needs.

The collectors must be oriented south for good exposure to sunlight. Anything within 15 degrees east or west of true solar south — not magnetic south — is ideal. The panels should be mounted at an angle that equals the average of the ideal angles for summer and winter. The rule of thumb is your latitude plus or minus 10 degrees (plus favors winter water heating, while minus favors summer heating). Remember, the panels will look best mounted on a portion of the roof that itself matches this ideal angle.

Ideally, the panels should get full dawn-to-dusk exposure to the sun; any shade will reduce their effectiveness. The most critical period is between ten in the morning and two in the afternoon, when the sunlight is at its most intense. At other hours, much of the sunlight is lost to heating as it's reflected off the panels' glazing.

A solar hot-water system for your house can set you back $3,000 to $5,000, but the payback time ranges from only six years to twelve years. The savings on a solar system that heats water for a swimming pool or spa are absolutely undeniable — solar costs as little as one tenth as much as a household hot-water system for this task.

Experience has shown that solar collectors for swimming pools usually need not be glazed; the cost of a glazed panel often far exceeds the benefits in heat gain in all but the coldest climates. The unglazed array is best located on a sunny slope below the pool or on the roof. Alternatively, it can be integrated into a handsome poolside arbor.

On-Demand Water Heaters

On-demand water heaters have been quite common in Europe and Japan for years. They're now widely available in the United States as well. Unlike the conventional water heater, in which energy is constantly required to keep a large tankful of water hot, on-demand heaters are tankless. When you turn on the hot water in the shower, sink, or laundry, a gas or electric heater comes on to heat only the water that actually flows through the pipes — resulting in an energy savings of up to 50 percent. A well-designed house would cluster all hot-water uses together so that the water would need to pass only a short distance from the on-demand heater through the walls; in a large house, several different heaters might be required.

Gas- or propane-fueled on-demand water heaters have a pilot light to ignite the burner whenever the hot water is turned on. Leaving the pilot flame off will conserve even more energy; it takes less than a minute to light the pilot before taking a shower or washing dishes.

Some super-energy-efficient on-demand heaters, such as the Japanese Paloma model, have two settings for the heating flame, high and low, allowing a measure of control over energy use. If the shower is not right next to the on-demand heater, you may need to use the high setting to get the water hot enough.

Many on-demand heaters are designed to generate a certain amount of heat regardless of the temperature of the incoming water. Some models, such as the French Aquastar, sense the temperature of the incoming water and add only enough energy to raise that temperature to a preset level. These models work especially well with solar hot-water systems, since they can boost the water temperature on overcast days, when the water heated by the solar system may be a bit too tepid.

■ Further Reading

Two of the best general references on home water conservation are *Water Efficiency for Your Home: Products and Advice Which Save Water, Energy, and Money* and *Water-Efficient Technologies for the Urban/Residential Sector,* both published by the Rocky Mountain Institute, Water Program, 1739 Snowmass Creek Road, Snowmass, Colorado 81654. The telephone number is (303) 927-3851.

Another booklet, *Stop the Five-Gallon Flush,* published in 1980 by McGill University School of Architecture's Minimum Cost Housing Group, in Montreal, Canada, is a good overview of many types of low-flush and composting toilets.

Tad Montgomery's *On-Site Wastewater Treatment Systems,* published in 1987 by the New Alchemy Institute, 237 Hatchville Road, East Falmouth, Massachusetts 02536, focuses on composting privies.

MATERIALS

A growing number of manufacturers and architects are pioneering alternatives to dozens of potentially health-threatening toxic building products from plywood to vinyl flooring. Natural materials such as solid wood, marble, and brick are both handsome and healthy.

When architects and interior designers choose materials for a project, they consider a number of variables, including how the materials will look, how much they will cost, how easy they are to find and install, and whether they're durable and easy to maintain. Until recently, however, no one considered the environmental impact of building materials.

One reason for this omission is that the study of building materials from an environmental perspective is still in its infancy. So-called life-cycle studies of the materials we use to build and decorate our homes — which evaluate and compare the entire range of environmental impacts of a product from manufacture through disposal — are just now getting under way. How much air and water pollution is created when the material is manufactured? How much energy is needed to make it and transport it to the homesite? Is it a potential health threat to either the builders or the inhabitants? Can it be recycled, or will it pose disposal problems in the future? These are a few of the questions these studies will address.

In a few years, we should have some of the answers. In the meantime, we can act on the knowledge we already have about the health impact of many common building materials. We have also become acutely aware of the ecological costs involved in our using certain woods. This chapter focuses on the products and practices that pose the most immediate threats to human health and to the survival of species and ecosystems. Alternative building products are also discussed. Suppliers are listed in Appendix A (page 221).

The cost of environmentally sensitive materials varies widely. Some of the new environmental paints cost less than more noxious products, while solid wood remains much more expensive than formaldehyde-laden plywoods or particleboards. Fortunately, in many cases, there are both reasonably priced and more expensive options. It's up to you to compare the risks and benefits as well as the costs of the various alternatives.

Materials and Health

In the past decade or so, as we've tightened up our houses and indoor air quality has become a concern, stories about dangerous home pollutants have been getting a lot of play in newspapers and magazines and on TV. By now, the health hazards of radon and asbestos have been so thoroughly publicized, and information about what to do if either one is a problem in your house has become so widely available, that there's no need to discuss them in detail here. What is new is the small but growing number of manufacturers and architects who are pioneering alternatives to the hundreds of potentially toxic building products, from plywood to paints, found in almost every house.

Plywood, Particleboard, and Other Composite Boards

Plywood — which consists of thin veneers of various woods bonded together with resin in a way that gives this material great structural strength — is ubiquitous in the modern house. Plywood is used for subflooring, to sheath exterior walls and the roof, and in kitchen cabinets. Plywood faced with a veneer of mahogany, oak, or other handsome wood is often used in paneling and furniture. Other composite wood products include particleboard, oriented-strand board, fiberboard, and flakeboard. All of these cheaper alternatives to plywood are also made of bits of softwoods bonded together with resin.

It's the resin that's the problem. Most composite woods in the United States are glued together with urea formaldehyde, a substance that the U.S. Environmental Protection Agency considers to be a probable cancer-causer in humans. Urea formaldehyde has also been linked to a host of other health problems, from headaches and dizziness to nausea and rashes.

One way to prevent urea formaldehyde from leaking out of your cabinets or subflooring and polluting the air in your home is to use only exterior-grade plywoods, such as CDX, which are glued with other resins. It is harder, but not impossible, to find particleboard and other composite boards that have been bonded with less toxic resins; the label should state specifically that the product contains no urea formaldehyde. If you prefer not to take a chance with any resin at all, you can build your house the old-fashioned way — with solid wood. In a number of the houses featured in this book, construction-grade pine installed on the diagonal for structural strength is used for wall sheathing, subflooring, and roof decking. However, this is apt to be a more expensive option. The least expensive course of action in existing houses is to seal all accessible plywoods and composite boards — in your kitchen cabinets, for example — with AFM water seal or any other product that can prevent the formaldehyde from polluting your rooms.

Pressure-Treated Woods

Pressure-treated wood is the stuff in lumberyards that has a greenish cast. Used outdoors for decks, balconies, gazebos, play sets, fences, and furniture, it has been treated with highly poisonous preservatives to make it less vulnerable to insects and rot. In 1984 the EPA warned consumers not to handle or walk on pressure-treated wood bare-skinned or barefoot. A few years later, the agency announced that it would restrict the sale of the three chemicals that account for 97 percent of the wood preservative used in this country — chemicals that have caused cancer and other illnesses in test animals — to certified professionals. If at all possible, avoid pressure-treated wood when building your pergola or garden bench.

In years past, redwood and other naturally rot-resistant woods were employed for outdoor construction. But these woods — especially the red-colored heartwood redwood so prized by woodworkers and so invulnerable to the weather — though still available, are very expensive. What's more, the profligate use of

Ordinary paints and wood finishes contain toxic preservatives and biocides, some of them suspected cancer causers. In this room, the wood finishes are made of beeswax and other time-tested natural materials.

heartwood redwood puts extreme pressure on remaining old-growth forests (see the section on old-growth woods, page 162).

Some forestry experts in the Pacific Northwest advise homeowners to use materials other than wood whenever possible — to build brick or flagstone patios, for example, instead of wood decks. Architect Paul Bierman-Lytle, the founder of Environmental Outfitters, a source of ecologically sound materials for building and remodeling, has had good success with some lesser-known woods from South America, such as pau lope and purpleheart. According to Bierman-Lytle, these species have a fine, even grain that rivals that of teak, and they require no preservatives, can last sixty years or longer, and don't contribute to rain-forest destruction. Still another option is to use ordinary lumber and treat it with one of the natural or less toxic preservatives now on the market.

Paints and Wood Finishes

The paints, stains, and varnishes used on almost every surface in the average house have more than one environmental problem. Paint containing lead, long recognized as hazardous, was banned for most uses in 1977, but mercury, barium, tin, and arsenic are still used as preservatives in many coatings, which also may contain mildewcides, fungicides, and bacteriacides, some of which the EPA classifies as suspected human carcinogens. Moreover, the petroleum-based solvents that are used to improve the application of coatings themselves contain volatile organic compounds (chemicals that volatilize, or become a breathable gas, at room temperature), some of which are suspected toxins, even carcinogens, and are extremely irritating to the estimated 15 percent of the population that is chemically sensitive. These solvents are also photochemically reactive — that is, they react to the ultraviolet rays in sunlight by producing ozone, a major component of smog. Both health concerns and the stringent air-quality regulations instituted in a number of states are turning the paint industry on its head.

Three German companies that now export their wares to the United States — Livos, Biofa, and Auros — have led the industry in the development of safer coatings by returning to natural ingredients. Their paints, for example, contain no toxic preservatives or biocides, only plant-derived resins and solvents such as citrus terpene, distilled from discarded citrus peels. Pigments come from plants and minerals. Only Auros, however, produces paints that are completely "natural"; the other two companies augment their citrus terpene with an isoaliphatic hydrocarbon that, although synthetic, is nonaromatic and caused fewer allergic reactions in workers than the totally natural solvents. The three companies also manufacture a host of other low-toxicity products, including lacquers, oils, waxes, varnishes, and shellacs. Some painters do complain that the German companies' water-based products, though not their oil-based enamels, are chalky.

In recent years, a few American companies, most notably Murco Wall Products, Miller Paint Company, and AFM Enterprises, have entered the field of environmental finishes. These companies have eliminated known toxic ingredients and either done away with or greatly reduced the biocides in their products. They do not use predominantly natural ingredients, however, opting instead for synthetics that are not irritating to most people with chemical sensitivities. A big advantage of the American paints is their price: they cost substantially less than their European counterparts and in some cases even less than conventional coatings.

Be sure to use even low-toxicity products only in well-ventilated areas.

Flooring

The most common floor coverings in the late-twentieth-century house are polyurethaned woods, vinyl linoleums, and wall-to-wall carpeting. Polyurethane contains urethane, which has caused cancer in test animals. Vinyl flooring off-gasses polyvinyl chloride, formaldehyde, and other volatile organic compounds. Most modern carpeting is made of nylon and other petroleum derivatives and is treated with fungicides, mildewcides, stain guards, and fire retardants. You don't have to be hypersensitive to chemicals to react badly to the stench of a newly carpeted room: wall-to-wall carpeting also harbors dust, dust mites, and other allergens.

What are the healthier alternatives? Wood floors are a good choice if they're coated with beeswax or one of the low-toxicity coatings available from the companies mentioned above. Natural linoleum, a Victorian innovation, doesn't off-gas toxic fumes, but it may be hard to find. Slate, marble, ceramic tiles, concrete, and brick, especially when installed with low-tox grouts and sealants, are other options. If you insist on wall-to-wall carpeting, stick to natural, untreated fibers with jute backings or Homosote cushions, made of recycled paper. All-natural carpeting is very expensive; area rugs made of untreated natural fibers, reed, or sisal are easier on the pocketbook, and they

can always go outdoors for a good shaking and airing.

Insulation

In the late 1970s, some of the first indications of what is now called the sick building syndrome came from residents of homes insulated with urea formaldehyde foam. Headaches, irritation of the eyes and the respiratory tract, and dizziness were common complaints. Formaldehyde levels in many of these homes proved to be unusually high. Urea formaldehyde foam insulation is no longer made in this country, but the sick building syndrome is proof positive that what you stuff between your walls can come back to haunt you.

Solid wood, natural linoleum, slate, marble, and ceramic tile are the floorings of choice in an environmental home. Area rugs made of untreated natural fibers are preferable to wall-to-wall carpeting because they can be taken outdoors for a good shaking and airing.

In a New England kitchen, local woods such as pine, maple, and butternut make handsome substitutes for species whose harvest threatens tropical rain forests and old-growth forests in the Pacific Northwest. Design: South Mountain Company.

None of the usual insulation materials is perfect from an environmental perspective. Fiberglass and mineral wool consist of tiny fibers that can be irritating to, among other things, the lungs. Manufacturers and installers are supposed to wear respirators, gloves, and other protective clothing when working with these materials, and there is some concern that the fibers can migrate through air ducts and into the house. Polystyrene boards and polyurethane, polyisocyanate, and phenolic foams release noxious fumes and produce deadly gases when they burn. Although cellulose insulation is made of innocuous-seeming pulverized newspaper, it is treated with toxic mildewcides and fire retardants. Cellulose and other kinds of loose insulation can produce airborne dusts and fibers that can infiltrate the house; they can also make for messy renovation and remodeling.

So what's left? Paul Bierman-Lytle recommends cork, a type of bark that can be installed either loose or in slabs. Cork is natural and nontoxic, but it is hard to find and quite expensive. Air-Krete, a cementitious compound typically made from magnesium oxide, a mineral derived from seawater, is a sprayed-in insulation used by Bierman-Lytle and a handful of other American architects. Air-Krete is noncombustible and insect-proof, doesn't release toxic fumes, and provides good R-value. But finding a trained local installer may be a problem.

◼ Tropical and Old-Growth Woods

Solid wood would seem to be the perfect material for the naturally elegant home. It's handsome. It's constantly renewed by nature. It links a home with the surrounding landscape, especially in forested areas. But it must be carefully chosen.

Some of the choicest woods come from rapidly disappearing rain-forest areas, while others come from threatened old-growth forests here at home. If you are building or remodeling a

house, it's important for you to make sure that your architect or contractor specifies wood whose harvest does not add to the destruction.

Sorting Out Tropical Woods

The tropical hardwood trade is big business — about $7 billion a year and growing. Most tropical woods come from Southeast Asia, especially Indonesia, Malaysia, and increasingly Papua New Guinea. Commercial logging has contributed greatly to deforestation in the region. Africa's tropical hardwoods have already been heavily exploited. In the Amazon, logging has so far been comparatively limited, but the potential consequences of indiscriminate hardwood production in this area are enormous. Japan is the largest importer of tropical hardwoods, followed by Europe and the United States.

American houses are built with a variety of

finished and semifinished products made of tropical woods. Hardwood plywoods used for decorative interior paneling, cabinetry, and furniture are made mostly from lauan, also known as meranti. The Rainforest Alliance, a conservation group, has singled out lauan as one of the most threatened tropical timbers. The plywood's lauan core is generally faced with veneers of such beautifully grained tropical species as mahogany and teak, two other tropical woods that are considered to be endangered or overexploited in all or part of their ranges. Even plywood faced with domestic wood veneers such as cherry or oak often contains a lauan core. Doors, door and window casings, flooring, moldings, and garden furniture are among the many other products made from tropical woods. The chart on pages 160–161 lists the tropical timbers that you should avoid whenever possible.

To reassure consumers, commercial logging in the tropics is often described as "selective" because only the most valuable hardwoods are cut down. In a few countries — most notably Guyana, Suriname, and Trinidad — valuable species are indeed harvested in this way, and the rest of the forest is not unduly damaged. Most of the time, however, you should take the term "selective logging" with a grain of salt. The careless tree felling, skid hauling, and road construction usually associated with selective logging inevitably results in unnecessary and wasteful damage to the rain forest. The logging roads open up previously inaccessible areas to slash-and-burn farmers. Because rain-forest soils are so poor, these landless farmers must move on in a few years to a new patch of forest, and the circle of destruction grows ever wider.

According to the Rainforest Alliance, a few tropical hardwoods are actually harvested with little or no damage to the rain forest. Rubberwood (*Hevea* spp.) grown on Malaysian plantations makes a suitable replacement for threatened ramin, especially in furniture. Virola (*Virola* spp.), which grows in Amazonian swamp forests, is a good all-purpose tropical

wood for veneer, furniture, moldings, and other uses. Teak grown on plantations is an environmentally sound alternative to teak taken from the rain forest, and it is difficult to distinguish between the two.

You can also feel confident about using tropical timbers labeled as Smart Wood. Having extensively researched the tropical hardwood trade and its ecological impacts, the Rainforest Alliance now certifies sources of Smart Wood and companies that sell Smart Wood products — that is, products made exclusively of certified woods. All sources of tropical timber are eligible for certification, including natural forest, plantations, large commercial timber concessions, and small community forestry projects. Until there are broadly accepted standards governing timber production in specific regions and types of operations, the Rainforest Alliance will continue to evaluate sources of tropical timber on a case-by-case basis, using the following criteria. First, the company must protect the ecological integrity of the tract of forest that the wood is taken from. This means, for example, that watersheds must be preserved and soil erosion

Using recycled wood not only conserves resources but also adds a mellow patina to renovated rooms.

Tropical Timbers to Avoid*

Common and Botanical Names	Origin	Primary Uses
Afrormosia *Pericopsis elata*	Africa, mainly Ghana	Wall paneling, furniture, decks
Amazaque *Guibourtia* spp. (also called shedua, mozambique)	Ivory Coast	Cabinetry
Andiroba *Carapa guianensis* (also called cedro macho, carapa, crabwood, tangare, bastard mahogany, para mahogany)	West Indies, Central America, Brazil	Cabinetry, flooring, furniture, millwork, decorative plywood
Avoidire *Turraeanthus africanus* (also called African white mahogany)	Ivory Coast	Cabinetry, fine joinery, paneling, veneer
Iroko *Chlorophora excelsa* (also called African teak, kambala)	Ivory Coast, Liberia, Ghana	Furniture, joinery, veneer
Kapur *Dryobalanops* spp. (also called Borneo teak, Borneo camphorwood)	Southeast Asia, Sumatra, Borneo	Joinery, construction, decking. Used in plywood, either alone or with lauan
Kempas *Koompassia malaccensis*	Malaysia, Indonesia	Flooring
Lauan *Shorea* spp. (also called meranti, Philippine mahogany)	Southeast Asia	Plywood, furniture, light structural work
Macawood *Platymiscium* spp. (also called macacaube, trebol, cristobal, Mexican tulipwood)	Trinidad, Mexico to Brazilian Amazonia	Furniture, cabinetry, veneers

*Adapted from *The Wood Users Guide,* by Pamela Wellner and Eugene Dickey.

must be controlled. Second, the company should harvest timber on a "sustained yield" basis — that is, the wood should not be cut down faster than it can be regrown or replaced by nature in the wild. And third, the operation should benefit local communities. Timber concessions are certified as Smart Wood sources according to how closely they meet these principles. A company that adheres strictly to them is classified as a "sustainable source," while one that at least demonstrates a strong commitment to them in its operations is classified as a "well-managed source." For a

list of Smart Wood companies and products, see Appendix A (page 221).

Some forest specialists believe that you can also take the pressure off overexploited tropical hardwoods by using lesser-known or even unknown species. By using these woods — and thereby creating a market where there currently is none — architects, interior designers, homeowners, and other wood users would increase the value of tropical forests in general and perhaps prevent them from being burned to the ground once the most valuable species have been removed. Anything that adds to the

Common and Botanical Names	Origin	Primary Uses
Mahogany *Khaya* spp.	West Africa	Furniture, veneers, interior finishes
Mahogany *Swietenia macrophylla*	Mexico, Central and South America	Cabinetry, furniture, interior trim, paneling, veneers
Merbau *Intsia* spp.	Southeast Asia	Flooring, furniture, construction
Okoume *Aucoumea Klaineana* (also called gaboon, samara)	West Africa	Plywood, furniture, paneling
Paduak *Pterocarpus* spp. (also called vermilion, pradu)	Africa, Thailand	Furniture, veneer
Ramin *Gonstylus bancanus*	Malaysia, Indonesia, Philippines	Furniture, molding, plywood, flooring
Rosewood *Dalbergia stevensonii, D. nigra, D. latifolia*	Brazil	Furniture, veneer
Sapele *Entandrophragma cylindricum*	Ivory Coast, Nigeria	Cabinetry, furniture, veneer
Spanish Cedar *Cedrela* spp. (also called cedro, cedrela)	Southern Mexico to Northern Argentina	Outdoor furniture, decking, paneling
Teak *Tectona grandis*	Burma, Thailand, Indonesia, Cambodia	Furniture, flooring, decking
Utile *Entandrophragma utile*	Ivory Coast, Ghana	Cabinetry, veneer, quality joinery
Wenge *Millettia laurenti* (also called panga panga, dikela)	West Africa	Cabinetry, furniture, paneling, flooring, interior and exterior joinery

value of the rain forest, the reasoning goes, strengthens the case for keeping it. See Appendix A for importers of these lesser-known woods.

Still another course of action is to substitute woods from temperate forests for threatened tropical species. For example, plywood made of domestic birch can be used instead of lauan plywood. The choice domestic species for architectural woodwork are oak, poplar, cherry, maple, alder, walnut, birch, and ash; for kitchen cabinets, walnut, maple, oak, cherry, birch, ash, alder, and hickory. Look for the Hardwood Manufacturers Association's "Solid Hardwood from the U.S.A." label.

In the words of Pam Wellner, author of the Rainforest Action Network's *The Wood Users Guide*, "Sometimes it's easy to do the right thing — for example, to substitute birch plywood for lauan plywood. But we recognize that other decisions are not so simple, and that there might not be a temperate wood that exactly fills the role of a tropical wood." She urges professionals to be imaginative and to experiment with alternative woods from temperate forests — for example, by exploring new ways to stain domestic woods. She also recommends that wood users seek out small-scale local milling operations that carry lesser-known but beautifully grained native woods.

The Old-Growth Dilemma

Redwood, Douglas fir, and Western red cedar, all widely used in home building and remodeling, often come from this continent's old-growth forests — so called because they are some of the most ancient forests in existence. The old-growth forests, primarily in the Pacific Northwest, are also some of the most diverse and complex biological systems on the planet, and they are easily disturbed. Only about 5 percent of North America's old-growth forest remains, but there is intense pressure to harvest magnificent still-standing specimens of redwood, Douglas fir, and cedar — some of the oldest trees in the world.

Redwood weathers exquisitely and is relatively impervious to rot. It is therefore used extensively for exterior siding and trim, decks, and outdoor furniture. Because Douglas fir is so strong and stable, it is a structural timber of choice and is also used for exterior doors and door and window casings. Western red cedar, like redwood, contains oils that repel water and insects, making it particularly suitable for wood shingles.

Much of the old-growth wood that is still available comes from residual patches of forest on relatively small, privately owned tracts of woodland, not from federally protected lands. However, conservationists and advocates of ecologically balanced forestry argue that these remaining fragments, rather than being harvested, should instead be the basis of efforts to restore larger, more viable tracts of old-growth forest, or at least to research which management techniques will do the least damage to the old-growth ecosystem.

What are the alternatives? Use second-growth and plantation-grown trees whenever possible. In many cases, quickly grown trees harvested from commercial forests cannot rival old-growth specimens in quality or rot resis-

tance, but there are exceptions: many woodworkers claim that second-growth Douglas fir is as good as old-growth (although it is reportedly slightly harder to nail). Look for salvaged old-growth timbers — recycled boards from demolished buildings or logs from abandoned logging sites, for instance. Look, too, for certified sources of old-growth timbers; see Appendix A (page 221) for a list of suppliers.

The truth is, however, that there isn't enough salvaged or certified old-growth wood to support our current uses of these magnificent trees. We simply must use less. We should substitute nonwood or aluminum-clad windows for redwood windows. Species of fir and cedar that don't come from old-growth forests can make quality windows, doors, and exterior trim, as can pine; cedar has natural rot resistance, and fir and pine can be painted or stained. We should seek out small, nearby mills that offer local species, and craftsmen who make furnishings out of native woods. For example, in nearly every county in the country there is someone who fashions benches, chairs, and tables from regional hardwoods. While most of these woods are not nearly as tough, rot-resistant, or long-lasting as teak or old-growth redwood, furniture made from them will probably last the rest of your life — and will help relieve the pressure on tropical and Californian woods. It will also add to your home's bioregional style and sense of place.

In short, we need a commonsense approach to building and decorating with old-growth woods as well as threatened tropical species. It is a waste to use teak as flooring when any number of handsome domestic woods could be substituted with durability and style. And why put old-growth redwood inside the house, where its rot resistance isn't needed? Whenever there is a viable substitute for old-growth timber, we should choose it — and reserve the problematic species only for those uses for which there are absolutely no alternatives.

■ Further Reading

First Cut: A Primer on Tropical Wood Use and Conservation, published by the Rainforest Alliance, is an excellent brief explanation of how the use of certain tropical woods contributes to rain-forest destruction. You can also get information on the Smart Wood certification program from the Rainforest Alliance by writing them at 270 Lafayette Street, Suite 512, New York, New York 10012.

The Wood Users Guide, by Pamela Wellner and Eugene Dickey, includes a comprehensive list of tropical woods used for building and remodeling, as well as plenty of information on alternative species and products. It's available from the Rainforest Action Network, 301 Broadway, Suite A, San Francisco, California 94133.

For more information on domestic hardwoods that can be substituted for tropical woods, write the Hardwood Manufacturers Association at 400 Penn Center Boulevard, Suite 530, Pittsburgh, Pennsylvania 15235. Ask for *The Finished Home: A Guide to Solid Hardwoods in Architectural Woodwork* and *The Heart of the Home: A Guide to Solid Hardwoods in Kitchen Cabinets.*

The Institute for Sustainable Forestry can provide a list of certified suppliers of old-growth woods as well as tanoak, madrone, and other species from Pacific Northwest forests. The Institute may also be able to hook you up with environment-minded suppliers of species indigenous to your area. The Institute's address is P.O. Box 1580, Redway, California 95560; the telephone number is (707) 923-4719.

The American Institute of Architects publishes the *AIA Environmental Resource Guide,* a series of quarterly documents that examine tropical woods, indoor air quality, and other environmental issues facing the home-building industry. The *Guide* also includes materials analyses to enable architects and designers to better understand the real environmental costs of materials they specify, and to help them identify viable alternatives. The AIA's address is 1735 New York Avenue NW, Washington, D.C. 20006; the telephone number is (202) 626-7300.

PART FOUR

DESIGNING A
Naturally Elegant Garden

There's no reason environmental home improvements must begin indoors. If your house is in decent shape and you love to garden, then outside is the best place for you to start.

So how do you create a garden that is bountiful and beautiful and helps promote biological diversity? Most of the naturally elegant gardens featured on these pages combine garden rooms or edible landscapes near the house with zones of natural vegetation toward the periphery of the property. There are plenty of other publications that will tell you how to plant a garden room, whether your taste runs to medieval knot gardens or lush herbaceous borders; that is not the focus of this book. This section will begin with a look at the two most unique areas of the naturally elegant garden: its natural and its edible landscaping. Various methods and techniques of environmental gardening will be discussed, including how to conserve water in the garden; how to compost food scraps and garden clippings the lazy way and still dramatically reduce the amount of trash you send to the local landfill; and how to design a landscape that will make your home both energy-efficient and comfortable.

In the garden, even those who already own a home can make major environmental changes for the better with a bit of ingenuity and muscle power and without a lot of money. The following is a list of "ten commandments" for naturally elegant landscapers. Use them as broad guidelines, tailoring them to your own needs and the natural character of your yard.

1. **Don't just let things go.** Simply mothballing the mower will give you a garden that's anything but natural and elegant. The "no-mow" approach is apt to produce a mess of aggressive weeds including ragweed, quack grass, bull thistle, and burdock. Because much of the native vegetation in most gardens has been removed and replaced with exotic plants, natural landscaping requires careful design and replanting, at least at first.

2. **Let your bioregion be your guide.** In this day and age, truly native landscapes are few and far between. But you can't re-create a natural landscape unless you know what the original looked like. To gather ideas for your garden, go out and explore natural areas nearby, with your field guide in hand. Become acquainted with the major plant communities in your bioregion and learn what species grow in them. If you can't find any natural areas, visit local botanical gardens and arboreta that feature native plant communities, or get help from native plant societies (most states have them), your local botanical club, or nurseries in your area that specialize in native species.

3. **Get to know your yard.** You should live in a new home for at least a year before you plan the permanent landscape. You'll learn countless things about soil types and drainage, wind, sun, and shade patterns, pests, noise, eyesores, and other annoyances. You'll also become more intimate with your landscape's best features — such as that rocky outcrop or intoxicating view that made you fall in love with the place. This act of willpower and self-restraint is often very difficult for avid gardeners. But proceeding with caution doesn't mean you must give up gardening entirely; quite the contrary. Gardening is the best way to discover nature's subtle clues about what will thrive where on your property. Just refrain from installing walls, paths, and other expensive architectural elements, and don't get too attached to where you plant things.

4. **Work with nature, not against it.** Theoretically, it's possible (if expensive) to level a hill or fill a low area, but as a rule, bulldozers and backhoes don't belong in the naturally elegant garden. In most cases, neither does topsoil, lime, or peat moss taken from another ecosystem. In a naturally elegant garden, you work with the local topography and soils, which in fact constitute the foundation on which you build your garden. Begin by choosing a native plant community that will do well in your particular conditions; don't buy plants from totally different environments and then work against nature's momentum to make them at home. Working with nature also means taking into account existing landforms and vegetation when siting a new home in order to moderate climate, or planting shade trees or vines to make your present home more comfortable and energy-efficient (see "Energy-Conserving Landscaping," pages 194–200).

5. **Preserve native vegetation.** If your property is in an undisturbed natural area — deep in a spruce and fir forest or surrounded by native chaparral — consider yourself lucky! Preserve as much of the native flora as possible. If your urban or suburban yard includes a fragment of native vegetation — say, a tiny patch of forest — make it a focal point of your garden.

6. **Where the native vegetation has been disturbed, restore it.** The vast majority of urban and suburban backyards have lost native vegetation to the bulldozer and are now covered with an unimaginative mix of plants from around the world. On these lots, native plant communities can be restored.

7. **Plant your edible landscape no farther from the kitchen door than you can throw your kitchen sink** — the old-fashioned cast-iron variety. There's a direct correlation between the distance from the kitchen to the vegetable bed and the latter's early demise.

8. **Put architectural garden elements close to the house.** From decks to terraces to pergolas, such elements ease the transition from architecture to nature. Putting garden rooms close to the house also makes entertaining or barbecuing a lot more convenient.

9. **The farther it is from the house, the wilder your landscape should be.** Blend your landscape into any surrounding native vegetation.

10. **Start small.** Unless you can afford to hire help or have a lot of fanatical gardener friends, develop your garden in phases. Begin, for example, with one zone of natural vegetation, so only as much area as you can care for will be a mess at any given time. As each area shapes up, you can move on to the next. As for the edible landscape, begin with an area of a hundred square feet or less. Make this vegetable patch picture-perfect, then add another hundred square feet a year until you've had enough. Don't let the edible landscape take over your life! Gardening should be great fun and therapy, not drudgery. Convert parts of your edible garden to lower-maintenance natural landscape if things get out of hand.

NATURAL LANDSCAPING

Zones of natural landscape are the backbone of the naturally elegant garden. Over the years, the term "natural landscaping" has had a variety of meanings. There's the "retire-the-lawn-mower-come-what-may" approach practiced by hopeful homeowners fed up with lawn care. There's a kind of "affirmative action" gardening that uses wildflowers in traditional ways — in Gertrude Jekyll–style perennial borders, for example. There's also a sophisticated kind of naturalistic gardening that mingles plants from similar environments worldwide with spectacular effect — elaborate rock gardens, for instance, which include rare and beautiful species from alpine settings around the globe. However, at a time when the planet is losing its biological diversity at a breathtaking clip, a stricter definition of natural landscaping now seems to be in order — one based on recreating native plant communities, or at least significant parts of them. Many urban and suburban gardens are far too small for full-fledged ecological restoration, but we *can* select and arrange plants in a way that expresses the essence of a natural area.

North America comprises a multitude of plant communities. On the largest scale, precipitation patterns, averages and extremes of temperature, the length of the growing season, and the amount of available sunlight combine to divide the continent into various plant provinces, or bioregions. In the East, for example, precipitation is not only plentiful but also fairly regular throughout the year, with no prolonged periods of drought. This kind of climate favors the development of deciduous forests. By contrast, conifers dominate the forests of western North America because they are superbly adapted to withstand extremes of cold, heat, and drought. In the North American grasslands, precipitation, which averages between ten and thirty-nine inches a year, is concentrated in peak periods; stretches of drought occur annually, and there are great fluctuations from year to year.

Plant communities also vary within each bioregion. Botanists divide the eastern deciduous forest, for example, into a number of smaller regions where various species predominate. In the moist forests of West Virginia, Ohio, Indiana, and Kentucky, called the central hardwoods region, maples, basswoods, buckeyes, beeches, and tulip trees form a dense canopy of rich and exuberant growth. In the Middle Atlantic states, oak forests with more open canopies predominate (although at the turn of the century, before the introduction from Asia of chestnut blight fungus, the American chestnut was probably the most common tree in these forests).

What's more, within each of these subregions, the contour of the land and the character of the soils can change in a matter of miles or yards, and with them the plant community. If you live in central Long Island, off the coast of New York, in the Middle Atlantic oak region, for example, your property could be full of oaks, tulip trees, hickories, and American beeches characteristic of the forests that blanket the glacial moraine that forms the island's spine. It could also be full of the swamp maples, tupelos, and sassafras typical of deciduous bottomlands and swamp forests; or the pitch pines of the pine barrens with their dry, sandy soils; or the straight-trunked cedars of the Atlantic white cedar swamps that dot Long Island's southern shore.

If you live in Illinois or Minnesota or Wisconsin, you live in a part of the Midwest that forms a transitional area, known as an ecotone, between the rich deciduous forests to the east and the drier grasslands to the west. Your area has the most dramatic range of plant communities in the eastern half of North America, including prairie, forest, and savanna, or open woodland.

Wherever you live, in order to create a natural landscape you must examine your property, determine what kind of habitat exists there, and then choose a local plant community that's suited to it.

Bioregions of North America*

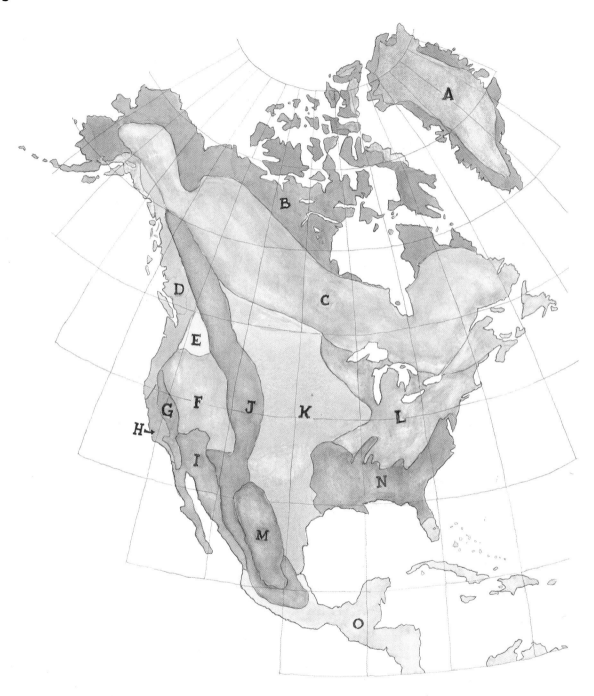

A	Ice	**E**	Palouse Prairie	**H**	Chaparral	**K**	Central Prairie	**O** Tropical Forest
B	Arctic Tundra	**F**	Great Basin	**I**	Mojave and	**L**	Eastern Deciduous	
C	Boreal Forest		Desert		Sonoran Deserts		Forest	
D	Pacific Maritime	**G**	Californian	**J**	Rocky Mountain	**M**	Chihuahuan Desert	
	Forest		Desert		Forest	**N**	Coastal Plain Forest	

*Adapted from *North American Terrestrial Vegetation*, edited by Michael G. Barbour and William Dwight Billings (New York: Cambridge University Press, 1988).

Living Garden Furniture

In the mid- to late 1980s, glossy garden catalogs were awash in teak chairs, benches, and tables. Since then, however, as the plight of rain forests around the world has become common knowledge, the problems associated not only with teak but also with mahogany and native redwood have made many people think twice about buying wooden garden furniture: nobody wants a bench that will hasten the demise of a forest (see "Materials," pages 154–163).

But it is possible to have wooden garden furniture that adds to, rather than subtracts from, the number of growing trees. Living garden furniture, or "bio-furniture," involves bending, tying, notching, wrapping, grafting, and pruning the young, supple shoots of a number of trees into one living unit with a useful shape. While most benches made from lumber will weaken with age, a well-tended living bench will actually build girth and strength over time.

There's little historical precedence for living

garden furniture. It's not topiary or espalier (trees trained to grow flat against a trellis or other framework), although some shaping and grafting techniques used to espalier trees are also used to train living furniture. Among these is an old European technique called pleaching, in which the limbs of two or more trees are joined, usually to form a sort of living arbor or trellis.

Some of the most important American examples of living furniture were created by Axel Erlandson in Scotts Valley, California. In the mid-1940s, Erlandson began training a small forest of sixty-seven oddly shaped, fantastically contorted trees that came to be called the Tree Circus. By carefully training trees on a framework and grafting

and pleaching them, he created, among other unbelievably complex and precise patterns, a working spiral staircase, two living chairs, and a perfect, crisscrossed, open lattice. Erlandson successfully merged architecture and horticulture. Most of his creations have been preserved and will be open to public view in the near future.

Living garden furniture is the ultimate horticultural challenge. Only gardeners with plenty of tree-pruning experience should attempt the pleaching and training required for a living garden structure. Your first project should be one that isn't designed to carry a load — for example, an arbor, gazebo, pergola, or shady extension of the roof. Save the living chair, bench, spiral staircase,

or jungle gym for later.

Regardless of the structure chosen, here are a few pointers for the budding practitioner of living furniture:

- The easiest trees to pleach are apple, pear, sycamore, hornbeam, hawthorn, and plum.
- Make a wooden or metal framework of the finished shape you hope to grow. Tie the supple young branches and tree trunks to it to train them.
- Vertical limbs will grow quickly and are less likely to sprout side branches.
- Cutting off vertical growth in winter will produce a number of side shoots that can eventually become horizontal elements.
- Horizontal limbs will grow slowly and sprout many vertical shoots.
- Slowly training a vertical limb to a horizontal position, over a period of months, will control the number of vertical shoots.
- You can speed the growth of a horizontal limb by tying it in a more vertical position.
- Unwanted growth is best controlled with summer pruning, after the end of July.

- Making a wide crescent-shaped notch just below the surface of the bark and below a bud will cause the bud to sprout into a limb. You can thus "place" a limb where you want one but the tree didn't.
- Late-summer T-budding (grafting a cutting onto a T-shaped cut) is another way to add a limb where one didn't naturally occur.
- Let the lower horizontal limbs fatten up before growing others above them.
- Branches will become pleached, or grow together, if they are twisted together and then tied.
- You can accelerate pleaching by scoring both limbs before twisting them together. Make sure the two scored limbs overlap as you twist and tie. You'll have a healed union in four to six weeks.
- Cross-bracing, diagonal pieces, and ornamental elements can be grafted onto the trees in winter. It's possible to graft both ends of a twig at the same time.

Opposite: Whether you're creating a living arbor, a bench, or a jungle gym, the technique is the same: trees are trained on a framework, and supple young branches are twisted together until they become entwined, or pleached.

Above: In time, after this living jungle gym builds girth and strength, generations of children will be able to climb it. Living garden furniture adds to, rather than subtracts from, the number of growing trees.

Natural Landscaping in Undeveloped Areas

Say you live in a relatively undisturbed natural area — perhaps you've just bought a house that's enveloped, Swiss Family Robinson–style, in a lush, subtropical Florida forest. How do you create your natural landscape? By doing as little as possible.

First study the site: what kinds of plant communities are growing there? You'll probably find that your tiny Garden of Eden has been invaded by plants that aren't native at all. People have been rearranging the planet's flora for so long that in North America you have to go to the remotest reaches of the Arctic to find ecosystems uncolonized by exotic plants. In many areas, some alien species have literally taken over. In Florida, for instance, the Brazilian pepper tree (*Schinus terebinthifolius*) is a most aggressive weed. In the Northeast, the Norway maple (*Acer platanoides*), first planted on this continent in the eighteenth century on a Pennsylvania estate, runs rampant throughout the deciduous forest. Below the Mason-Dixon line, the kudzu vine (*Pueraria lobata*), a Japanese import, has choked off so much native vegetation that it's known as the plant that ate the South. Iceplant (*Mesembryanthemum crystallinum*), meanwhile, is so drought-tolerant it has outcompeted many natives and overrun countless acres of California chaparral. The list goes on and on: Canada thistle, autumn olive, Japanese honeysuckle, purple loosestrife, multiflora rose, Oriental bittersweet, porcelainberry, and the casuarina tree are but a few of the interlopers. Left unchecked, these most aggressive weeds of the global garden can swamp native ecosystems. In most cases, the best thing to do is get rid of them.

But that's just janitorial work. If your urge to garden is strong, you can restore native species that have been smothered by the invaders, instead of waiting for wild volunteers. Some careful but creative pruning can enhance a view or let in light so that a richer ground flora can become established. Or you can cre-

Right: Patrick Chassé's deft native planting on Mount Desert Island replicates the generous massing, colors, and textures of plant associations in the wild: cushion mosses with a backdrop of New York fern, *Thelypteris noveboracensis.*

Below: A natural rock outcropping became a focal point of a Mount Desert Island garden after Patrick Chassé peeled away extraneous vegetation. Water trickles down the exposed granite and plunges into a small pool below. Photograph: Peter C. Jones.

ate a meandering path to heighten appreciation of your patch of forest, prairie, or chaparral — and encourage the weeding. Alternatively, you can grow flowers and edibles in containers, which leave no permanent mark on the land and can be moved around with the sun.

Natural Landscaping in Cities and Suburbs

In most of our yards, bulldozers have turned the soil into cement. Natural landforms have been leveled, and the native vegetation has been ripped out and replaced with lawn or, worse, asphalt. In cities, the only place to garden is often an abandoned lot strewn with splintering boards, old pipes, and plaster. The silver lining in this cloud is that you can start from scratch and have the freedom to design

with imagination and gusto — unlike gardeners in wilder areas, which should be treated with the utmost respect.

So where do you start?

Do a site analysis. This is landscape-architect talk for the process of examining the physical environment of your yard, with special attention to such factors as soil, moisture levels, and microclimates, areas that are especially windy, hot, and dry (a southern slope, for example, or the south side of the house), or moist and cool (a northern slope, a low area, or the north side of the house).

The soil — its pH (alkalinity or acidity), drainage, moisture content, and degree of organic matter — is the most critical factor in the choice of a native plant community or communities. Water is such an important factor that botanists classify communities according to their moisture preferences, from dry (xeric) to wet (hydric). On Long Island, for example, very dry, sandy soils are usually colonized by the pitch-pine communities; less xeric upland soils favor the forests dominated by oaks; and moist bottomlands are filled with swamp maples and other moisture-loving species.

You can learn a lot about your soil by simply digging several holes to check soil depth and texture (to determine how rich or sandy the soil is), wet and dry areas, and possible drainage problems, often caused when soil is compacted by construction equipment. An easy way to test soil drainage is to dig a hole about two feet deep and fill it with water. After it drains, fill it again. If the water takes

A Natural Landscape for Mount Desert Island, Maine

When landscape architect Patrick Chassé was called to consult on this spectacular property, a circular driveway severed the house — which sits on a coastal ledge and was designed by architect George Howe in 1938 — from the surrounding spruce-fir forest. Chassé knitted the house and forest back together with artfully placed stones (matched carefully in size, shape, and color to existing rocks on site) and "native sod," a combination of native bunchberry, wintergreen, and haircap moss rescued from a blueberry farm. Now the owners stroll from the parking area to the house down a handsome path strewn with pine needles. The designer left one small clearing near the front entrance of the house and edged it with a lush herbaceous border. In this secluded area, drifts of blue-gray foliage pick up the silvery tones of lichens in the boreal forest, while astilbes and other flowering plants add bright splashes of color. A side path leads to an intimate circle of granite benches close by the exposed granite ledge at the water's edge, where 'Hyperion' daylilies and other ornamentals mingle with the native species. Scattered throughout the woodland garden are lanterns, birdbaths, and other objects likewise chiseled from granite.

(Photographs of this garden appear on the opposite page and on pages 24–25 and 174.)

Selected Native Plants

Arrowwood	*Viburnum dentatum*
Bar Harbor juniper	*Juniperus horizontalis* 'Bar Harbor'
Bayberry	*Myrica pensylvanica*
Bearberry	*Arctostaphylos uva-ursi*
Bigleaf aster	*Aster macrophyllus*
Bluebead lily	*Clintonia borealis*
Bunchberry dogwood	*Cornus canadensis*
Christmas fern	*Polystichum acrostichoides*
Cinnamon fern	*Osmunda cinnamomea*
Creeping juniper	*Juniperus communis depressa*
Haircap moss	*Polytrichum commune*
Hay-scented fern	*Dennstaedtia punctilobula*
Highbush blueberry	*Vaccinium corymbosum*
Hobblebush	*Viburnum alnifolium*
Huckleberry	*Gaylussacia baccata*
Jack pine	*Pinus banksiana*
Lowbush blueberry	*Vaccinium angustifolium*
Male fern	*Dryopteris filix-mas*
Marginal shield fern	*Dryopteris marginalis*
Meadow rue	*Thalictrum polygamum*
Moose maple	*Acer pensylvanicum*
Mountain cranberry	*Vaccinium vitis-idaea*
New York fern	*Thelypteris noveboracensis*
Paper birch	*Betula papyrifera*
Pitch pine	*Pinus rigida*
Red maple	*Acer rubrum*
Red pine	*Pinus resinosa*
Red spruce	*Picea rubens*
Rock fern	*Polypodium virginianum*
Shadbush	*Amelanchier canadensis*
Sheep laurel	*Kalmia angustifolia*
Sweet fern	*Comptonia peregrina*
Violets	*Viola* spp.
White pine	*Pinus strobus*
White spruce	*Picea glauca*
Wild lily of the valley	*Maianthemum canadense*
Wild raisin	*Viburnum cassinoides*
Winterberry	*Ilex verticillata*
Wintergreen	*Gaultheria procumbens*

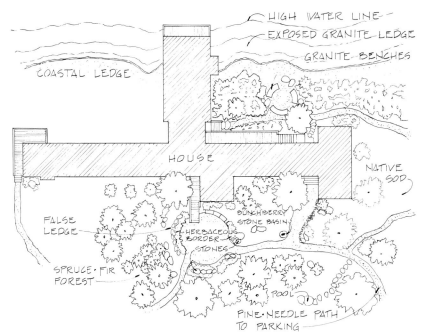

This secluded clearing is edged with a lush herbaceous border. Drifts of blue-gray foliage pick up the silvery tones of Mount Desert Island's boreal forest.

more than an hour to drain this second time, you've got a problem. You have two choices in this case. If it's the site of the future kitchen garden, you'll have to improve drainage by adding coarse sand and organic matter (see "Soil-Conserving Landscaping," pages 211–220); if it's part of the natural landscape, you can plant a native community of moisture-loving species.

Soil pH is easy to check with an inexpensive test kit available at most garden centers. For a few dollars more, soil laboratories will test samples, and they can also tell you whether salts or other elements are present in amounts high enough to be toxic to plants.

Make note of all these special areas in your garden.

Your site analysis should also include an inventory of the existing vegetation. Weeds are another clue to what kinds of plant habitats are in your yard. The presence of Queen Anne's lace, for example, is an indication that the soil is sandy and alkaline and not very fertile, whereas stinging nettle prefers wet, acidic soils. Note, too, all major native and nonnative plants on your property; at some point, you'll have to decide which will stay, which will move, and which will be made into compost or mulch.

Compile a wish list. What do you want from your garden? A tranquil retreat for strolling, contemplation, and other quiet pursuits? privacy from a busy street? a place for the kids to play? the world's best barbecue and lots of healthy, fresh produce? formal dinners on a flagstone terrace enclosed by a boxwood hedge or fragrant drifts of lavender?

Once your wish list is complete, it needs to be looked at in relation to the information you've gleaned from exploring your backyard environment — with some old-fashioned common sense thrown in for good measure. Areas where the soil is often soggy don't make the greatest playgrounds. You don't want to be carting elaborate entrees to a far-flung terrace. You're more apt to tend a clump of arugula if it's close to the kitchen door or a well-traveled path. But you must also keep in mind that many edibles require at least half a day of sunlight every day.

Native plant communities can serve some of your needs, especially for privacy or views, energy conservation, and outdoor comfort. A swath of shortgrass prairie or meadow (an area of grassland in an area dominated by forest) can preserve a view. If you live in the southern pinelands and need an evergreen community to screen your house from the street, and your soil is shallow and sandy, you can plant long-leaf pine (*Pinus palustris*) and other species native to the pine barrens of the region. If you have moister soil, you could use loblolly pine (*Pinus taeda*), oaks, and hickories. In cold northern climates, an evergreen community with balsam fir (*Abies balsamea*) or eastern hemlock (*Tsuga canadensis*) can provide an effective windbreak. On dry limestone ridges in subtropical Florida, communities of slash pine (*Pinus elliottii*) can shade your house from the relentless sun.

You'll also need a system of pathways to direct traffic, add shape, and invite closer scrutiny of the wild areas of your garden.

Choose appropriate plant communities. You've done your homework: you've studied the physical characteristics of your site as well as your family's wants and needs, and you've spent some time exploring the forests, prairies, or open shrublands near your home. Now you're ready to choose a native plant community or communities. This is of fundamental importance in the natural landscape. The basics of your site — soil types, landforms, and microclimates — will dictate which communities you can grow.

Often, more than one native plant community will be appropriate on any given site. So how do you decide whether to plant grassland, open woodland, or dense forest if they're all suited to your topography and soils? Functional considerations — for example, the need to screen out an eyesore in your neighbor's yard — will usually narrow down the choice. If not, you're free to pick any one you like. Keep in mind, though, that not all plant communities are equally easy to establish, and some are harder to maintain than others. A prairie or meadow typically takes only three or four years to mature, while a forest or woodland can take ten times that long. On the negative side, prairies need periodic mowing or controlled burning to keep down Eurasian weeds and brushy vegetation.

You're still not sure how to go about choosing suitable plant communities for your yard? Consider the following hypothetical situation: You've just bought a house in the heart of suburbia in East Meadow, Long Island. Most of the island's natural vegetation has long since disappeared, and the vegetation on your property is no exception. Your research into the natural history of the area has turned up the fact that East Meadow, as its name suggests, was once on the edge of one of the East Coast's largest prairies, the Hempstead plains. After chatting with ecologists who are trying to reestablish native prairie in a nearby park, you decide to replace the lawn struggling in poor soil in your front yard with wild grassland. You buy seed of big bluestem (*Andropogon gerardii*) and other grasses and wildflowers from a local nursery specializing in native plants. You prepare to till and then disk the soil in fall and spring to destroy weeds before seeding the area. You also decide to hasten

your pocket prairie by adding some established, container-grown plants.

Your backyard is also mostly turf. However, unlike your front yard, it consists of darker, richer soil that runs down to a corridor of wet woods of swamp maple and white oak, straddling a stream that parallels one of the island's major parkways. You resolve to return part of your backyard to this forest ecosystem; the added woodland will also add a bit more

Top: A cedar deck extends an Illinois home into the surrounding prairie and pond created by P. Clifford Miller.

Above: Beyond the parking court, on a gentle knoll built out of spoils from the pond area, Miller planted a bur-oak savanna.

A Natural Landscape for Illinois

On this five-acre site in Lake Forest, Illinois, landscape designer P. Clifford Miller had to contend with a large, wet prairie area that was being overrun by woody plants. Miller restored the grassland community and put a pond where the vegetation was too degraded to recover. Today, marsh phlox and Michigan lily tumble onto the long wooden walkway that connects the pond to the cedar deck of a handsome wood-and-stone prairie home. Somewhat drier, or mesic, areas were planted with such Midwest grassland denizens as prairie dock and pale purple coneflower. In Illinois, bur oaks will colonize the prairie if fire does not keep them at bay. Miller planted a bur oak savanna on a gentle knoll created out of spoils from the pond area. This planting helps screen the house from the public road. Existing stands of aspen, which colonizes the upland edges of wet prairie areas, were left to screen the house from adjacent properties. However, Miller did remove alien understory plants and is presently coaxing prairie species to move in around the edges.

(Additional photographs of this garden appear on the previous page and page 22.)

A great blue heron presides over the water garden that wraps around one corner of the handsome wood-and-fieldstone prairie house.

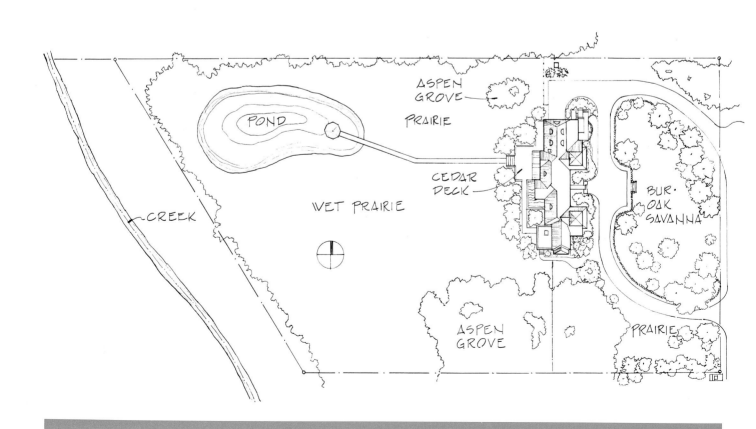

Selected Native Plants

Wet Prairie

Blue flag	*Iris virginica* var. *shrevei*
Cordgrass	*Spartina pectinata*
Great blue lobelia	*Lobelia siphilitica*
Joe-pye weed	*Eupatorium maculatum*
Marsh phlox	*Phlox glaberrima*
Michigan lily	*Lilium michiganense*
Prairie blazing star	*Liatris pycnostachya*
Tussock sedge	*Carex stricta*
Turtlehead	*Chelone glabra*

Mesic Prairie

Bergamot	*Monarda fistulosa*
Big bluestem	*Andropogon gerardii*
Bottle gentian	*Gentiana andrewsii*
Golden alexander	*Zizia aurea*
Indian grass	*Sorghastrum nutans*
New England aster	*Aster novae-angliae*
Pale purple coneflower	*Echinacea pallida*
Prairie coneflower	*Ratibida pinnata*
Prairie dock	*Silphium terebinthinaceum*
Spiderwort	*Tradescantia ohiensis*
Sweet black-eyed susan	*Rudbeckia subtomentosa*

Savanna

Black-eyed susan	*Rudbeckia hirta*
Bur oak	*Quercus macrocarpa*
Canada wild rye	*Elymus canadensis*
Elm-leaved goldenrod	*Solidago ulmifolia*
Shooting-star	*Dodecatheon meadia*
Smooth blue aster	*Aster laevis*
Switch grass	*Panicum virgatum*
Thimbleweed	*Anemone cylindrica*
Wild geranium	*Geranium maculatum*

Aspens, which colonize the upland edges of wet prairie areas, were left to shade the deck and screen the house from adjacent properties. Miller removed the alien plants that were growing underneath and is now coaxing prairie species to move in around the edges.

buffer between your house and the major traffic artery. You plan a sweep of forest that begins at the existing woods and curves around the northwest side of your house, where it will at least partially screen the peeling old wooden boat rotting on blocks in your neighbor's yard. Local nurseries sell most of the appropriate trees and shrubs. You'll have them plant the trees and plant the shrubs yourself: sweet pepperbush (*Clethra alnifolia*), shadbush (*Amelanchier canadensis*), spicebush (*Lindera benzoin*), and highbush blueberry (*Vaccinium corymbosum*). As the forest develops, you'll fill in with wildflowers such as the brilliant, carmine-red cardinal flower (*Lobelia cardinalis*) and with native ferns propagated by a local botanist.

Imitate nature's design. Your native planting should look as natural as possible. In the words of natural landscape pioneer Darrel Morrison, dean of the School of Environmental Design at the University of Georgia in Athens, "We can't design gardens that will equal the order, complexity, integrity, and beauty of the typical undisturbed natural landscape. But we can learn about design from the process and forms [that occur there]."

A good way to begin designing a natural planting is to study the key species that occur together in your chosen plant community in the wild. First, note the dominant species — that is, the major plants that form the backbone of the native plant community. In the tallgrass prairie, these are the grasses such as the stately big bluestem, which can reach six feet in autumn. In the pinyon-juniper woodlands of the Southwest, the major plants are the species of juniper and pinyon pine, which vary somewhat from state to state. In the Pacific coastal forest, the conifers — including the redwood, *Sequoia sempervirens,* and the Douglas fir, *Pseudotsuga menziesii* — dominate.

Next, note which species are most common in the native community you're trying to recreate. Then pay particular attention to other species that may not be present in the same numbers as others but that are nonetheless

Above the septic drain field, Stephen K. Domigan planted yellow coneflowers and purple horsemint, which stand out against a canvas of green grasses, including side oats gramma, the state grass of Texas.

Selected Native Plants and Cultivars

Drain-Field Area

Black-eyed susan	*Rudbeckia hirta*
Firewheel	*Gaillardia pulchella*
Little bluestem	*Schizachyrium scoparium*
Purple horsemint	*Monarda citriodora*
Sideoats grama	*Bouteloua curtipendula*
Standing winecup	*Callirhoe digitata*

Natural Areas

Drummond sundrops	*Calylophus berlandieri*
Gayfeather	*Liatris pycnostachya*
Maximilian sunflower	*Helianthus maximilianii*
Twisted-leaf yucca	*Yucca rupicola*
Western spiderwort	*Tradescantia occidentalis*

Trees

Deciduous yaupon	*Ilex decidua*
Plateau live oak	*Quercus virginiana* var. *fusiformis*
Texas persimmon	*Diospyros texana*
Yaupon holly	*Ilex vomitoria*

Shrubs

Agarita	*Mahonia trifoliata*
American beautyberry	*Callicarpa americana*
Anisacanthus	*Anisacanthus wrightii*
Compact cherry laurel	*Prunus caroliniana* 'Compacta'
Coralberry	*Symphoricarpos orbiculatus*
Dwarf yaupon	*Ilex vomitoria* 'Nana'
Green cloud sage	*Leucophyllum frutescens* 'Green Cloud'
Salvias	*Salvia greggii*
	Salvia azure var. *grandiflora*
Spanish bayonet	*Yucca aloifolia*

critical to the visual character of the community. Morrison calls these important plants "visual-essence" species.

Once you have a good feel for the key plants in the community, the next step is to observe how and where they grow. Plants form horizontal and vertical patterns in a plant community. Each species in a forest, for example, occupies a position in the canopy (or tallest layer of vegetation), the understory layer of smaller trees, the shrub layer, or the ground layer.

Study the way horizontal masses of plants form soft shapes, the way forest paths flow in gentle curves, the way deserts are etched by arroyos. Note whether a plant grows only at the edges of the woods, or deep in the forest community, or both; whether it's usually present only as an individual, in loose colonies, or in dense clumps. The natural growth patterns of individual species, which serve as a useful guide to planting, are generally determined by the way the plants reproduce. Trees, shrubs, and grasses that reproduce mainly by seed, for example, appear in random, scattered patterns

A Natural Landscape for Austin, Texas

The owner of this property, a nature photographer, wanted her garden to attract as many species of wildlife as a one-acre site just outside the city could accommodate. Landscape architect Stephen K. Domigan and restoration contractors Environmental Survey Consulting obliged, creating a variety of habitats, a kind of biological crossroads like east-central Texas itself, where the prairie bumps up against the coastal plain forests and the Desert Southwest. The septic drain field was revegetated with thirty species of wildflowers and native grasses, including sideoats grama, the state grass of Texas, and bright red and yellow firewheel. On the periphery of the property, zones of natural landscape were restored with a bright tapestry of wildflowers and succulents, among them Maximilian sunflower and twisted-leaf yucca. Scattered around the house are plateau live oak, Texas persimmon, and other native trees, as well as clusters of native shrubs and wildflowers and a few exotics and annuals. A tiny aquatic area near the master bedroom provides yet another refuge for both humans and wildlife.

(Additional photographs of this garden appear on the previous page and on pages 26–27.)

Wildflowers spill onto a limestone wash in one of the restored natural areas on the property.

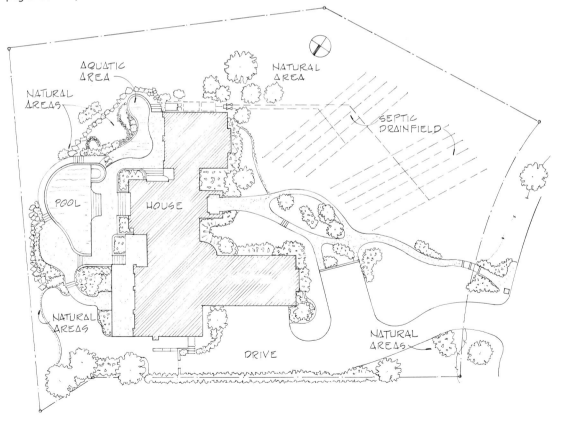

A Natural Landscape for Mesa, Arizona

The aim of landscape architect Steve Martino was to preserve the ecological integrity and natural character of this undisturbed five-acre Sonoran Desert site on Usery Mountain, elevation 1,850 feet, with a 220-degree view of the Valley of the Sun. Outdoor patios follow the natural descent of the hillside on a series of levels. During construction, the owners stood guard to make sure that the cement trucks stayed on the driveway and did not stray onto the desert. All areas scarred by construction were restored. Close by the house, located between two arroyos, the garden is based on a native plant palette associated with the lush flora of the desert wash. Blue palo verde and other trees provide cooling shade, while ocotillos, hedgehogs, prickly pears, and barrel cacti, many moved from the path of construction, add striking desert shapes and textures. Native wildflowers and species from similar deserts around the world — including red-flowering *Salvia greggii* from the nearby Chihuahuan Desert — ensure a year-round procession of color.

(Photographs of this garden appear on the following pages and on page 20.)

Selected Native Plants

Arizona yellowbell	*Tecoma stans*
Barrel cactus	*Ferocactus wislizenii*
Blue palo verde	*Cercidium floridum*
Brittle-bush	*Encelia farinosa*
Catclaw acacia	*Acacia greggii*
Cholla	*Opuntia acanthocarpa*
Chuperosa	*Justicia californica*
Creosote bush	*Larrea tridentata*
Desert willow	*Chilopsis linearis*
Hedgehog	*Echinocereus* spp.
Indigo bush	*Dalea bicolor* var. *argyraea*
Ironwood tree	*Olneya tesota*
Jojoba	*Simmondsia chinensis*
Mesquite	*Prosopis* spp.
Ocotillo	*Fouquieria splendens*
Palo verde	*Cercidium microphyllum*
Penstemons	*Penstemon* spp.
Pink penstemon	*Penstemon parryi*
Prickly pears	*Opuntia* spp.
Saguaro	*Carnegiea gigantea*
Verbenas	*Verbena* spp.
Wolfberry	*Lycium fremontii*

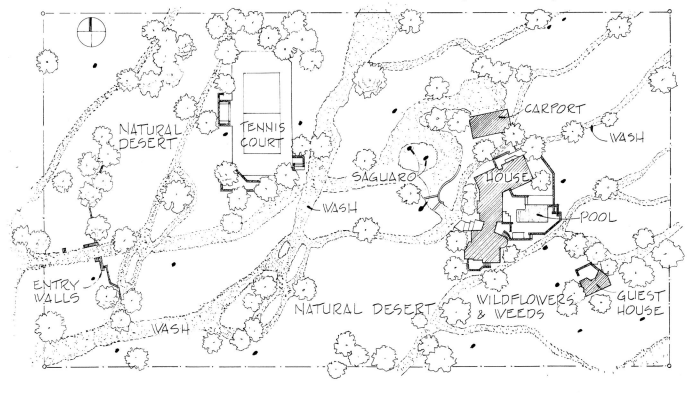

The Mesa, Arizona, garden designed by landscape architect Steve Martino is unmistakably of the Sonoran Desert. Squiggly multi-stemmed ocotillo, tall, columnar saguaro cactus, and other sculptural desert plants cast intricate shadow patterns on walls and walkways.

in the landscape. Those that reproduce vegetatively — that is, either by means of suckers or by running roots — occur in ever-expanding clumps. However, other factors may also influence growth patterns. In the desert, for instance, plants are often spaced relatively far apart because there is intense competition for water and nutrients. (No matter which community you're trying to re-create, keep in mind that initially you probably shouldn't plant at the same density as nature. You'll want to leave room for the plants to fill in and can mulch any temporary spaces between plants or groups of plants.)

Does all this mean that the natural landscaper has no freedom of choice, no room for artistic expression? Not at all. As noted above, in the section on choosing plant communities, you'll often have a choice of communities suited to your site. And in nature, no two communities are alike. That means that once you've settled on a plant community, you'll also have a choice of which of its species — particularly the nondominant ones — to feature in your yard. Here's where you can let your imagination run wild, choosing species for their form, seasonal color, interesting bark, or eye-catching contrast — just as you would if you were designing a traditional garden.

Pay special attention to the edges of your natural landscape. Try to ease the transition from one zone of the garden to another. Forest, for example, should not end abruptly in manicured lawn. Observe the composition of woodland edges in nature: younger, shorter shrubs are usually found along the perimeter, and certain transitional species tend to predominate. If there's room, try to re-create this transitional effect in your yard. But in any case, don't make edges meet in straight lines; try to emulate the undulating effect of the soft edges of nature.

Steve Martino's garden plantings are based on plant associations in the wild. Hedgehog, prickly pear, barrel cactus, saguaro, and other cacti rise up from masses of lower-growing vegetation.

Desert willow, blue palo-verde, catclaw acacia, and other desert trees provide cooling shade throughout the Arizona garden. Pink penstemon blooms behind the chaise.

Many of the naturally elegant gardens featured in this book blend some of the showier exotics of traditional landscapes with native plants, especially at the junctions between more formal garden rooms or kitchen gardens and the natural zones of vegetation. Here it's especially important not to choose invasive exotic species that will be tough to eradicate once they get a foothold in the native plantings.

Make paved areas and paths look as natural as possible. This means using materials native to the area. Pine needles or shredded bark can be used to "pave" forest paths, for example, while regular mowing can create a meandering route through a meadow or prairie. Crushed stone from a local quarry can blaze an effective trail through a rock garden. In the East, flagstones make for an attractive terrace, especially when wildflowers are planted in clumps among the stones.

This principle extends to other architectural elements of the landscape as well. In many desert gardens, low adobe walls shelter garden rooms or edible landscapes from the harsher environment beyond. An adobe pillar and "coyote" fence made of native juniper logs and edged with santolina-like native rabbitbrush (*Chrysothamnus nauseosus*) form a handsome roadside entrance in the pinyon-juniper scrub-

land around Santa Fe. Rustic Adirondack-style furniture enhances the sense of place in the Eastern deciduous forest. If you're really ambitious, you can even create living garden furniture by pleaching and grafting young trees (see pages 170–171).

Buy native plants only from reputable nearby dealers. The natural areas of North America are not only threatened by pollution, development, and invasion by exotic species; to make matters worse, many of the rarest and most beautiful species are also threatened by private and commercial plant collectors who dig them from the wild. This is not an isolated problem. Cactus rustlers in the Sonoran Desert imperil the saguaro (*Carnegiea gigantea*), and illegal digging is decimating wild populations of the Venus's-flytrap (*Dionaea muscipula*), the insectivorous plant native to boggy areas in the Carolinas. One of the eastern deciduous forest species most threatened by overcollecting is the large-flowered trillium (*Trillium grandiflorum*). Unfortunately, many of the native species sold at garden centers and by mail-order nurseries have been taken from the wild. Part of the problem is that native plants tend to be difficult to propagate; some, such as the trilliums, don't reach bloom size for years.

When you shop for native species, be sure to ask whether they have been grown in the nursery from seed, cuttings, or tissue culture. Be aware, though, that there are nurseries that take plants from the wild, pot them up, and then tell buyers they're nursery-grown. Ultimately, you must rely on a nursery's good reputation. Your persistence will pay off: nursery-propagated plants do better in gardens than those taken from the wild, which often never recover from the shock of being dug up.

Botanists are also concerned that the genetic integrity of local plant communities is being compromised by the introduction of the same species from other regions. While local plants have adapted for thousands of years to the precise conditions of your area, plants of the same species from other areas have no doubt adapted to different conditions. More than just

A Natural Landscape for Sun Valley

This garden on a two-and-a-half-acre site, designed by landscape architect Robert Murase, links a striking solar home to the surrounding sagebrush steppe. The design incorporates native flora almost universally ignored by other Sun Valley residents: the ubiquitous sagebrush, a dozen native grasses, and wildflowers commonly found along ravines. About half of the property was left in its natural state. A series of formal terrace gardens lined with stands of quaking aspen runs like a riverbed down the south side of the house. These elegant outdoor terraces terminate in a group of artfully placed boulders brought in from a neighboring farm, which echo rock outcroppings on nearby hills. Using native and naturalized species as well as a few cultivars, Murase planted intensively among these boulders and around the two paths that encircle the house. Sprays of shrubby cinquefoil (*Potentilla fruticosa*) are interlaced with prairie flax and wild geranium. Beyond, wilder patches of grass and wild white yarrow bleed freely into the scrubby vegetation of the Sawtooth foothills.

(Photographs of this garden appear on the following pages and on page 21.)

Selected Native Plants

Wildflowers

Beard-tongue	*Penstemon cyananthus*
Oregon sunflower	*Balsamorhiza sagittata*
Prairie flax	*Linum perenne*
Scarlet gilia	*Ipomopsis aggregata*
Sulphur flower	*Eriogonum umbellatum*
Wild geranium	*Geranium viscosissimum*
Wild sunflower	*Helianthus annuus*
Wild white yarrow	*Achillea millefolium* var. *lanulosa*

Grasses

Sheep fescue	*Festuca ovina*

Trees and Shrubs

Basin sagebrush	*Artemisia tridentata*
Beech leaf mountain mahogany	*Cercocarpus montanus*
Golden currant	*Ribes aureum*
Orange globemallow	*Sphaeralcea munroana*
Oregon boxwood	*Pachistima myrsinites*
Oregon grapeholly	*Mahonia repens*
Quaking aspen	*Populus tremuloides*
Rabbitbrush	*Chrysothamnus nauseosus*
Red-osier dogwood	*Cornus sericea*
Sand cherry	*Prunus besseyi*
Serviceberry	*Amelanchier alnifolia*
Shrubby cinquefoil	*Potentilla fruticosa*
Wood rose	*Rosa woodsii*

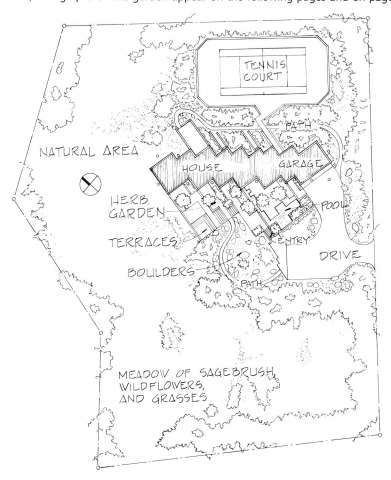

A series of formal terraces tumbles like a riverbed down the south side of a solar house outside Sun Valley, Idaho. Robert Murase ringed the terraces with stands of aspen and artfully placed boulders. (See the landscape plan on page 183.)

genetic integrity is at stake here, since nonlocal plants may not perform as well in your garden as true natives. The swamp maple, for example, is known for its spectacular scarlet foliage in fall. However, a swamp maple planted, say, in Minnesota but adapted to the soils and climate of Georgia may not color as brilliantly or for as long as it would in its native habitat. Unfortunately, most mail-order nurseries do not list the geographic origins of the parents from which the plants in their catalogs have been propagated. Seek out local nurseries propagating native species from populations growing naturally within fifty miles of your garden.

Follow nature's clues on when to plant. After you've selected a native plant community or communities and tracked down reputable sources of native species for your natural landscape, it's time for you to get down to the actual planting. The best time to plant will vary from region to region. The best planting time for most forest species, for instance, is in the early to middle spring and fall, while the best time to plant natives of the California chaparral is in the fall, right before the rains begin, because the plants will then have time to develop strong root systems before the dry season commences. If you're not sure about the best time to plant a natural garden in your area, check with other gardeners and with local nurseries that specialize in native plants.

Be vigilant about maintenance for the first few years, then relax. If your natural landscape has been designed properly, and if you've chosen a plant community that is suited to your soil and climate, you'll be rewarded with a garden that not only enhances the biological integrity of your bioregion but also conserves water and energy — especially *your* energy. An expanse of prairie, for instance, needs mowing only once a year, while a conventional lawn needs mowing once a week during the growing season.

A natural landscape will demand some investment of time and energy during the first few years. In a forest garden, you'll most likely

have to water and weed until the young trees, shrubs, and herbaceous plants become established. Mulching will retain moisture and discourage weeds while enriching the soil; after several years, your patch of forest should be producing most of its own mulch as it sheds its leaves and needles. Watering is absolutely critical in desert and chaparral gardens if many new plantings are to take hold. The first three years or so are critical for a re-created prairie or meadow; during that time, you'll have to weed diligently to keep down exotic weeds. After the first few seasons, you'll need to mow or burn occasionally to discourage woody vegetation and keep your grassland from reverting to woodland.

■ Further Reading

In a book of this scope, it's impossible to provide nitty-gritty detail on how to create gardens modeled after plant communities in all the various bioregions. Fortunately, the number of publications geared to gardeners in particular regions is increasing. The following books devoted entirely to natural landscaping are good places to start:

Janet Marinelli, ed., *The Environmental Gardener* (Brooklyn: Brooklyn Botanic Garden, 1992). This handbook includes in-depth how-to articles by experts from all over the continent who specialize in natural landscaping.

William H. W. Wilson, *Landscaping with Wildflowers and Native Plants* (San Francisco: Ortho Books, 1984). A good introduction to the subject, this volume includes information on natural gardens for bioregions across the country, from the eastern deciduous forest to the Sonoran Desert to the California chaparral. Sections on each bioregion end with a bibliography that lists other sources. An extensive list of sources for native plants and seeds is also included.

John Diekelmann and Robert Schuster, *Natural Landscaping: Designing with Native Plant Communities* (New York: McGraw-Hill, 1982). This is the definitive book to date on designing natural landscapes in the Northeast forest bioregions and in the Midwest prairie states. It's currently out of print but is worth hunting for.

The New England Wild Flower Society publishes *Sources of Propagated Native Plants and Wild-flowers,* the most exhaustive list available of conservation-minded nurseries that either propagate their own stock or rescue native plants from the path of development. To obtain a copy, write to the Society at Garden in the Woods, 180 Hemenway Road, Framingham, Massachusetts 01701.

Above: This lush planting, comprising mostly native and naturalized species from the surrounding Sawtooth foothills, spills onto the red tile banding that flows effortlessly from the outside to the inside of the house.

Above left: Strollers are drawn down the circuitous path that winds around the house through rocks and drifts of wildflowers. In the foreground and at center is yellow shrubby cinquefoil (*Potentilla fruticosa*).

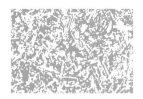

EDIBLE LANDSCAPING

The earliest gardens were edible. They were also rather formal in design. Since the dawn of civilization, in the Fertile Crescent, humans have harvested fruits and vegetables from square, fenced-in plots. Now, thousands of years later, we still have a fondness for the formal kitchen garden. In recent years, a new kind of free-form foodscaping that rejects straight lines and mingles edibles with ornamentals throughout the garden has come to the fore. No matter which style you prefer, however, there are a few important guidelines to consider:

1. Start ever so small. Keep your kitchen garden as compact as possible. This will reduce weeding, watering, and other maintenance chores, which in the edible landscape can be time-consuming indeed. Dwarf fruit trees, compact vegetables, and small fruiting shrubs are easiest to tend. Starting small and gradually expanding your edible area is far more gratifying than planting a huge garden and feeling guilty when you can't cope with it. Ultimately, yards with less than 2,400 square feet should have no more than 50 percent of the area planted to edibles; yards of more than 2,400 square feet should be less than 20 percent edible. And these are ambitious figures.

2. Don't segregate the edibles. Informal edible landscapes dissolve the boundary between the vegetable garden and the rest of the yard. The idea is to have a productive landscape without banishing the beans and squash to a camouflaged corner out back. Instead, food plants and ornamental plants chosen for their color, form, fragrance, and texture should be creatively combined. Even the classic formal kitchen garden, which reached its pinnacle in seventeenth-century France, included a dazzling array of fruits and vegetables — and flowers.

3. Keep the herbs and salad plants close to the house. The most distant portions of an edible landscape return to weeds the soonest. Use the farthest reaches of your yard for windbreaks and natural landscape.

4. Use double-duty plants. To keep the garden compact and richly textured, use as many multipurpose plants as possible. For example, upright rosemary makes a lovely dark-green hedge about four to six feet tall, comes in handy for Italian and other types of Mediterranean cooking, and attracts pollinating bees in early spring.

5. Choose low-maintenance plants. Choose your plants carefully. Cosmopolitan tastes developed in high-priced gourmet markets can lead the beginning gardener astray. Homegrown, tree-ripened apricots dripping with sun-warmed nectar, for example, are far cheaper than the ones found in gourmet stores — and far superior to those greenish-orange golfballs passed off as apricots at supermarkets. But in some areas, apricot trees are attacked by four or more serious diseases, even though, a mere sixty miles away, they may thrive with a fraction of the care. The moral of the story is to know which crops in your area are plagued by pests and which are not. Vulnerable vegetables and fruits should be attempted only by the most dedicated or masochistic gardeners. (For advice on pest-resistant plants, consult your local nursery or Cooperative Extension agent. The number of this federally funded gardening adviser — most counties have at least one — should be listed in the phone book.)

■ Getting to Know Your Yard

Start your edible landscape with annual vegetables and flowers only, and try not to get too dogmatic about where you grow them. The first year's bed of lettuce may ultimately prove to be the best place for a dwarf fruit tree. Any soil improvements you make in the first year will be most appreciated by subsequent plants, so you can't lose.

Once you've learned the sun and shade patterns of your yard, you'll know exactly where to put some of the planting areas. The best sunny spots should be reserved for those vegetables and fruits that require lots of heat to fully ripen — tomatoes, peppers, eggplants, citrus, peaches, and nectarines, for example. Many salad greens are quite adaptable to various levels of shade, up to 50 percent. In partial shade, salad greens will grow more slowly, but their foliage may actually get bigger. Shady spots are also the best places to grow salads in climates with ferociously hot summers.

Contrary to popular belief, not all fruits require full sun to mature with a full flavor. While peaches are not forgiving of shade, apples and pears will ripen to full sugar in much less light than most people would expect — as little as two hours of direct sunlight during the middle of the day. Reduced light levels will delay ripening, though. For this reason, you shouldn't plant late-season fruits in shady places; use early- to mid-season varieties instead. Cane fruits such as blackberry, raspberry, and ollalie berry are also well adapted to less than full sun; indeed, in areas with hot summers, shade is essential to good berry production. By placing the cane fruits to the east of tall trees or buildings so that the fruit will be shaded by early to midafternoon, you can prevent the fruits from getting dehydrated and shriveling up.

Next, look to see what the yard's topography has to offer. If, for example, all the spring's cold night air settles into a low area, consider it a plus for fruit trees such as 'McIntosh', 'Jonathan', and 'Northern Spy' apples and cherry trees, which require more winter chilling. But this wouldn't be the place for low-chill apples such as 'Beverly Hills', 'Granny Smith', and 'Winter Banana', since late frosts might catch the tree in full bloom and destroy the season's crop.

Study the movement of air and wind throughout your yard. Where the wind is too intense or cold, you may want to plan a windbreak to shelter a portion of the edible landscape. Basically, there are no limitations to

A raised flagstone terrace dotted with ground-hugging thyme and alpine plants links a formal herb garden in Connecticut with the house. 'New Dawn' and 'White Dawn' roses clamber over arbors and the surrounding picket fence.

your property, only limitations to your own ability to imagine the benefits of each microclimate and environmental nuance.

Likewise, you can work with whatever soil you've inherited, though you may have to adjust your expectations as to what you'll grow. Many homes are built upon exposed clay subsoil. Peach tree roots, for one, hate heavy, poorly drained clay soil and often quickly die in it. On the other hand, pear (both European and Asian), quince, standard apple, and plum roots can tolerate the heavier soils. This means that the rootstock of a fruit tree is one of the most important "design criteria" for you to take into account when planning an edible landscape. Most peach and nectarine trees are sold with peach rootstocks; planting them as is in heavy, gumbo clay is like throwing away money. But peach and nectarine varieties can be grafted onto plum roots, which have more of a chance of success in clay soil. If your local

In the bed at center, pink beebalm forms a lush mounded backdrop for alternating lavenders 'Jean Davis,' 'Hidcote', and 'Munstead'.

nursery can't supply peaches and nectarines on plum rootstocks, you can graft your own. With a little practice and a couple of years' patience, you can make your own fruit tree with a rootstock that is appropriate for your yard's soil. Vegetables' tolerance for heavy clay soil varies, but it doesn't take long to improve a small area for intensive vegetable production. You can get off to a fast start by purchasing a custom-blended topsoil for the initial small area of raised vegetable beds. Then use compost, green manures, and cover crops to slowly develop areas that will be planted to food in the not-too-distant future (see "Soil-Conserving Landscaping," pages 211–220).

■ Designing Your Edible Landscape

Herbs

Add herbs to your edible garden. Dried herb seasonings are some of the most expensive and most overpriced products in the supermarket — and the most tasteless, when compared to their fresh, homegrown counterparts. Many herbs are gathered overseas and sprayed for insects at border crossings; they may travel for up to two years before reaching your vinaigrette or marinara sauce.

The classic herb garden illustrated on the

opposite page is quite elaborate and elegant, with precisely laid-out beds of billowing edible and ornamental herbs and flowers. However, herbs can grow quite happily in small containers on a deck or balcony, or the sill of a sunny south-facing window. All herbs are comfortable in attractive terra cotta pots. Plan to keep some of your favorite kinds as close to the kitchen sink as possible. This is especially important during inclement weather: if you don't have to get soaked to harvest your herbs, you're more likely to add heaps of the fresh, savory leaves to your culinary creations.

Some good herbs to start with are rosemary, thyme, lavender (which can be used in place of rosemary in Mediterranean cooking — just add three to four times more finely minced lavender leaf than the rosemary called for in the recipe), perennial garlic chives, oregano, and regular chives. Be sure to use a well-drained potting mix, and in cold climates, bring the potted herbs indoors for the winter. Many herbs thrive in rocky, poor soil, so their potting medium need not be particularly fertile; these include sage, rosemary, oregano, the saffron crocus, and marjoram. Chives, tarragon, mints, lovage, and garlic, among others, prefer a richer potting mix.

When planting an herb garden in the ground, be sure to group the plants according to their water, soil, and fertility requirements. Drought-tolerant herbs such as lavender, rosemary, sage, oregano, and marjoram lose some of their flavor if they're grown with the same nutrients and water as salad greens. Besides, it's a waste of precious water and compost. While mints love water and fertility, you shouldn't plant them in the salad garden because they'll take over. Such herbs as lovage, French sorrel, dandelion, borage, calendula, chives, nasturtium, and tarragon either prefer or happily tolerate fertilized soil and ample water.

The Salad Garden

Next turn your attention to the salad patch. Growing your own salads can be a big

A Formal Edible Landscape

This sixty-by-seventy-foot garden, a former parking lot transformed, traces its lineage back hundreds of years to monastic gardens in which culinary herbs were mingled with others grown solely for their beauty or fragrance. Sage, dill, thyme, savory, chives, rosemary, lovage, bay, and other edible herbs tumble onto the paths that divide the garden into four perfectly symmetrical quarters, each one further divided into four planting beds. In perimeter borders, 'New Dawn' and 'White Dawn' roses and several varieties of clematis clamber over arbors and the surrounding picket fence. A raised flagstone terrace dotted with ground-hugging thyme and alpine plants links the garden with the house. Designed by landscaper Andrew Hogan at his family's Connecticut home with the help of his friend Jim Marchand, this formal herb garden is not only traditional and elegant but also original and quirky — one of the geometric-shaped beds, for example, is devoted to such species as mayapple and foxglove, reflecting the family's interest in poisonous plants.

(Photographs of this garden appear on the previous pages and on pages 22–23.)

I. Alternating lavenders: *Lavandula angustifolia* 'Jean Davis', 'Hidcote', and 'Munstead', with pink and white *Monarda* at center

II. Annual herbs, including scented geraniums edged with boxwood

III. Heathers (*Calluna vulgaris* cultivars), heaths (*Erica* spp.) and thymes (*Thymus* spp.)

IV. *Dianthus* 'Blazing Star', rue (*Ruta graveolens*), blue mist caryopteris (*Caryopteris* x *clandonensis* 'Blue Mist')

V. Lady's mantle (*Alchemilla vulgaris*) edged with germander (*Teucrium chamaedrys* 'Prostratum')

VI. Artemisias (*Artemisia* spp.)

VII. Upright germander, scented geraniums, chives (*Allium* spp.) summer savory (*Satureja hortensis*), yarrow

VIII. Upright germander, feverfew (*Chrysanthemum parthenium*), annuals

IX. Lavenders, lemon verbena (*Aloysia triphylla*), rosemary, bay (*Laurus nobilis*)

X. Lavenders, scented geraniums

XI. Upright germander, Roman chamomile (*Chamaemelum nobile*), flax (*Linum perenne*), tansy (*Tanacetum vulgare*), Scotch broom (*Cytisus scoparius*)

XII. Fairy rose, lemon balm (*Melissa officinalis*), borage (*Borago officinalis*), lovage (*Levisticum officinale*), marsh mallow (*Althaea officinalis*), comfrey (*Symphytum officinale*)

XIII. Thymes, with meadow rue (*Thalictrum speciosissimum*) at center

XIV. Knot design, including *Lavandula angustifolia* and rue

XV. Germander, scented geraniums, santolina (*Santolina* sp.), costmary (*Chrysanthemum balsamita*)

XVI. Poisonous plants, including monkshood (*Aconitum fischeri*), lily of the valley (*Convallaria majalis*), and mayapple (*Podophyllum peltatum*)

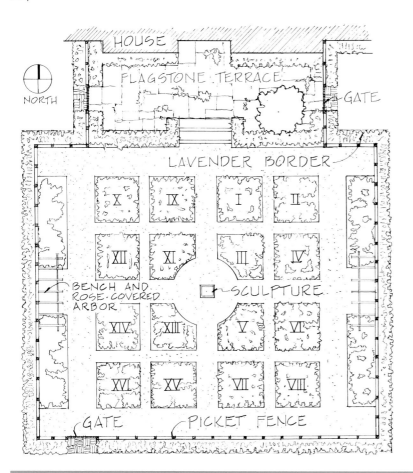

In this informal edible garden, annual vegetables are grown in raised beds in a sweeping curve to keep maintenance manageable. Beyond is a vineyard with Zinfandel and Cabernet Sauvignon grapes.

The Vegetable Area

Slightly farther from the kitchen is the place to plant those vegetables that take up a lot of room, are used in quantity for canning, or are not the most attractive of plants. Examples include paste tomatoes, eggplants, vining squashes, potatoes — and corn. Tall, somewhat ratty-looking in late summer, with a low yield per square foot, corn doesn't belong in the foreground, in full view of the house. Plant it instead behind an attractive hedge of upright rosemary, behind a vine-covered trellis, or on the little-traveled side of the house. You can still be adventurous: have you ever noticed that all that fancy, gourmet produce with the "wrong" color costs more? Blue-grained corn, 'Hopi Blue', costs considerably more than its conventional cousins yet requires no extra effort to grow — in fact, 'Hopi Blue' requires much less care and less precious water than regular corn. It also tastes superior, with a richer, nuttier flavor than traditional yellow grinding corn.

Beds and Pathways

What shape should your salad and vegetable beds be? Some designers believe that straight lines are a sin in the edible landscape. They abhor straight lines when it comes to annual vegetables because they're too reminiscent of the linear design of conventional agriculture. Instead, these designers plan sweeping beds of vegetables that curve throughout the edible garden. Such beds are often bordered by a soft-looking mulch or a dense, mounding ground cover such as ornamental chamomile. If you favor classic kitchen gardens, you can reserve one or two of the round, square, or hexagonal beds — the ones closest to the kitchen — for salads, and mingle other vegetables, herbs, and flowers in other beds according to shape, color, and texture. You can also compromise by planting rectangular-shaped beds arranged, for example, in a sweeping curve and edged with handsome foliage and flowers to mask their boxiness.

boon to your food budget, especially if you're partial to radicchio, arugula, and other gourmet greens. Commercially grown nonorganic salad greens are sprayed with all kinds of pesticides, and while these pesticides are regulated, enforcement is limited at best. The safest salads are those grown within view of the kitchen table.

It's a good idea to design each edible landscape with an area of intensive salad cultivation. If you scatter your lettuce plants randomly throughout your flower beds, you're bound to forget where they are until they bolt and poke up their flower stalks — and by then they'll be too bitter to eat.

Raised beds are useful in an edible garden of any style. They make planting, weeding, and harvesting less backbreaking and guarantee good drainage even during a spell of wet weather. They can be made of two-by-twelve-inch rot-resistant planks, with aviary wire underneath to protect the plants from gophers, and can measure from three to three and a half feet wide and from six to eight feet long apiece.

Whenever possible, leave a four- or five-foot-wide pathway along a length of raised beds to allow for easy access with a wheelbarrow or garden cart whenever you bring in manure or compost or haul out the harvest. The beds should be at least eighteen inches apart. Since the beds are only six to eight feet long, wheelbarrow access along more than one side isn't necessary.

Berries and Cane Fruits

Strawberries and all cane fruits require plenty of care if you're to get continued good yields while maintaining some semblance of propriety. But they taste too good to resist. To reduce the amount of effort involved, try alpine strawberries, with their little nuggets of intense strawberry flavor. Alpine strawberry plants have two important advantages over more traditional runner strawberries: they fruit well in half shade, and they are clumping plants and don't make a tangle of runners in all directions. (Alas, they do lose their vigor after three to five years and must be replaced.)

One of the least pleasurable parts of growing cane fruits is the tedious task of finding and clipping out the previous year's canes each fall. There is an easier way — one that requires twice as much space but saves countless hours of work. First, plant double the number of rows you'd like to harvest. Each fall, you simply cut all the canes in one row flush to the ground with a scythe or power weed cutter and leave the next row unpruned. The cutback row will bear a crop in two years, after which you'll cut it to the ground again. Each

A close-up view of one of the raised vegetable beds with its bounty of lettuce and herbs.

year, you'll cut half of the rows down and leave the others alone.

Cane fruits send out vigorous runner roots. To prevent them from invading other beds in the garden, make sure the cane fruits are in their own separate area. Use drip irrigation — not a sprinkler — near the base of the plants, and leave a strip of unirrigated native plants to serve as a dry buffer between the berries and the rest of the edible landscape. To head off runner roots between the rows of your cane-fruit patch, consider putting in a permanent pathway.

All berries and cane fruits like a relatively acid soil. Your site analysis should tell you whether any area of your property is suitably acidic. If your soil is naturally alkaline or not sufficiently acidic, cluster your cane fruits and berries, especially blueberries, in a separate area where it will be easy to adjust the soil's pH.

An Informal Edible Landscape

Located in Sonoma County wine country, some ninety miles north of San Francisco, the Preston Vineyard is well known among wine aficionados for its Zinfandels and Cabernet Sauvignons. Sue and Lou Preston wanted a small edible landscape with an Italian peasant-garden ambience between the house and winery to reinforce the link between wine and food in the minds of visitors and to supplement staff lunches. Low maintenance and enough open space to entertain 200 to 250 people outdoors were other important design criteria.

To keep maintenance manageable, landscape designer Robert Kourik created seven raised vegetable beds — each only three by six feet — in a sweeping curve. The raised beds allow for crucial winter drainage and have wire bottoms to keep out pesky gophers. The more informal perennial planting scheme outside the beds includes Mediterranean herbs, artichoke plants, and an Italian terra cotta fountain. Purple-leaved sages, purple-flowering wisterias, and red-berried Alpine strawberries bring out the "Zin" and "Cab" theme.

Kourik ensured low maintenance by making the annual vegetable beds small, siting a permanent gravel pathway along the north end of the beds, installing an automatic irrigation system, and planting as many drought-resistant perennials as possible. The lawn "piazza" at the core of the design is composed of low-maintenance, drought-resistant turf grasses.

(Photographs of this garden appear on the previous pages and on page 23.)

Selected Plants

Artemisia	Artemisia schmidtiana 'Silver Mound'
Artichoke	Cynara scolymus
Bay	Laurus nobilis
Cardinal flower	Lobelia cardinalis
Chinese wisteria	Wisteria sinensis 'Purpurea'
Daylilies	Hemerocallis spp.
Dwarf blood oranges	Citrus sinensis 'Tarocco', 'Moro'
Florence fennel	Foeniculum vulgare var. azoricum 'Giant Bronze'
French lavender	Lavandula dentata
Japanese iris	Iris japonica
Japanese wisteria	Wisteria floribunda 'Longissima'
Lady Banks rose	Rosa banksiae 'Alba Plena'
Lavender	Lavandula angustifolia 'Hidcote'
Marjoram	Origanum vulgare
Mullein	Verbascum thapsus
Rock rose	Cistus salviifolius
Rosemary	Rosmarinus officinalis
Salvia	Salvia officinalis 'Purpurascens'
Salvia	Salvia officinalis 'Tricolor'
Society garlic	Tulbaghia violacea
Spanish lavender	Lavandula stoechas
Veronica	Veronica spicata 'Icicle'

WALNUT

MIXED EDIBLE AND ORNAMENTAL BORDER

LAWN

HOUSE

RAISED VEGETABLE BEDS

WINERY

MIXED EDIBLE AND ORNAMENTAL BORDER

ALPINE STRAWBERRIES

ROSE-COVERED ARBOR

POMEGRANATES

DWARF BLOOD ORANGE

MEDITERRANEAN BORDER

Fruit and Nut Trees

Farther still from the salad garden is the place for fruit and nut trees. Some people design their edible landscapes with a mixture of ground covers, herbs, ornamentals, edible perennials, and fruit trees all planted together. But that means that when you harvest or prune a large apple tree, for example, you either step all over the smaller shrubbery and crush the ground-cover plants or else spend an inordinate amount of time stepping gingerly around each plant. More important, fallen apples hide beneath the foliage of the lower plants and are difficult to find during fall cleanup; left to rot on the ground, they guarantee more codling moth "worms" the following year, as well as scab, mildew, and other pests and diseases. If water-loving ornamentals are planted beneath or near the fruit trees, the trees get more water than they really need, which may stimulate pest or disease problems or, at the very least, dilute the ripening fruit with water and thus reduce its flavor. While these multilayered designs are intriguing and full of complexity, they're quite difficult to maintain. If you leave some space beneath and around the fruit trees, you'll be able to harvest, prune, manage pests, and water with much greater ease.

Formal kitchen gardens can be punctuated dramatically with dwarf fruit trees, either grown in pots or espaliered on a trellis. You can also cluster the fruit trees in naturalistic groves — like small aspen groves, but with more openness and fewer trees. Nowhere is it written in stone that fruit trees must be laid out in straight lines as in an orchard. Mulch the area inside the dripline of each tree's eventual mature foliage with a permanent mulch (the dripline, on the ground, corresponds to the outer edge of a tree's foliage). The chipped material from a local tree-trimming service makes a good mulch because its random sizes and shredded leaves lend a natural woodland effect. (Do make sure, however, that the chips aren't from trees that can sprout from small pieces, such as willows or aspens, or trees with plant-suppressing compounds, such as black walnut or eucalyptus.)

Native Edibles

Don't forget about native edibles, not only when you're designing your edible area but also in your zones of natural landscape. Any gardener who is put off by the difficulty of growing peaches and other ordinary fruits should definitely try natives, most of which are ignored by pests and many of which don't require pruning. The very uncommonness of most native fruits is another good reason to grow them — you won't find pawpaws (*Asimina triloba*), for example, at the fruit stand. Called the banana of the north because of its yellow, brown-speckled skin and creamy-white, bananalike flesh, the pawpaw grows naturally in rich, moist soils from New York to Florida and Texas. The flavor has hints of vanilla custard, pineapple, and mango. Like most native fruits, it's easy to grow, needs little pruning, and harbors few pests.

■ Further Reading

Rosalind Creasy's *The Complete Book of Edible Landscaping* (San Francisco: Sierra Club Books, 1982) was the first book on the subject, with a focus on design and a good listing of edibles. In Creasy's *Cooking from the Garden* (San Francisco: Sierra Club Books, 1988), the emphasis is on growing edible landscapes around a food theme. The book also contains plenty of tasty recipes.

Designing and Maintaining Your Edible Landscape Naturally by Robert Kourik (Santa Rosa, Calif.: Metamorphic Press, 1986) is full of cultural tips and stresses the organic planting and care of an edible landscape.

Kate Gessert's *The Beautiful Food Garden* (Pownall, Vt.: Garden Way, 1987) gives a good overview of the aesthetic qualities of many annual vegetables.

ENERGY-CONSERVING LANDSCAPING

The natural and edible landscape surrounding your home can be more than just pretty to look at or tasty to eat: it can also keep your house cooler in summer and warmer in winter. An energy-conserving landscape utilizes hedges, screening, shrubs, vines, and trees to provide cool summer shade as well as insulation against heat loss in winter and overheating in summer. It can funnel cool breezes into your living spaces during the dog days of summer and deflect winter's heat-robbing winds. Landscaping, indeed, can be your third skin — after the real skin of your body and the insulating skin of your house. Energy-conserving landscaping can perform other functions, too. A windbreak, for example, can define the space in your yard or your patio while blocking blustery winds. And by using plants as a living air-conditioner or an insulating blanket, you can soften your house's hard architectural edges while improving its performance.

What's more, an energy-conserving landscape can slash your utility bills. According to the U.S. Department of Energy, "strategically placed landscaping materials" (that is, plants and structures such as walls, berms, and fences) can save homeowners as much as 30 percent on utility bills. In the hot, dry Sacramento Valley in California, according to the Sacramento Municipal Utility District, shade trees can reduce attic temperatures by twenty to forty degrees, equaling the effect of several room-size air-conditioners. In a study in South Florida, properly placed shrubs and trees reduced overall energy use for air-conditioning in a double-wide mobile home by 60 to 65 percent after only one year of growth. In areas with colder winters, the energy savings for the heating season from a windbreak alone can range from 3 to 34 percent. In central Pennsylvania, thanks to energy-saving landscaping, the winter heating needs of a mobile home were reduced by 8 percent, and summer cooling needs by 75 percent. In Logan, Utah, scale-model studies projected an astounding 98 percent reduction of one home's summer cooling requirements when light shade was cast over the entire house by a honey locust tree.

Energy-conserving landscaping also saves money. In the Florida study mentioned above, researchers calculated a four-year payback for a landscape installed by a contractor, with the payback time being shortened drastically if the homeowner did his or her own planting. This study also concluded that planting an energy-conserving landscape cost only one tenth as much as delivering kilowatts from a new power plant. Calculations for a house in Mesa, Arizona, showed an annual cooling-season savings of $154.50 when trees were planted on the east side of the house, $10.62 when they were planted on the south side, and $63.90 when they were planted on the west side. A maturing landscape can add to your home's value: by some estimates, good landscaping with energy-conserving shade trees may increase a property's worth by as much as 15 percent.

◼ How to Shape the Sunlight

To cool your home in summer, start with nonliving shade. Plants take a while to grow; in the interim, use structural devices such as awnings, curtains, louvered shutters, lattice, and patio umbrellas to moderate hot sunshine. Some of these will always be useful, as plants can't solve every solar problem and can't be as finely adjusted as, say, an awning (see "Natural Climate Control," page 93).

Next, turn your attention to annual vines, which grow quickly and can cover a large area by middle to late summer. Annual vines are best located very close to, but not actually up against, the walls of the house. A wooden lattice put up to support the vines will itself lend a measure of shade from the very start. Keep the trellis a foot or more away from the house to allow for enough air circulation to keep the house's exterior free of mildew and rot. Use drip irrigation, not a sprinkler, to water the vines, for the same reason (see "Water-

In summer, vines clamber up the trellis of a picturesque cottage on Martha's Vineyard, providing cooling shade.

Conserving Landscaping," pages 204–207). You can plant either vigorous, fast-growing edible vines such as scarlet runner beans (*Phaleolus coccinea*), winter squashes, and luffa squashes, or ornamental vines such as hyacinth bean (*Dolichos lablab*) and moonflower (*Ipomoea alba*).

At the same time, you can plant perennial vines, which may take two or more years to cover a trellis as tall as a home's walls. Be sure the trellis for any perennial vine isn't under the eaves of the house; you want any hot air that builds up between the trellis and the siding to vent out the "top" of the trellis. Edible perennial vines include grapes, chayote, kiwi, and passion fruit. Good ornamental covers include clematis and fragrant jasmine. And don't forget native vines such as Dutchman's pipe (*Aristolochia durior*), a rapid grower indigenous to areas from Pennsylvania to Georgia and Kansas.

Large shrubs and trees take much longer to fill in but provide the best cooling shade. Be sure to plant the varieties best suited to your soil and climate. This is a long-term investment, so seek advice from plenty of nurserymen, landscapers, and Cooperative Extension agents.

▮▮Where to Shape the Sunlight

Placing trees for summer shade and winter sunshine is more complicated than it would first appear. What you want is a cooling device for summer that won't block out warming winter sunlight. That means you can't just plant a bunch of trees along the south side of the house. (In fact, trees on the south side of the home — even deciduous varieties — can actually *increase* your energy bills.) Instead, you'll need to leave a "solar corridor" on the south side — that is, an area with no shade trees. To determine how wide your solar corridor should be (in areas south of 45 degrees north latitude), extend an imaginary line due south from the southeast and southwest corners of the house, then draw a line 45 degrees east of the southeast line, and another one 45 degrees west of the southwest line. The entire area between the second two lines should be free of trees tall enough to shade the wall or roof.

The east and west sides of the house are crucial in moderating summer heat, but exactly where should you plant the trees on those sides? To figure out the best placement, use old utility bills to determine when the hottest

It's important to leave a solar corridor on the south side of your house — an area with no trees, not even deciduous varieties, whose trunks and limbs would block the warming winter sun. In addition, the area between 45 degrees east of the southeast corner of the house and 45 degrees west of the southwest corner should be free of any trees tall enough to shade the wall or roof.

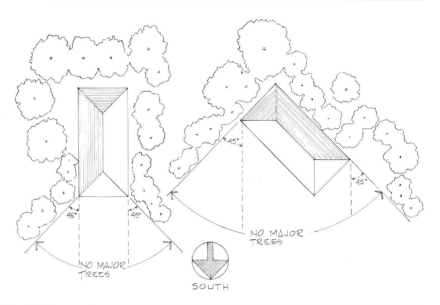

part of summer is in your area, then look in sun charts at your local library to find the angle of the sun in midafternoon during that period. Use this angle as you did above to calculate the solar corridor. For example, the hottest period in St. Louis, Missouri, is usually the last week of July, when the midafternoon sun is 75 degrees high in the sky. Trees should thus be planted along a line 75 degrees east or west of solar south.

Remember, annual and perennial vines and large shrubs can do a lot to shade and cool your home's walls while the shade trees are maturing. To boost your energy savings in the meantime, plant small trees or large shrubs near your air-conditioner to keep it shaded during the hottest months. But be certain that no falling leaves or twigs can interfere with the unit's fan or the flow of air.

■ Shaping the Wind for a Warmer House

Although it's more difficult to shape the wind with plantings than to shape the sunlight, it is possible to keep the house warmer

in the winter by blocking the chilling effects of the wind, or to cool the house or yard in the summer by capturing prevailing breezes. The most common way to shape the wind is to plant a windbreak or a hedge, but wooden fences and other garden structures can also help sculpt breezes.

Many suburban yards are not big enough for a windbreak, a stand of trees designed to block prevailing winds. To be effective, a mature windbreak, or shelterbelt, must be of a certain length and height. A good windbreak should be at least eleven times longer than its mature height. The windbreak should also extend at least fifty feet on both sides of the area or house it protects. To protect a single-story home, the windbreak must be at least fourteen to twenty feet high if it's close to the house and even taller if it's some distance away. A windbreak twenty feet tall should be 220 feet long. If your yard can't accommodate such a long line of trees, consider installing a hedge or fence instead. The shelterbelt's height should be one twentieth to one fifth the distance to be protected. While a windbreak can reduce the wind's speed by 50 percent over a distance up to twenty times its height, the area

Even on the blustery northern California coast, a windbreak can keep a house warmer by deflecting chilling winds.

of best protection is usually five to ten times the height of the windbreak. This means that even an eight-foot-high hedge or fence can protect a considerable distance — up to eighty feet. Choose trees for your shelterbelt on the basis of their eventual, mature height.

All windbreaks, whether constructed or cultivated, work best when their long side is perpendicular to the prevailing winds. They needn't have an angled slope of short to taller trees to be effective; in fact, one row of the right tree is much more effective than a wide, multirow planting.

When sculpting the wind, even if your yard is big enough for a full-sized shelterbelt, be sure to start with structural elements. A wooden fence or trellis will begin blocking the wind as soon as it's built. Some air should be able to pass through a windbreak, whether wooden or living; a completely solid windbreak will cause some of the wind to whip up over the top and down, creating a sort of sideways tornado that will slam into the house instead of lofting over it. When the windbreak is partially permeable, some of the wind can slip

through to form a gentle buffer that will help keep the brunt of the blast aloft for a much longer distance. The most effective windbreaks are 50 percent permeable; for a slat fence being used as a wooden windbreak, this means that every other slat should be missing.

There are a number of other important points to consider in designing a windbreak:

■ Evergreen trees provide the best protection from frigid winter winds.

■ Don't leave any large gaps in the windbreak, or the wind will be funneled through at a speed up to 20 percent greater than normal.

■ Make sure the windbreak is far enough away from the house that it will not cast a shadow on south-facing windows in winter.

■ You can reduce the speed of the wind by 75 percent as it hits the sides of the house by planting tall shrubs twice as far from the wall as they are high (that is, a five-foot-tall shrub should be ten feet from the wall).

■ Most edible trees make poor windbreaks. A couple of exceptions are wild plum and hackberry.

■ The roots of a windbreak are one and a half

to three times wider than the foliage and will compete for water and nutrients with other plants, so water and feed accordingly.

■ The illustration of a windbreak below assumes a house built on flat land. If your property is hilly, carefully observe the wind's patterns, and plan accordingly.

■ Planting a Windbreak

Healthy, sturdy plants are essential to a good windbreak. If one or more trees die, the resulting hole will allow wind to whip through. Here are some guidelines to follow when planting a windbreak:

■ Always choose those trees that are best suited to your soil and climate. Choose only pest-free trees. A windbreak shouldn't become another maintenance problem.

■ Plant small seedlings with healthy root systems. Large plants in small containers aren't the good deal they appear to be because the roots become permanently damaged when they circle the bottom of the container. A small plant with an undisturbed root system will easily outgrow the initially larger but rootbound plant within two to five years. Pull the young tree out of its container and make sure that no

roots are circling around the bottom. The best tree seedlings for windbreaks are grown in narrow, deep tubes. Typically, these tube-grown seedlings are a mere three to six inches tall apiece.

■ For a more immediate effect without the expense of a wooden structure, plant some fast-growing shrubs or small trees. They will fill in quickly and eventually either blow over or be overgrown by the permanent windbreak trees. Plant the fast-growing plants at the recommended intervals for a normal planting. At the same time, in clusters around them and twice as close as the usual suggested spacing, transplant two to four tube-grown seedlings. The fast-growing plants will nurse along the seedlings, even buffering the wind to help them grow. After the seedlings in each cluster have grown for several years, cull out the slower-growing ones, leaving only the best specimen.

■ Don't add fertilizer or compost to the planting hole, since that will only encourage the roots to stay close to the trunk. Trees, especially container-grown transplants, don't usually have deep taproots. Most trees have a wide network of roots in the top two to three feet of the soil, ranging from one and a half times larger in diameter than the branches (called the dripline) in heavy clay soils to three

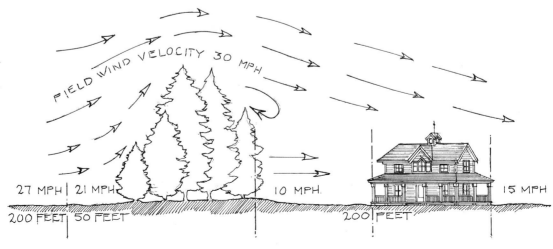

A windbreak can reduce the wind's speed by half. It should be one twentieth to one fifth as high as the distance to be protected, and at least eleven times longer than its height at maturity. Ideally, the windbreak should also extend fifty feet on either side of the house.

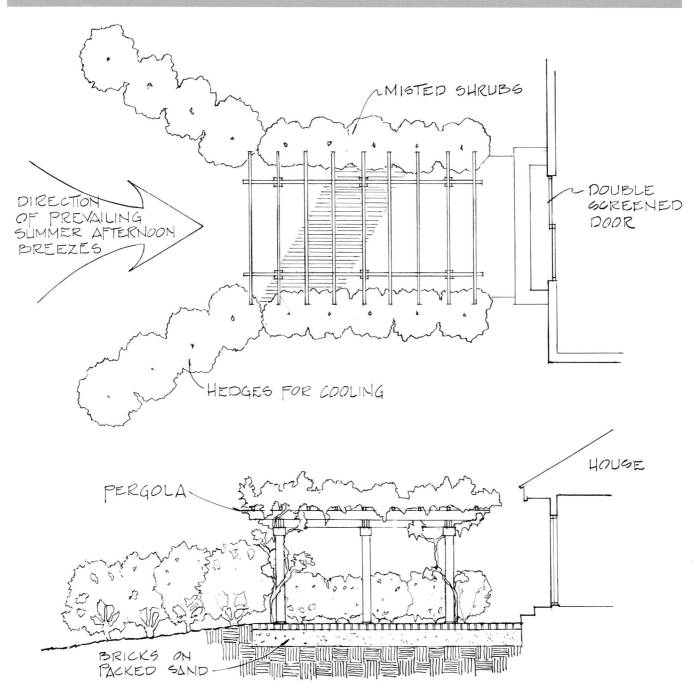

MISTED SHRUBS

DOUBLE SCREENED DOOR

DIRECTION OF PREVAILING SUMMER AFTERNOON BREEZES

HEDGES FOR COOLING

HOUSE

PERGOLA

BRICKS ON PACKED SAND

Trees and hedges can be used not only to block the wind but also to funnel breezes toward the house or patio. They should be planted parallel to the prevailing summer air currents, in a funnel shape, with the narrow side closest to the house. In arid climates, the air will feel cooler if it passes over a moist brick patio or sprinkled shrubs.

times larger in sandy loam soils. From these horizontal roots, deep sinker roots can grow down many feet to anchor the tree. You want the roots to grow far beyond the dripline to help anchor the tree against the worst winds. If you've selected the correct tree, you won't need to add any fertilizer.

■ Dig a planting hole that is deep enough only to fit the roots without your having to bend or twist any of them when backfilling the hole. Dig with a spading fork so you don't compact the sides of the hole; if you use a shovel, be sure to break up the hole's sides with a spading fork or garden pick to allow the roots to easily spread into the surrounding soil.

■ If the planting area tends to be soggy or flood easily, plant the seedlings — even those with roots adapted to these conditions — on a raised mound for extra drainage. For each cluster of seedlings, construct a well-drained mound of native soil three to four feet wide and up to eighteen inches high. Fracture the soil in the area where the mound will be by heaving, not inverting, the soil with a spading fork.

■ Never stake a windbreak tree. If you're planting the right-size tree, it will not be tall enough to require staking. Trees that bend and blow in the wind develop thicker, sturdier trunks than those bound to a confining stake.

■ Shaping the Wind for a Cooler Home

If you live in an area where prevailing summer and winter winds come from different directions, the same windbreak dynamics applied in reverse can be used to help cool your house or garden in the summer. Instead of fending off the wind, windbreaks and hedges can funnel afternoon breezes toward the house or patio. Such windbreaks are placed nearly parallel to the prevailing summer air currents, in a funnel shape that is wider away from the house and narrower closer up. This configura-

tion can increase the breezes by up to 20 percent and can be designed to force the air through the house's open windows.

In arid climates, the air can be made to feel cooler if it passes over a moist brick patio or sprinkled shrubs. The channeled breezes pick up some of the moisture and become cooler as it evaporates.

■ Further Reading

Anne Moffat's and Marc Schiler's *Landscape Design That Saves Energy* (New York: William Morrow, 1981) is still the most thorough book on the topic.

The U.S. Department of the Interior's *Plants, People and Environmental Quality* (Washington, D.C.: U.S. Printing Office, 1972) is an inexpensive introduction to the subject.

Hedges, Screens and Espaliers, by Susan Chamberlain (Tucson: HP Books, 1983), is a good, brief overview of the basics of design, with plenty of horticultural information on the best trees and shrubs for all parts of the country.   ■

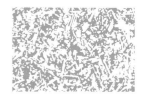

There are an estimated 9,780,000,000,000 gallons of fresh water on earth, but securing enough pure water for our homes is an increasing problem. Since the yard accounts for as much as 50 percent of all the water used by the average family, it's a good place to start looking for ways to conserve this most essential resource. Even if you don't live in the water-short West, a water-conserving landscape offers many benefits: reduced garden maintenance, lower water bills, and surroundings as beautiful as any — if not more beautiful.

Every water-thrifty landscape requires both "hardware" and "software." The hardware includes low-volume lawn sprinklers, drip irrigation, automatic irrigation controllers, cisterns, and graywater systems. The software includes savvy planning, soil improvement, drought-resistant plants, and mulches. It makes sense to consider the software first.

■ Planning to Conserve Water

A water-conserving landscape begins with planning. That first year in your house, when you're doing your site analysis, pay particular attention to drainage patterns. Observe where standing water collects after a rain — a sign of heavy clay soils. Note which plants are the first to wilt after watering, a possible indication of the rapid drainage of rocky, gravelly, or sandy soils. Be attentive to which trees harvest, via condensation, the most rain or fog. The rainfall under tall trees can be twice that in a nearby open field, or even more; that's where to plant the more water-loving plants.

■ Planning Zones of Water Use

Early on, when you sketch your future landscape on paper, group plants and landscape structures together in "irrigation zones" according to similar water needs as well as comparable fertilizer requirements. Don't plant a water-loving, fertilizer-dependent rosebush

among a clump of water-thrifty, sand- and rock-tolerant rosemary. Bog-loving plants should be clustered with other water-loving plants, next to a small ornamental pool and in a spot that gets afternoon shade (to limit evaporation). This oasis of high water use, carefully sized to offer the sensuous appeal of water without actually using too much of the precious liquid, might be sited, for example, in a private courtyard garden outside the master bedroom. (Yes, a water-conserving landscape can have a small water feature to attract wildlife that a dry garden would never harbor, and to add another dimension of visual interest and sound that soothes the soul. Just keep it small.) A small lawn for the children to tumble on might be placed outside their bedroom. The next-most-water-intensive area, the edible landscape, should be located just outside the kitchen door. The rest of the yard should consist of beds of colorful, drought-resistant shrubs and flowers and zones of natural landscape, which is by definition adapted to the rainfall in your area.

■ Limiting the Lawn

At every opportunity during the planning process, limit the size of your lawn! Many a suburban property has a lawn spilling over onto the next property like green waffle batter oozing off the edges of a griddle. Across the country, the lawn soaks up the lion's share of outdoor water. Lawns need be only a fraction of their traditional size to function as sitting areas and places for barbecues, to provide evaporative cooling near a bedroom window, or to offer an oasis of verdant green. A smaller lawn also means fewer hours spent trying to get the lawnmower started, mowing the lawn, and bagging up the stuff you just cut.

Some lawn grasses, such as the fine-bladed Kentucky bluegrasses and bentgrasses, need copious infusions of water and fertilizer to look healthy and green, while others, such as creeping red fescue, blando brome, zoysiagrass,

Common mullein guards a walkway that winds through a water-conserving landscape in Santa Barbara, California, designed by Dennis Shaw — a model of environmental sensitivity for the more intensively designed areas of the naturally elegant garden.

and tall fescues, require 20 percent less water and 50 percent less fertilizer for virtually the same pastoral look.

Improving the Soil

Planning takes time; in the interim, you can work on improving your soil. Remember, in the natural landscape it's best to work with your existing soil, restoring those plant communities that are best adapted to it. However, in selected, highly cultivated areas such as the kitchen garden, you can follow the guidelines in the chapter on soil-conserving landscaping (pages 211–220) and enrich the soil with cover crops, green manures, and compost. Adding organic matter and compost to sandy soils will help them hold on to moisture.

Choosing Appropriate Plants

Proper selection of plants is critical for a water-conserving landscape. Well-chosen zones of natural landscape are intrinsically suited to the natural precipitation patterns of your area and won't require massive infusions of water. But even for the rest of the garden, it's important that you pick only those plants that are best suited to the local climate. On the East Coast, azaleas and rhododendrons, including such spectacular natives as *Rhododendron canescens* (Piedmont azalea) and *Rhododendron vaseyi* (pinkshell azalea), thrive without supplemental irrigation. A landscape in coastal Louisiana could easily support some water-loving bog plants without additional irrigation, while a garden in the higher elevations of the Rocky Mountains would feature alpines and coniferous trees. Along the West Coast, various forms of Mediterranean and indigenous chaparral plants thrive in spite of a six-month seasonal drought. More and more water districts and Cooperative Extension offices are planting demonstration "xeriscapes," the increasingly popular form of landscape that requires either

Below: The vines that are being trained to clamber over the pergola cast cooling shade on the house. Feathery fern palms are planted underneath.

Right: The water-conserving xeriscape includes an intriguing assortment of plants native to California and similar climates around the world, including lavender and rosemary from the Mediterranean region. Mulched planting beds predominate here, not thirsty lawn.

no supplemental irrigation or 75 percent less water than a conventional landscape; call to see if there's one nearby. Talk to local landscapers and nurseries about which plants are well adapted to your area. Most important, don't just focus on flower color when you plan your garden; be sure to select plants that are suited to your yard's soil and climate.

Exotic plants from similar climates elsewhere in the world may be well suited to your yard, but do be careful to avoid those exotics that are *so* well adapted that they become rampant pests, choking off native vegetation. Purple loosestrife (*Lythrum salicaria*) is a colorful exotic that easily colonizes moist soils in bogs and beside ponds. This aggressive foreigner spreads so quickly that it's often mistaken for a native; it has even shown up on the cover of a book on natural landscaping. In contrast, French lavender (*Lavandula dentata*), a Medi-

terranean shrub, is indispensable in the warm-winter areas of the dry West, where it blooms longer than most native plants and doesn't spread because it produces very little viable seed.

Mulching

A drought-resistant planting without a water-conserving mulch is like a new fuel-conserving car with only half the specified oil in the engine: it'll work for a little while but soon fail. Mulch is any material placed on top of the soil to conserve moisture, suppress weeds, or keep the soil cooler. Mulches of hay, straw, or leaves slowly break down to become a very mild fertilizer. Other mulches, such as gravel or shredded redwood bark, save water but do nothing to improve the soil. Some mulches provide an attractive finish for any planting; compost, shredded leaves, bark, and bark chips are in this category. Still other mulches, such as shredded paper, conserve moisture but make your garden look like something straight out of a Li'l Abner cartoon strip. Most mulches should be at least two inches and at most four inches thick; unless you're using a very loose mulch such as straw or hay, you're probably wasting your time and money if your mulch is thicker than that. Keep the mulch four to six inches away from the stem of each plant to prevent crown rot.

Once you've mastered the planning, or software, of your water-conserving landscape, it's time for you to consider the hardware.

Sprinkling the Lawn

Lawn sprinklers come in five basic forms: impulse, oscillating, revolving, traveling, and fixed. Each type has a different spray pattern. For ease and efficiency, make sure the sprinkler's pattern matches your lawn's shape. To see if the sprinkler distributes water evenly and to determine how long it takes your sprinkler to apply an inch of water, set out some randomly placed empty cat-food or tuna-fish cans. Run the sprinkler until a number of the cans contain about an inch of water. Note the elapsed time, then measure the water in all of the cans with a ruler. This will tell you where the dry spots are in your sprinkler's pattern and how long to run the sprinkler to apply an inch of water. More and more newspapers now carry a weekly chart, usually on or near the weather page, estimating how many inches of water you'll need to apply to your lawn in the week ahead. You can also ask your local Cooperative Extension for guidelines on weekly watering rates. Be sure to dig up a few spots in the lawn to make sure the water is penetrating deeply.

Fixed lawn irrigation systems are becoming increasingly popular, especially in the arid West. Permanent sprinkler systems may cost much more than a movable sprinkler and hose, but they offer the advantages of ease, convenience, and automated control. To ensure even coverage, every square foot of the lawn should be overlapped two or three times. Each sprinkler head puts out water in a given radius; the risers (the vertical pipes that supply the sprinkler heads) should be installed no more than a radius apart, or closer. Every year, new low-volume spray heads are introduced that distribute water more effectively. Buy the most current hardware. Be sure to purchase the low-angle spray heads; their lower trajectory loses less water to the air and wind. Check the consistency of the spray pattern and the time needed to apply one inch of water in the manner described above.

Drip Irrigation

The most efficient way to water your landscape is with drip irrigation, in which water dribbles from emitters attached to tubing that

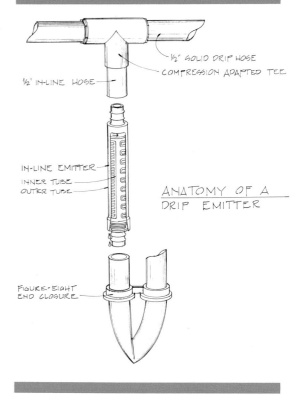

½" SOLID DRIP HOSE
COMPRESSION ADAPTED TEE

½" IN-LINE HOSE

IN-LINE EMITTER
INNER TUBE
OUTER TUBE

ANATOMY OF A
DRIP EMITTER

FIGURE-EIGHT
END CLOSURE

The most efficient way to water your landscape is with drip irrigation, whereby water dribbles from emitters at a rate of as little as half a gallon per hour. All of the water soaks slowly down through the soil to the root zone, where it does the most good.

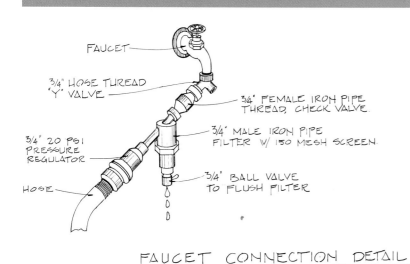

FAUCET

3/4" HOSE THREAD "Y" VALVE

3/4" 20 PSI PRESSURE REGULATOR

HOSE

3/4" FEMALE IRON PIPE THREAD, CHECK VALVE.

3/4" MALE IRON PIPE FILTER W/ 150 MESH SCREEN.

3/4" BALL VALVE TO FLUSH FILTER

FAUCET CONNECTION DETAIL

Every drip irrigation system should have a check valve, a filter, and a pressure regulator threaded together at an existing hose bib. The check valve prevents dirt and manure from being sucked into the drip tubing and into the water pipes inside the house. The filter screens particles that could easily clog the tiny emitter openings. The regulator reduces water pressure from 40 to 60 pounds per square inch (normal pressure inside a house) to 25 psi or less.

runs on top of the soil throughout the landscape — hence the name. A drip irrigation system costs more than any movable sprinkler and, with its array of tubing and parts, is more complicated to install. However, most people find that with some guidance, they can install their own water-thrifty drip irrigation system.

The benefits of such systems are many. Your plants will grow better. You will enjoy a water savings of 50 to 70 percent over sprinklers, since most drip systems use as little as one half gallon per hour (gph) per emitter. Water-related diseases such as rust, mildew, and crown rot will be greatly reduced or even eliminated. Even where summer drought isn't a chronic problem, vegetable and fruit yields will increase. Saline irrigation water will be easier to manage. Weeding will be minimized in dry summer climates.

Drip irrigation systems can be automated for convenience. Drip is the best way to evenly water steep slopes and can help prevent the compaction that comes from overwatered soils. The most serious drawback to drip irrigation, aside from the initial cost and all the widgets, is the fact that you can't use it on the lawn because the tubes and emitters would get in the way of mowing. Drip systems can also be very awkward to use in annual beds of flowers and

vegetables. What's more, gophers occasionally perforate the tubing to steal water.

Because drip emitters distribute water so slowly, none is wasted to the air; instead, all of the water soaks slowly down to the root zone, where it does the most good. People unfamiliar with drip irrigation are often confused by the system's appearance: on the surface, they see only a moist circle around the emitter and lots of dry soil along the length of drip hose until it reaches another emitter, where there's another wet spot. The relatively large dry area on the surface is deceptive, however; just beneath the soil, the moist zone below each emitter is much wider. In rapidly draining sandy soils, the wet zone is shaped like a carrot, while in clay soils the water spreads in a shape resembling that of a fat turnip. In any type of soil, the roots get much more moisture than surface appearances would seem to indicate.

Many drip irrigation systems are available at local hardware stores and nurseries, but they may not have all the parts you need, or else the parts they have may not be of high quality. Make sure you get several favorable references for the particular system you're thinking of buying.

Every system should have three important parts: a backflow preventer, a filter, and a pres-

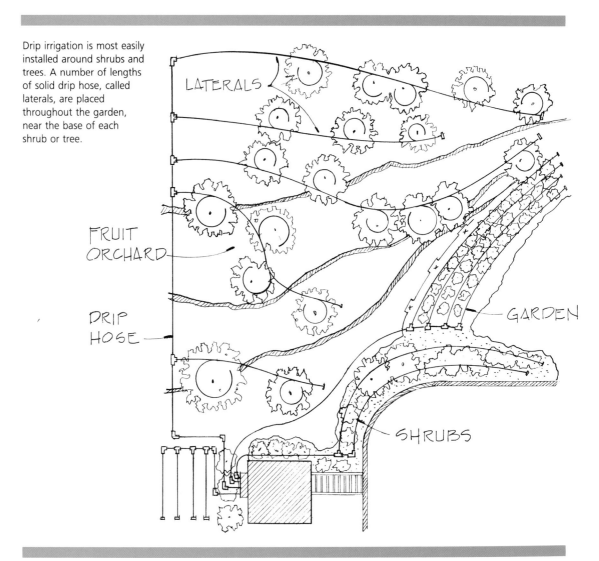

Drip irrigation is most easily installed around shrubs and trees. A number of lengths of solid drip hose, called laterals, are placed throughout the garden, near the base of each shrub or tree.

LATERALS

FRUIT ORCHARD

DRIP HOSE

GARDEN

SHRUBS

sure regulator. These parts are threaded together at an existing hose bib and are called the main assembly. The backflow preventer protects your family's health by stopping the siphon action that can occur whenever you shut off the system. Without a backflow preventer, dirt, manure, compost, or tiny bugs could be sucked into the drip tubing and from there into the water pipes inside your house. The emitters have very small openings (much smaller than those in most sprinklers), which could easily become clogged and useless without proper filtration. Use a filter with at least a 140-mesh metal screen. Drip-system tubing is joined together with simple fittings that re-

quire no wrenches, no messy thread sealers, and no toxic glues. But these simple-to-use fittings can't take the same pressure as your house plumbing. Normally, house water pressure is forty to sixty pounds per square inch (psi). A pressure regulator is essential to keep the drip irrigation system's pressure at or below 25 psi. The pressure regulator should always be installed *after* the filter; that way, you can use the full 40 to 60 psi pressure to flush the filter clean during routine maintenance.

Drip irrigation systems are most easily installed around shrubs and trees. To set up your system, after adding the main assembly to a hose bib, place a number of lengths of solid

vals. After adding the emitters, flush the system again with the ends of the hose open to ensure that any dirt is removed. Finally, cap the ends of each lateral. Your drip irrigation system is now complete.

Graywater Gardening

The design and plumbing of a graywater system is described in the earlier chapter on bathrooms (pages 146–149). Here, the discussion will focus on how to use the recycled water from your shower, bathtub, bathroom sinks, and laundry in your garden. However, it is worth repeating that graywater systems are illegal in all but a few forward-thinking — and drought-stricken — communities.

For your family's safety, all graywater should be applied *below* the surface of the soil. One way to guarantee that graywater stays below the surface is to construct two or more mini–leach fields — shallow trenches of gravel with perforated drainpipes that allow the wastewater to trickle down into the soil. The best time to install a mini–leach field is before you plant a new area of the landscape. Make each trench twelve to eighteen inches deep and six to twelve inches wide, add four to six inches of one-inch-round gravel, and lay a ten-foot length of rigid pipe with its two lines of holes facing down. After making sure that the drainpipe is perfectly level, add a ninety-degree elbow at one end and a length of pipe extending to just above the soil's surface (this is where the hose from your graywater system will hook up with your mini–leach field). Add round gravel to the top of the trench and then cover it with landscape fabric and a decorative mulch.

Usually, it's not advisable to add mini–leach fields to an existing planting. Instead, you can use inverted flowerpots over small pockets of gravel, which are much easier to install. Make pockets in several locations around the dripline of each tree or shrub, adding only enough

drip hose, usually one half inch in diameter, on the ground throughout the garden and then cover them with mulch for appearance' sake. These hoses, called the laterals, should run near the base of each new shrub or tree. Next, turn on the hose bib for a few minutes to flush out any dirt that may have gotten inside. Add two emitters, each ten to eighteen inches long, on either side of a young plant. Don't be tempted to put the emitter right at the base of the stem or trunk, as this is an invitation for crown rot. For larger shrubs or trees, place a ring of solid drip hose around the dripline of the plant and add emitters every twelve to twenty-four inches, depending on the soil. Sandy soils usually call for emitters every twelve inches to fully moisten the root zone, while clay soils allow for greater inter-

While drip irrigation systems are most easily installed around permanent plantings, they can also be used in vegetable and flower beds.

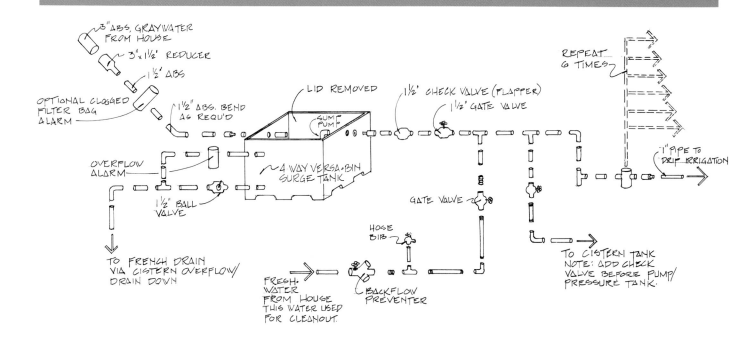

GRAYWATER SYSTEM SCHEMATIC
·NOT TO SCALE·

round gravel so that the bottom of the flowerpot is visible just above the soil. Use solid, half-inch drip irrigation hose to supply each flowerpot. The drip hose should protrude through the pot's drainage hole but not into the gravel itself; the gap of air between the hose and the gravel will prevent roots from growing into the hose. Add a simple, inexpensive drip irrigation ball valve to each flowerpot to adjust the flow of water, especially on hills.

Drip irrigation is the most efficient way to apply any type of water, even graywater. However, graywater contains an enormous amount of particulates, lints, and general grunge, and it's not easy to design a system that can filter it enough to prevent clogging of the emitters. Currently, there is only one graywater system available that can inexpensively filter out enough of the suspended solids (see Appendix A, page 221). It may be worth your while to

look into it: five to ten times more plants can be watered with a graywater drip system than with mini–leach fields or flowerpots.

No matter how you irrigate with graywater, be sure to distribute the recycled water to different sections of the landscape every couple of days, depending on your soil's structure. It can't be emphasized enough that you should not apply too much graywater to the same spot all at once: the soil will become sodden and may begin to smell bad or, worse, become a health hazard, and the saturated soil may cause the roots of your plants to rot. The constant infusion of water could also lead to soil compaction and might even permanently damage your soil structure. All of this can be prevented with a set of simple manual valves in the landscape, which will enable you to rotate the graywater to a different area as often as necessary. This interval will vary according to how much graywater you and your family generate and how well your soil drains; at most, it will be a week or two.

Since most soaps and detergents are slightly alkaline, avoid using graywater on the most acid-loving plants. Most shade plants prefer an acid soil, as do blueberry, heather (*Erica* spp.), spruce (*Picea* spp.), pin oak (*Quercus palustris*), crape myrtle (*Lagerstroemia indica*), lily of the valley (*Convallaria* spp.), holly (*Ilex* spp.), mountain ash (*Sorbus* spp.), and hemlock (*Tsuga* spp.). This is not a rigid rule; many people in southern California have successfully used graywater to irrigate acid-preferring citrus trees for over a decade. If you must use graywater on acid-loving plants, watch them carefully and till in compost and acid fertilizers if necessary.

Plants that are irrigated properly with graywater actually grow better than those watered with municipal or well water. Consequently, graywater makes good sense in any climate — when it is legal.

■ Cisterns

When people start running out of water, they often turn to cisterns, large holding tanks for rainwater captured from the home's roof. Cisterns are far from a new technology; many old houses have them. And cisterns of stone and brick can easily be blended into the design of contemporary houses.

In most climates, a home's roof can provide most if not all of the water that a landscape will ever need. By capturing runoff in gutters linked to a cistern, every 1,200 square feet of roof can "harvest" 748 gallons of water for each inch of rain; if the seasonal rainfall is fifteen inches, that means approximately 11,220 gallons of free, soft rainwater. A twenty-inch season would net nearly 15,000 gallons.

The catch is in the catching — or more specifically, in the storing. The cost of a cistern to store all this free water is usually the limiting factor. The cheapest possible storage usually costs at least fifty cents per gallon. But this is for ugly black plastic tanks, built above ground and in desperate need of camouflage. Typically, cisterns are set below ground or beneath the house, where the water can be kept cool and refreshing. Tanks discreetly buried below ground can cost fifty cents to two dollars per gallon of storage.

Ironically, cisterns are least appropriate in some of the places that need them the most — especially large estates. For example, Santa Barbara, California, has a six- to seven-month drought each year and gets less than fifteen inches of winter rain. It's not uncommon for a three-acre estate in Santa Barbara to use 400,000 gallons of water for year-round irrigation. Few if any of these estate homes have roofs big enough to capture that much water with only fifteen inches of rain — it would take nearly an acre of roof! Furthermore, the storage tank would have to be seventy-six feet around and thirty tall and would cost $400,000 or more — hardly a practical solution. Cisterns do, however, make sense where rains occur all summer, even if erratically.

It isn't wise to use cistern water for drinking or washing, since rain washes down every type of pollution in the sky. Recently, the U.S. Geological Survey found a number of herbicides in rainwater throughout the Northeast and Midwest. While the *average* concentrations for all twenty-three states where herbicides were detected were below recognized hazardous levels, no one is testing the rainwater at your house. Reserve your cistern water for the landscape, or possibly for any toilets plumbed separately from your potable water supply.

Even if the cistern is reserved solely for irrigation, your roof can really clog up the works with debris, leaves, dirt, and soot during a dry spell. Take some protective measures. First, mount screens over all the gutters that feed into it. Build a divert valve into the downspout plumbing. Allow the first few rains to dump as they did before you installed the cis-

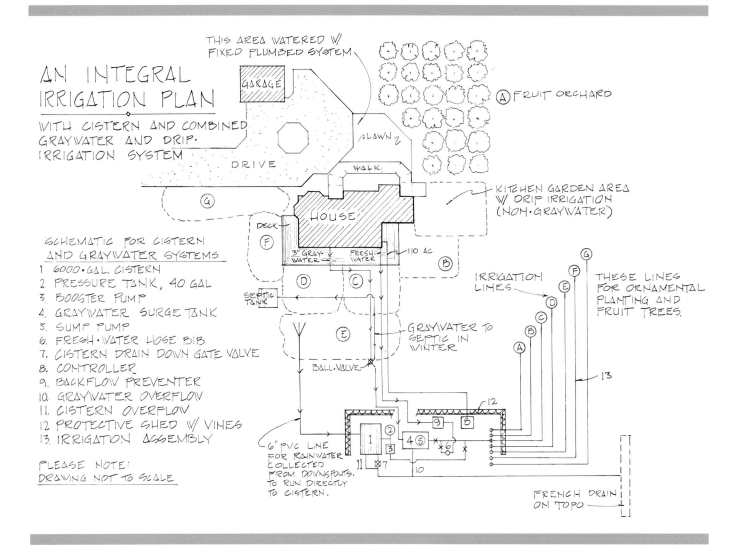

AN INTEGRAL IRRIGATION PLAN

WITH CISTERN AND COMBINED GRAYWATER AND DRIP. IRRIGATION SYSTEM

THIS AREA WATERED W/ FIXED PLUMBED SYSTEM

GARAGE

Ⓐ FRUIT ORCHARD

LAWN

DRIVE

WALK

KITCHEN GARDEN AREA W/ DRIP IRRIGATION (NON-GRAYWATER)

Ⓖ

HOUSE

DECK

Ⓕ

110 AC.

SCHEMATIC FOR CISTERN AND GRAYWATER SYSTEMS

1 6000-GAL. CISTERN
2 PRESSURE TANK, 40 GAL
3 BOOSTER PUMP
4 GRAYWATER SURGE TANK
5 SUMP PUMP
6 FRESH-WATER HOSE BIB
7 CISTERN DRAIN DOWN GATE VALVE
8 CONTROLLER
9 BACKFLOW PREVENTER
10 GRAYWATER OVERFLOW
11 CISTERN OVERFLOW
12 PROTECTIVE SHED W/ VINES
13 IRRIGATION ASSEMBLY

PLEASE NOTE: DRAWING NOT TO SCALE

3" GRAY-WATER   FRESH-WATER

SEPTIC TANK

Ⓓ   Ⓒ   Ⓑ

Ⓔ

BALL-VALVE

GRAYWATER TO SEPTIC IN WINTER

IRRIGATION LINES

THESE LINES FOR ORNAMENTAL PLANTING AND FRUIT TREES.

Ⓖ
Ⓕ
Ⓔ
Ⓓ
Ⓒ
Ⓑ
Ⓐ

13

6" PVC LINE FOR RAINWATER COLLECTED FROM DOWNSPOUTS TO RUN DIRECTLY TO CISTERN.

FRENCH DRAIN ON TOPO

tern; this will clean the roof of much of the stuff that has settled on it. Now turn the valve to the cistern. Attach a wire mesh basket over the tank to catch any stray leaves or sticks, and install the outlet pipe a foot or more above the bottom of the tank so particulates can settle out. Finally, make sure your cistern has an outlet port flush with the bottom of the tank to allow for flushing and cleaning. Cleaning will be even easier if the tank has a lid big enough to allow you to climb into it.

■ Further Reading

Plants for Dry Climates: How to Select, Grow and Enjoy, by Mary Rose Duffield and Warren Jones (Tucson: HP Books, 1981), is a good introduction to xeriscaping.

Gary Robinette's *Water Conservation in the Landscape* (New York: Van Nostrand Reinhold, 1984) is an excellent overview, albeit a little too technical in places for the average homeowner.

Bob Perry's *Trees and Shrubs for Dry California Landscapes* (San Dimas, Calif.: Land Design Publishing, 1981) contains the best list of drought-tolerant plants for the American Southwest. The plants are described and listed according to various criteria.   ■

Topsoil, with its living matrix of microorganisms, minerals, organic matter, and invertebrates, is an essential element of any healthy home garden. True topsoil takes hundreds of years to evolve into its crumbly, dark, nutrient-rich form; it's not something you want to squander. If you can get your hands on good topsoil for your yard, it's hard to rationalize the fact that it has been ripped off from somewhere else. Many nurseries sell "topsoil" that is concocted from dirt (which can be quite clayey, gravelly, or full of weed seeds) and fillers such as ground-up bark or sand and some manure — a far cry from the wonderfully complex, fertile loam it's meant to replace. What it all boils down to is that when it comes to protecting this precious resource, you're largely left to your own devices.

The fundamentals of creating a soil-conserving landscape are simple: you must build up your soil to hold and retain water, nutrients, and soil particles; allow as much of the landscape as possible to percolate and absorb water; attempt to knit the soil together with living roots to discourage erosion; and protect the soil surface from the direct impact of rain by mulching. Taking care of one problem will often solve others at the same time.

▪️ Improving Your Soil

While there is a native plant community for almost any soil, it's often necessary to improve the soil of your future kitchen garden or cutting garden. There are two major categories of soil amendments: those that improve the soil's tilth and those that provide nutrients. Good tilth is that crumbly, loamy structure typically found in the soil of an old forest; it allows for good drainage but at the same time binds the soil together to prevent erosion.

Sand is an example of an amendment used solely for tilth. When added in moderation to clay soil, it will enhance drainage, but it will add little in the way of fertility. Blood meal is the other extreme: it adds plenty of valuable nitrogen but does little to improve tilth or prevent erosion. The ideal soil amendment both provides nutrients and improves tilth. It is high in organic matter and humus.

Why are organic matter and humus so vital to your garden's soil? Organic matter, the residue of dead plant and animal life, is as important to soil health as dietary fiber is to human health. When organic matter decays, due to the actions of soil microorganisms, it releases valuable minerals and nutrients, literally feeding the soil life as it helps retain moisture without making the soil sticky or waterlogged.

Ultimately, much of the organic matter decomposes into humus, a complex dark-brown substance with an enormous capacity to retain moisture and nutrients. Humus acts like a diffuse, elastic glue to hold the soil's particles together in a loose aggregate. In clay soils, humus's plastic nature keeps particles apart to enhance drainage, while at the same time holding them together to deter erosion. In sandy soils, humus helps retain moisture and nutrients.

Unfortunately, humus doesn't last forever. It oxidizes in a silent, flameless combustion. Consequently, you must constantly renew organic matter to keep your soil healthy. Compost, green manures, and cover crops provide the best means of enhancing your soil's organic matter and therefore its humus content.

▪️ Composting

Compost — dark, loamy, sweet-smelling material that resembles rich forest soil — is the Porsche of garden amendments because it combines organic matter, stabilized humus, nutrients, and minerals. For best effect, compost should be thoroughly dug into the soil; it's easier to incorporate it before planting than to try to insert it around existing plants. Using compost as a mulch is like serving filet mignon at a kid's birthday party: it's too valuable and will most likely go unappreciated.

At the height of the organic gardening

movement of the 1970s, compost was believed to be the cure for all gardening ills. To devotees, watching the four-foot piles steam in the crisp early morning air was an almost mystical experience. But for many, the ardor soon wore off, and constructing the carefully layered piles and religiously turning them every three to five days became, to put it bluntly, a pain in the neck.

Alas, gardens still need compost; in fact, the problems that first sparked the interest in composting ten or twenty years ago have only gotten worse. Landfills across the country are approaching capacity, and new sites are increasingly hard to find. In any case, with yard waste comprising almost 20 percent of the average landfill, more and more cities are banning it from the trash can or charging a premium for its disposal. Many homeowners

are therefore stuck with having to do some form of backyard composting to comply with the new garbage guidelines.

The Lazy Gardener's Guide to Composting

There are two extremes in the spectrum of composting techniques: the cool, passive method and the hot, active process.

Compost Heaps   The most passive compost pile is just a big mound that develops little if any heat as the assorted yard wastes heaped upon it slowly rot. It's characterized as "passive" because you don't have to spend a whole lot of time combining the right materials; instead, you just leave it alone — no watering, no turning, no fussing. This is also known as the "cool" method because only bacteria, fungi, insects, slugs, and worms that

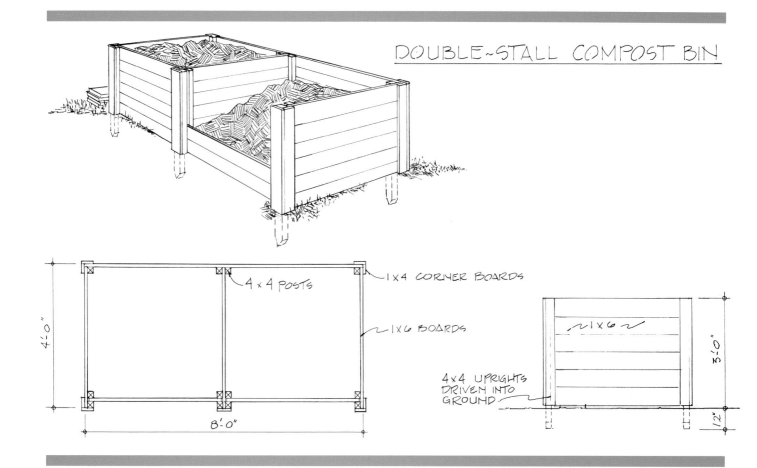

DOUBLE-STALL COMPOST BIN

1 X 4 CORNER BOARDS

4 X 4 POSTS

1 X 6 BOARDS

1 X 6

4 X 4 UPRIGHTS DRIVEN INTO GROUND

4'-0"

8'-0"

3'-0"

12"

thrive at low temperatures decompose the pile. In time — perhaps as much as two to four years — the heap will become high-fiber material for use as a mulch or soil amendment. Passive composting is a form of decomposition suited to active life-styles — all you do is add the latest batch of clippings to the heap. But unlike compost made the active way, it won't be a significant source of nutrition for your plants, as rainfall will leach away valuable nutrients while the heap sits around rotting. And you'll want to keep out the kitchen scraps, which tend to attract creatures of the rodent persuasion.

Hot Composting It was hot, active composting that overtaxed gardeners in the 1970s. In this approach, the industrious gardener must carefully build a one-cubic-yard pile of just the right types of compostable materials. Layers of premoistened high-carbon materials (straw, wood chips, corn stalks, or dry leaves) must be alternated with moist high-nitrogen refuse (freshly mown grass or manure) in an approximate ratio of thirty to one. The materials must then be judiciously moistened, and the pile turned every three to seven days for about a month. The pile gets very hot — up to 160 degrees — due to heat-loving bacteria and fungi. The heat kills weed seeds, diseases, and pests; kitchen scraps are acceptable. The process even speeds the breakdown of some chemical pesticides. Better yet, compost produced this way provides a dose of the "big three" plant nutrients — nitrogen, phosphorous, and potash — as well as micronutrients and plenty of organic matter. But considerable effort and plenty of compostable materials are required to maintain an active compost program.

Bastard Trenching "Bastard trenching" is an easy alternative if you're trying to improve the soil in a new garden. Given its moniker by the English, it is a remarkably simple way to compost kitchen scraps. All you have to do is dig a hole deep enough so that the scraps will be covered with at least six inches of soil; if critters are a problem, make it twelve

to eighteen inches. Soil microorganisms and earthworms will digest the garbage and turn it into rich organic matter for whatever you intend to plant there in the future. Bastard trenching is not a great way to recycle garden clippings, however; the sheer volume of mowed grass, pruned branches, and leaves would necessitate more trenches than a war zone.

Sheet Composting If you're not using kitchen waste loaded with meat scraps, sheet composting is an even easier way to improve garden soil — with no strenuous digging or time-consuming turning. Simply apply thin layers of compostables over the soil as you would a mulch, alternating layers of high-carbon and high-nitrogen materials up to one foot deep. Finish with a good-looking mulch and you'll improve your soil from the top down while recycling large quantities of kitchen scraps and garden clippings.

Worm Composting Somewhat different from all of the above approaches is vermicomposting, or worm composting. This approach is used primarily with kitchen scraps and fresh garden wastes that are high in nitrogen. All you need is a light-tight and fly-tight bin or box containing thousands of worms.

If kitchen scraps are added to a cool, passive

When you need to replenish the soil in your kitchen garden or cutting garden, use compost. Compost provides essential organic matter and nutrients, and is made up of recycled leaves, lawn clippings, and other "wastes" that would otherwise end up at an overburdened landfill.

compost pile, the food can go rancid and attract flies and vermin. Scraps can be quickly digested in a hot, active compost pile, but you must always have a fresh pile to bury them in — a particular problem in cold-winter climates, where the pile must be much larger than normal in winter to insulate it from the cold. Worms may be a viable alternative: they can rapidly digest an amazing amount of kitchen wastes and save you the bother of building and turning a hot compost pile. And unlike a compost pile, they produce a very rich, concentrated fertilizer for houseplants, vegetables, ornamental flowers, shrubs, and fruit trees. One effective way to separate the fertilizer from the worms is to move the digested, ready-to-use material to one side of the box and add a fresh batch of food wastes on the other side. In no time, the hungry worms will wiggle over, and you can transfer the compost — or more technically, the worm "castings" — to your garden.

Some Easy Alternatives

Composting is an ecosystem that includes you, the composter. Before plunging into composting, consider which method is best for you. How much free time do you have? What kind of finished compost do you want? Often you'll have to trade one off against the other. For example, a passive compost pile requires less effort than an active one, but the final product will be less nutritious. You'll also need to take a good look at the materials you'll be composting and choose the best place in your yard for the pile.

The average American lawn is a major source of organic matter. While the typical lawn can be a source of fresh greens for composting, one of the new mulching mowers may be an easier way for you to deal with grass clippings. You can also convert some of these mowers to capture, in a removable bag, the clippings for the compost pile. Thus they give you a choice: you can collect compostables when you wish and use the mower to help keep the lawn fertile the rest of the time.

While leaves make a wonderfully rich, black, loamy compost once they have fully decomposed, their initial volume can be overwhelming. You can skip the effort involved in hot composting by heaping the leaves in a wire-mesh cylinder in some hidden corner of the yard. Although you'll have to wait a couple of years, minimal effort is required, and the end product will be a choice mulch and an excellent addition to any potting soil. Another option is to rent or buy a mechanical leaf shredder, which will turn the leaves into a valuable mulch.

You needn't compost all yard wastes. Woody prunings from trees and shrubs, which take forever to break down in a passive heap, can be chopped into small pieces by another gizmo called a chipper and used to cover a pathway or as mulch in a woodland garden.

Kitchen scraps accumulate year-round. Unfortunately, it's difficult to compost outdoors during cold, snowy winters when the ground is frozen solid. Instead of sending kitchen refuse to the dump all winter, you can compost with a worm bin in a garage or basement that stays between fifty-five and seventy-five degrees. Regardless of the season, worm bins can be odor-free and simple to care for, and can quickly transform table scraps as well as used newspapers into rich fertilizer. Another alternative for kitchen scraps is one of the new kitchen-waste digesters. These cone-shaped containers have holes in the bottom that are designed to be submerged in the soil outdoors. The top flips open so you can deposit the food wastes. Over time, the volume of kitchen scraps is reduced by dehydration and is at least partially digested by bacteria and earthworms. What's left can be easily buried in your garden.

Choosing a Location for Composting

Don't treat the composting area as an afterthought; it should be planned as carefully as any other structural portion of the landscape. Plan to compost as far away as possible from both your house and your neighbor's. A well-managed compost pile is relatively odorless, but neglected piles do occasionally smell foul. As most compost piles aren't the most attractive part of the garden, try to locate yours behind a fence or some evergreen ornamental shrubs.

If you'll be composting kitchen scraps, the location of the compost bins is particularly important. The idea is to make frequent trips to the compost bin as painless as possible. Remember, at times kitchen scraps need to be taken out in rainy weather, so arrange to compost near a carport, pergola, or covered walkway. If you're using a worm bin, it can be conveniently located in the basement, garage, garden shed, or carport or beneath a wide porch or eave, as long as the worms won't freeze in the winter.

The ideal location for a compost pile is different in each bioregion. Drying winds and sunlight can either improve or impede the process. In areas with hot and dry summers, it's best to place the compost in a spot that's shady all day. In hot and moist regions, morning sun and afternoon shade are the optimal conditions. In cool, moist summer climates, a sunny location will help reduce heat loss and keep the exterior of the pile from getting too soggy. If you're mostly composting leaves in the fall, you may want to build a compost pile in a sunny area to extend the biological activity further into the fall and early winter.

When in doubt, compost in the shade of a large tree. But be aware that some types of tree roots can invade your compost pile and rob it of valuable nutrients. Trees with particularly invasive roots include coastal redwood (*Sequoia sempervirens*), *Ficus benjamina*, tree of heaven (*Ailanthus altissima*), willow (*Salix* spp.), black locust (*Robinia* spp.), alder (*Alnus* spp.), and eucalyptus (*Eucalyptus* spp.). Where invasive roots are a problem, build the compost pile on a concrete slab, or use wooden bins with wooden bottoms.

Whichever composting method you choose, be sure to leave lots of working space around the pile or bins. You'll be using long-handled pitchforks and a wheelbarrow or garden cart,

so allow for a minimum of six to eight feet of access on at least two sides of the pile or in front of each bin.

◼ Green Manures

Some plants, called green manures, are grown simply to be tilled into the soil within a matter of months. These plants have many of the advantages of compost. Quite often, legumes such as clover, alfalfa, and vetch are used as green manures because of their high nitrogen content. Nonleguminous green manure plants include young grasses, buckwheat, and mustards. Green manuring, like composting, is best done either before planting a new landscape or on a seasonal or rotating basis to renew parts of the vegetable garden. It is a considerably easier way to improve soil than making and turning a compost pile.

Green manure is nearly a free fertilizer, if you discount the cost of a few seeds and some elbow grease. Green manures improve soil drainage in clay soils, retain moisture in sandy soils, and are a readily available fertilizer in all soils. The additional fiber also helps to bind the soil together, protecting it against the ravages of wind and water.

Green manures, grown to be tilled under, improve the structure of the soil and prevent erosion. Bacteria that live on the roots of leguminous green manures such as crimson red clover are additionally able to "fix" atmospheric nitrogen gas into free fertilizer.

Grasses for Fiber

The best green manure plants for sheer bulk of fiber are members of the grass and cereal families. They have a very extensive, fibrous root system that helps loosen clay soil. As the grasses and cereals grow, the extensive network of roots aids in preventing wind and water erosion.

Grasses and cereals are not as shallow-rooted as is commonly thought. Grains such as wheat, rye, and barley have a bulky root system that can grow down from five to seven feet in a good loamy or sandy soil. When roots die in the deeper soil, the tissue rots and "deposits" organic matter much deeper than any type of tilling could. The fibrous root systems of annual rye, oats, barley, sudan grass, winter wheat, and fescue are better than legumes at loosening tight clay soils and increasing the moisture retention of sandy soils.

Legumes for Nitrogen

The bacteria that live on the roots of legumes have the ability to "fix" atmospheric nitrogen gas into fertilizer. Thinking they'll get a bigger dose of nitrogen to fertilize their soil, many gardeners grow only legumes, leaving out other kinds of green manure crops. While legumes are important in a green manure mix, they should always be part of a mixture that also includes fibrous-rooted plants.

Mixing Legumes and Grasses

The best approach to green manuring is to have both — grasses and legumes. One classic green manure blend is a combination of oats (or ryegrass) and the leguminous crops vetch, bell beans, and Austrian peas. Some version of this blend was the nutrient backbone of many farms long before chemical fertilizers were invented. The mix is usually composed of about 20 percent Oregon annual ryegrass (or oats) and the following legumes: 40 percent bell beans, 20 percent Austrian field peas, and 20 percent purple vetch.

Planting

For germination, legumes require calcium and phosphorous. Many legumes also prefer to sprout in a slightly alkaline soil. Lime or oyster-shell flour will take care of both needs; use the amount recommended for your area. Initially, legumes will not grow well if the soil is low in phosphorous. Use a single application of colloidial phosphate, bone meal, or rock phosphate to adjust the phosphorous content of the soil; once they're established and growing, the legumes will accumulate plenty of phosphorous themselves and won't require any extra.

Tossing green manure seeds onto untilled soil is a waste of time and seed. The soil for all green manures should be prepared as for crops such as beans, corn, and carrots. Big seed such as that for beans requires only a rough seed bed, while fine seed such as that for ryegrass germinates better if the soil is prepared, as in a carrot bed. In all cases, cover the seeds with a layer of soil equal to three times their diameter.

Timing

The best time to till under a green manure crop for maximum nitrogen is just prior to bloom or before 20 percent of the blossoms open (see the table on the following page for a list of green manures and when to sow and till them). You must sacrifice beautiful blossoms for the optimal amount of nitrogen. Turning under young succulent growth is the quickest way to release the largest amount of nutrients; older growth is woodier and more resistant to decomposition by soil bacteria.

Growing All Your Fertilizer

For hundreds of years, farmers have used green manures in rotation with fallow periods as their sole source of nutrients. In the kitchen garden, with a fallow of one or more seasons to allow nutrients to accumulate, you can grow all your own fertilizer.

Green Manures

Legumes	Seed Rate (lbs. per 1,000 sq. ft.)	When to Sow	When to Turn Under	Winter Hardy	Comments
Alfalfa *Medicago sativa*	1/2–1	Spring	Prebloom, 4–12" tall	Yes	Use phosphorous to germinate, water when dry; dislikes wet soils; don't let it turn into a pesty perennial
Austrian peas *Lathyrus hirsutus*	2–5	Fall	Prebloom, next spring	No	Best for mild winter climates; takes some frost; doesn't like heat; helps to smother weeds
Bell bean *Vicia faba*	2–5	Fall	Prebloom, next spring	No	Makes massive amount of foliage; hardy to 15°F; grows in acid soils
Crimson clover *Trifolium incarnatum*	1/2–1	Fall in mild climates; spring in cold climates	Prebloom	No	Not hardy north of New Jersey; tolerates shade; beautiful blossoms
New Zealand white clover *Trifolium repens*	1/2–1	Spring, summer	Prebloom, 4–12" tall	Yes	Heat-resistant; attracts beneficial insects; good bee plant
Purple vetch *Vicia benghalensis* or *V. atropurpurea*	1–3	Fall in mild climates; spring in cold climates	Prebloom	No	Vining plant, can climb trees and shrubs; germinates and grows in acid soils; good bee plant
Nonlegumes					
Annual ryegrass *Lolium multiflorum*	4–8	Fall in mild climates; spring in cold climates	When 4–12" tall	No	Best grass for mild winter areas; not hardy; massive root system
Oats *Avena sativa*	2–2 1/2	Spring	When 4–12" tall	No	Less cold-hardy than ryegrass; tolerates wet soils
Sudan grass *Sorghum sudanense*	1/2–1	Spring, summer	When 4–12" tall	No	Very drought-resistant; needs warm soils to germinate, doesn't like wet soils; suppresses weeds; reduces nematodes; fast grower
Winter wheat *Triticum* sp.	1–2 1/2	Fall	When 4–12" tall	Yes	Best nonlegume for cold winter areas; massive root system
Buckwheat *Fagopyrum esculentum*	1–1 1/2	Spring, summer	Prebloom, 4–12" tall	No	Summer crop only; very sensitive to frost; crowds out weeds; flowers attract beneficial insects
Mustard and rapeseed *Brassica* spp.	1/4–1/2	Fall in mild climates; spring in cold climates	Prebloom, 4–12" tall	No	Best for germination in cool, wet soils; mix with other green manure seed to keep from stunting crops/plants

■ The Permeable Landscape

Anywhere there is a solid surface in your yard, water will gain both volume and velocity as it runs down it. The amount and sometimes the speed of the water as it reaches the edge of the hard surface can cause soil erosion. The average downspout is a classic example of this: few lawns or flower beds can stand up to the power of a downspout's deluge. To control this source of erosion, place a splash plate or trough beneath the spout to spread the water. You can also use a pile of riprap stones to scatter the water, or attach a roll of perforated tubing to the spout to unfurl and dissipate the water's momentum. More complicated solutions that may require consultation with a landscape professional include piping the water underground to the sewer or off the property (which doesn't allow you to collect the water for the landscape), constructing a French drain to disperse the water underground, or building dry well boxes that allow the water to slowly percolate into the soil.

Nonpermeable driveways and pathways can also cause erosion. If you must have an impermeable path or driveway, design it to slope slightly to alternate sides a number of times

For an environmentally sound driveway, sidewalk, or path, use a permeable, mortarless surface such as the interlocking pavers at right and below, made by Balcon, Inc. They are durable and come in a variety of shapes and colors, and because water can percolate down between the blocks, they also prevent runoff and erosion.

over its length. This will impede the velocity and momentum that increase moving water's destructive power. Also, if you crown the center of the path or road — that is, make the middle somewhat higher than the edges — half the water will flow to each side, reducing its erosive potential. For garden walkways, use a porous material such as wood chips, crushed rock, bricks set in sand, or slatted wooden decking whenever possible to allow as much rain as possible to soak into the soil. For an environmentally sound driveway, use one of the many types of load-bearing turf block — also called lawn pavers, grassroads, geoblock, turfstone, or grasscrete. These are concrete or plastic grids of various designs with gaps where plants, particularly turf, can grow. From a distance, an area with turf blocks looks like lawn, but it can support any vehicle. The turf blocks are installed in an interlocking grid. At a cost of more than three dollars per square

foot, they aren't cheap, but they do reduce
runoff by 50 to 80 percent. Areas covered with
turf block are also cooler than those paved
with concrete or asphalt.

Mulching Away Erosion

The first line of defense against erosion
caused by falling rain is the protective canopy
of either a plant or a mulch. The impact of a
speeding raindrop is not to be discounted: the
tiniest amount of visible erosion can account
for a loss of fifteen tons of valuable topsoil per
acre per year! Placing a leaf or a bit of straw in
the way of the droplet will scatter the water
and dissipate some of its momentum.

If the plants in your landscape have a dense
canopy, mulch may not be necessary. If they
do not, mulch the entire landscape with two
to six inches of organic matter. Mulches with
stems, straw, or lengthy fibers will grab the
soil and not "walk away" and leave the soil
bare. Loose, pebbly mulches wash away, slide
down gentle slopes, and more readily allow
weeds to germinate. Use seed-free mulches —
mushroom compost, seaweed, sand, gravel,
shredded bark, wood chips, or shredded
leaves — to minimize weeding. Keep the soil
bare for six to eighteen inches from the base of
your plants, depending on their size.

On steeper portions of your landscape, soil-
conserving mulch is especially important, but
most any mulch will have a tendency to slip
downhill. What you should do in this case is
mulch the soil surface thoroughly — before
planting — and then install erosion-control
netting. There are two types: a loose netting
made of woven fiber and a "blanket" made of
two layers of photodegradable plastic netting
filled with wheat straw or coconut fiber or a
combination of the two. The woven fiber netting is the more traditional material, but each
roll is very heavy and difficult to work with on
steep slopes, and the fiber is impregnated with
a toxic rodenticide to prevent damage. The
lightweight rolls of erosion blankets are a

The mulch in this wood-
land garden looks elegant,
conserves water, and keeps
weeds down. It also helps
prevent erosion.

breeze to install, especially on steep terrain, but although the netting does photodegrade, tiny bits of plastic are left behind.

Both netting and blankets can be used on hills with slope-to-height ratios of up to 1:1 (meaning that the slope gains a foot in height for every horizontal foot), or an angle of 45 degrees. With the netting, you should apply a layer of two to four inches of mulch before rolling out the material. The blanket comes with its own mulch, but there's no reason you can't add more. Both varieties are held in place with landscape pins, six inches long for clay soil and nine inches long for sandy soil. The pins are hammered in at different intervals, depending on your slope and soil type; ask your supplier for the specifics. Once the netting is installed, make small holes where necessary to insert your plants, or if you prefer, you can overseed the netted slope. Be sure to water consistently and at a rate that will encourage germination without causing erosion.

■ The Roots That Bind

Next to organic matter and humus, the best soil binder is a matrix of living roots. Once a plant begins to grow, its minute root hairs hold on to soil particles, maintain and improve soil drainage, and absorb valuable nutrients that might otherwise have leached away. Not all roots are alike: some are woody, rather sparse, and deep, while others are more fibrous, shallower, and distinguished by a mat of tiny roots closer to the surface. Roots of the latter type are common to the members of the grass family, rushes, sedges, various tip-rooted ground covers, and sunflowers. Those plants with extensive surface networks of fibrous roots are the best for safeguarding soil and preventing surface erosion, while most trees and many shrubs have roots too deep and

woody to protect the shallow portions of the soil. A zone of native prairie or meadow is therefore an excellent means of erosion control for any areas of your property where erosion is a serious problem.

■ Further Reading

E. W. Russell's *Soil Conditions and Plant Growth* (Englewood Cliffs, N.J.: Prentice-Hall, 1974) includes good detail on green manuring and cover crops.

Soils and Men: Yearbook of Agriculture 1938 (Washington, D.C.: U.S. Department of Agriculture, 1938) is still the best treatment of the subject, although from an agricultural perspective. It's worth looking for in used bookstores or from book antiquarians.

Appendix A:
SUPPLIERS

Architects and Builders

Amsler Woodhouse MacLean Architects Inc.
65 Long Wharf
Boston, MA 02110
(617) 523-0442

Anderson Mason Dale
1615 Seventeenth Street
Denver, CO 80202
(303) 294-9448

Obie G. Bowman Architect
1000 Annapolis Road
Post Office Box 154
The Sea Ranch, CA 95497
(707) 785-2344

Thomas Brown, Architect
945-A Main Street
Stevens Point, WI 54481
(715) 341-8672

Arne Bystrom Architect
1617 Post Alley
Seattle, WA 98101
(206) 443-1011

James Cutler Architects
135 Parfitt Way SW
Winslow, WA 98110
(206) 842-4710

Design Guild
6 Riedesel Avenue
Cambridge, MA 02138
(617) 426-0432

Drerup Armstrong Ltd.
P.O. Box 130
Carp, Ontario, Canada K0A 1L0
(613) 836-1494

David Easton
Rammed Earth Works
1350 Elm Street
Napa, CA 94559
(707) 224-2532

Dagmar B. Epsten Architect
The Epsten Group
303 Ferguson Street
Atlanta, GA 30307
(404) 577-0370

Ford Powell & Carson Inc.
1138 East Commerce Street
San Antonio, TX 78205
(512) 225-1246

Jersey Devil Design/Build
Steve Badanes, Architect
Box 145
Stockton, NJ 08559

Fay Jones & Maurice Jennings Architects
619 West Dickson Street
Fayetteville, AR 72701
(501) 443-4742

Lake/Flato Architects
311 Third Street, Suite 200
San Antonio, TX 78205
(512) 227-3335

Line and Space
Les Wallach, Architect
645 East Speedway
Tucson, AZ 85705
(602) 623-1313

William McDonough
116 East Twenty-seventh Street, Twelfth Floor
New York, NY 10016
(212) 481-1111

The Masters Corporation
12 Burtis Avenue
Post Office Box 514
New Canaan, CT 06840
(203) 966-2807

Jonathan Poore
Architectural Design and Restoration
965A Washington Street
Gloucester, MA 01930
(508) 281-6071

Antoine Predock Architect
300 Twelfth Street NW
Albuquerque, NM 87102
(505) 843-7390

Santa Fe Design
Passive Solar Rammed Earth and Adobe Homes
2855 East Grant Road
Tucson, AZ 85716
(602) 623-2784

John Silverio Architect
Chimney House Designs
RFD 1, Box 169
Lincolnville, ME 04849
(207) 763-3885

Solar Design Associates
Harvard, MA 01451-0242
(508) 456-6855

South Mountain Company, Inc.
Architectural Design and Construction
South Road
Chilmark, MA 02535
(508) 645-2618

Southwest Solaradobe School
Post Office Box 153
Bosque, NM 87006
(505) 252-1382

William Turnbull Associates
Pier 1 1/2 The Embarcadero
San Francisco, CA 94111
(415) 986-3642

Donald Watson, Architect
2 Irving Place
Troy, NY 12180
(518) 273-5051

Helmut Ziehe
International Institute for Baubiologie and Ecology
Post Office Box 387
Clearwater, FL 34615
(813) 461-4371

Landscape Architects and Designers Who Specialize in Natural Landscaping

Patrick Chassé, Landscape Architect
Post Office Box 1007
10 Main Street
Northeast Harbor, ME 04662
(207) 276-5674

John Diekelmann, Landscape Architect
1705 Heim Avenue
Madison, WI 53705
(608) 238-7794

Stephen K. Domigan, Landscape Architect
609B West Thirty-Second Street
Austin, TX 78705
(512) 453-5545

Ecohorizons, Inc.
22601 SW 152nd Avenue
Goulds, FL 33170
(305) 248-0038

Edmund Hollander, Landscape Architect
21 East Fourth Street, Suite 608
New York, NY 10003
(212) 473-0620

John Longhill, Landscape Architect
Swans Nest Farm
Star Route Box 246
Marble Hill, GA 30148
(404) 523-4005

Steve Martino & Associates
225 West University #102
Tempe, AZ 85281
(602) 967-0307

P. Clifford Miller & Associates
177 N. Washington Road
Lake Forest, IL 60045
(312) 234-6664

Murase Associates
1300 NW Northrup
Portland, OR 97209
(503) 242-1477

Peter Strelkow, Landscape Architect
6834 SW Seventy-eighth Terrace
Miami, FL 33143
(305) 669-0008

Stroudwater Design Group
1258 West Brook Street
Portland, ME 04102
(207) 871-1524

Plants and Tools for the Naturally Elegant Garden
All catalogs are free unless otherwise noted

Balcon, Inc.
P.O. Box 3388
Crofton, MD 21114
(410) 721-1900
Alternatives to nonpermeable driveways and pathways, including interlocking pavers in a variety of shapes and colors.

The Cook's Garden
Box 65050
Londonderry, VT 05148
(802) 824-3400
Vegetable and flower seeds, especially lettuces and radicchios (catalog $1.00).

Gardener's Supply Company
128 Intervale Road
Burlington, VT 05401
(802) 863-1700
An excellent selection of tools and hardware.

Harmony Farm Supply
Post Office Box 460
Graton, CA 95444
(707) 823-9125
Irrigation and drip-irrigation hardware, fertilizers, tools, and seed for organic gardeners; also landscape netting and cover crop and green manure seeds (catalog $2.00).

Lawyer Nursery
950 Highway 200 West
Plains, MT 59859
(406) 826-3881
Bare-root seedling trees in many sizes for planting windbreaks in all climates.

A. M. Leonard, Inc.
6665 Spiker Road
Post Office Box 816
Piqua, OH 45356
(800) 543-8955
Source of erosion-control netting and staples (pins), as well as quality garden tools.

Natural Gardening Company
217 San Anselmo Avenue
San Anselmo, CA 94960
(415) 456-5060
Tools, hardware, and irrigation systems exclusively for organic gardeners, including a nonclogging drip-irrigation system for ornamental trees and shrubs as well as vegetables; also organically grown vegetable and flower seedlings.

Necessary Trading Company
New Castle, VA 24127
(703) 864-5103
Premixed cover-crop and green-manure seed combinations and organic fertilizers.

Peaceful Valley Farm Supply
P.O. Box 2209
Grass Valley, CA 95945
(916) 272-4769
Tools, fertilizers, and seed, including green-manure seed, for the organic garden (catalog $2.00).

Seeds Blüm
Idaho City Stage
Boise, ID 83707
(208) 336-8264
Heirloom vegetable seeds, including a number of unusual potato tubers (catalog $3.00).

Shepherd's Garden Seeds
6116 Highway 9
Felton, CA 95018
(408) 335-5311
Gourmet vegetables and some unusual ornamental flowers (catalog $1.00).

The Urban Farmer Store
2833 Vicente Street
San Francisco, CA 94116
(800) 753-3747
Drip-irrigation hardware.

Natural Climate Control

Photovoltaics:
Real Goods Trading Corp.
966 Mazzoni Street
Ukiah, CA 95482
(800) 762-7325
Extensive listing of photovoltaic products. Their *Alternative Energy Sourcebook* provides design guidelines.

Rumford Fireplaces:
Superior Clay Corp.
Box 352
Uhrichsville, OH 44683
(800) 848-6166

Masonry Heaters:
Biofire Inc.
3220 Melbourne
Salt Lake City, UT 84106
(801) 486-0266

Dietmeyer, Ward & Stroud
P.O. Box 323
Vashon, WA 98070
(206) 463-3722

European Heat & Design
416 Pinehurst Avenue
Salisbury, MD 21801
(301) 742-3771

Hearth Warmers
Box 36B, Route 112
Colrain, MA 10340
(413) 624-3363

Serge Levasseur
2030 RR2
Val-David, Quebec, Canada J0T2N0
(819) 322-1315
Masonry heater builder. Conducts workshops for do-it-yourselfers.

Lightning Arrow Stoveworks
Box 161
Norwich, VT 05055
(802) 649-8818 eves

Maine Wood Heat Company, Inc.
RFD 1 Box 640
Norridgewock, ME 04957
(207) 696-5442

Royal Crown European Fireplaces, Inc.
333 East State, Suite 206
Rockford, IL 61104
(815) 968-2022
Olenych Masonry
Bovina Center, NY 13740
(607) 832-4373
Vesta Masonry Stove Company of North Carolina
373 Old Seven Mile Ridge Road
Burnsville, NC 28714
(704) 675-5247

Sunspaces and Outdoor Rooms

Selected Sunspace/Greenhouse Manufacturers
Creative Structures, Inc.
1765 Walnut Lane
Quakertown, PA 18951
(215) 538-2426
Four Season Solar Products Corp.
5005 Veterans Memorial Highway
Holbrook, NY 11741
(800) 368-7732
Habitat Solar Rooms
Habitat/American Barn
123 Elm Street
South Deerfield, MA 01373
Janco Greenhouses
J. A. Nearing Company, Inc.
9390 Davis Avenue
Laurel, MD 20723
(800) 323-6933
Lindal Cedar Sunrooms
4300 South 104th Place
P.O. Box 24426
Seattle, WA 98124
(206) 725-0900
Machin Designs USA
557 Danbury Road
Wilton, CT 06897
(203) 834-9566
Northern Light Greenhouses
128 Intervale Road
Burlington, VT 05401
(800) 356-4769
Pella Windows and Sunrooms
102 Main Street
Pella, IA 50219
(515) 628-1000
Solar Additions, Inc.
Route 40
P.O. Box 241
Greenwich, NY 12834
(800) 833-2300
Sun Room Company, Inc.
322 East Main Street
P.O. Box 301
Leola, PA 17540
(800) 426-2737

Vegetable Factory, Inc.
P.O. Box 2235
New York, NY 10163
(800) 221-2550

The Kitchen

Superefficient Refrigerators:
Sun Frost
P.O. Box 1101
Arcata, CA 95521
(707) 822-9095

Convection Combo Steamer/Oven:
Groen
1900 Pratt Boulevard
Elk Grove Village, IL 60007
(312) 439-2400

For other manufacturers of pressure steamers, contact the National Association of Food Equipment Manufacturers, (312) 644-6610

For suppliers of faucet aerators, see "The Bathroom," below

The Bathroom

Clivus Multrum
21 Canal Street
Lawrence, MA 01840
(508) 794-1700
Composting toilets and optional hardware.
Composting Toilet Systems
1211 Bergen Road
Newport, WA 99156-9608
(509) 447-3708
Composting privies.
Co-op America
2100 M Street NW, Suite 403
Washington, D.C. 20063
(202) 872-5307
Low-flow showerheads and toilet-tank devices.
Ecological Water Products, Inc.
102 Aldrich Street
Providence, RI 02905
(800) 926-NOVA
Low-flow showerheads, aerators, and toilet dams.
EcoSource
9051 Mill Station Road, Building E
Sebastopol, CA 95472
(800) 688-8345
Environment-friendly products, including low-flow showerheads and faucets and toilet dams.
The Real Goods Trading Corporation
966 Mazzoni Street
Ukiah, CA 95482
(800) 762-7325

A mail-order catalog offering on-demand water heaters, solar water heaters, water purifiers, compost privies, toilet dams, low-flush toilets, and low-flow showerheads and faucets. Also available is the *Alternative Energy Sourcebook,* by John Schaffer, Robert Sardinsky, Randy Wimer, and Jim Cullen, on designing integrated environmental systems.
Resource Conservation Technology, Inc.
2633 North Calvert Street
Baltimore, MD 21218
(301) 366-1146
Several models of ultra-low-flush toilets.
Seventh Generation
Colchester, VT 05446-1672
(800) 456-1177
Catalog of environment-friendly products, including low-flow showerheads and faucets, toilet dams, and one ULF toilet.
The Water Cycle Company
P.O. Box 1841
Santa Rosa, CA 95402
(707) 874-2606
A graywater system designed to filter laundry water sufficiently for use with a drip-irrigation system.

Materials

Air-Krete, Inc.
P.O. Box 380
Weedsport, NY 13166
(315) 834-6609
Insulation.
Environmental Outfitters
12 Burtis Avenue
P.O. Box 514
New Canaan, CT 06840
(203) 966-2807
A variety of environmentally sound building and remodeling materials.
Homasote Company
Box 7240
W. Trenton, NJ 08628
(609) 883-3300
Manufacturer of composite board products made from recycled materials that don't off-gas formaldehyde, including insulating boards, ceilings, partition walls, floor decking, interior paneling, roof underlayment, and carpet backing.
Rivenite Corporation
National Headquarters
6121 Highway 98 North
Lakeland, FL 33809
(813) 858-8299
Manufacturer of Rivenite, a product composed of wood fiber and scrap plastics without added chemicals or toxins, an alternative to pressure-treated woods for outdoor use.

Rodman Industries
P.O. Box 76
Marinette, WI 54143
(715) 735-9500
Resin-core particleboard made without urea
  formaldehyde.

Low-Toxicity Paints, Finishes, Preservatives,
and Strippers:
AFM Enterprises, Inc.
1140 Stacy Court
Riverside, CA 92507
(714) 781-6860
Various products.
Auro Natural Paints
Distributed by Sinan Company
P.O. Box 857
Davis, CA 95617-0857
(916) 753-3104
Various products.
Biofa Naturprodukte
Distributed by Bau, Inc.
P.O. Box 190
Alton, NH 03809
(603) 364-2400
Various products.
**Environs Control and Containment
  Products, Inc.**
1400 Brook Road
Richmond, VA 23220
(804) 649-0007
Citrus mastic removers.
Livos Plantchemistry
1365 Rufina Circle
Santa Fe, NM 87501
(505) 438-3448
Various products.
Miller Paint Company
317 SE Grand Avenue
Portland, OR 97214
(503) 233-4491
Various products.
Murco Wall Products, Inc.
300 North East Twenty-first Street
Fort Worth, TX 76106
(817) 626-1987
Various products.
Preserva-Products, Inc.
P.O. Box 744
2955 Lake Forest Road
Tahoe City, CA 95730-0744
Wood and concrete preservatives and sealers.
3M D-I-Y Division
P.O. Box 33053
St. Paul, MN 55133
(800) 548-6257
Low-toxicity stripper.

Woods:

**Sources of Woods Certified as Smart
Woods by the Rainforest Alliance**
Lynn-Nusantara Marketing Company, Inc.
Agents for the State Forestry Corporation, Java,
  Indonesia
21 East 28th Avenue, Suite D
Eugene, OR 97405
(503) 686-9886
Mahogany, teak, pine, and rosewood available
  in semifinished or finished products.
Plan Piloto Forestal, Quintana Roo
Contact Plan Estatal Forestal
Henning Flachsenberg
Infiernillo 157, Esqu. Efrain Aguilar
Chetumal, Quintana Roo, Mexico
011 (52) 983-24424
Mahogany and other species available in sawn-
  wood.
Proyecto Desarrollo Bosque Latifoliado
(Broadleaf Forest Development Project)
P.O. Box 427
La Ceiba, Honduras
(504) 43-1032
Various species available in sawnwood.

**Smart Wood Companies Selling
Products Made Exclusively of Smart
Woods**
Kingsley-Bate Ltd.
P.O. Box 6797
Arlington, VA 22206
(703) 931-9200
Outdoor furniture in mahogany and teak.
Latitude 16 Designs
c/o French Harbor Yacht Club
Isla Roatan, Honduras
(504) 45-1460
Wholesaler of outdoor furniture made of lesser-
  known tropical woods.
Mahogany Craft
16 East Patrick Street
Frederick, MD 21701
(301) 663-4611
Retailers of fine reproduction Chippendale
  furniture in mahogany.
The Plow & Hearth
301 Madison Road
P.O. Box 830
Orange, VA 22960
(800) 627-1712
Outdoor furniture in teak.
Victorian Reproductions
P.O. Box 54
La Ceiba, Honduras
(504) 42-0342
Outdoor furniture and accessories made of
  lesser-known tropical species.

**Other Companies Selling Smart Wood
Products**
Smith & Hawken
25 Corte Madera
Mill Valley, CA 94941
(415) 383-4415
Mail-order retailer of teak planters and outdoor
  furniture in Honduran cedar.
Summit Furniture
P.O. Box S
Carmel, CA 93912
(408) 394-4401
Fine furniture in teak and mahogany.

**Other Ecologically Minded Suppliers of
Tropical and Old-Growth Woods**
Berry Sawmills
Cazdero, CA
(707) 923-2979
Second-growth redwood and Douglas fir.
Big Creek Lumber
3564 Highway 1
Davenport, CA 95017
(408) 423-4156
Second-growth redwood and Douglas fir.
Champion Ridge Lumber Company
P.O. Box 272
Whitehaven, CA 95489
Salvage redwood and Douglas fir.
John Curtis
P.O. Box 697
Healdsburg, CA 95448
Contact for retailers of lesser-known tropical
  hardwoods grown and harvested responsibly
  by the Yanesha forestry project in Peru.
Michael Evenson
P.O. Box 202
Redway, CA 95560
(707) 923-2979
Salvage redwood and Douglas fir.
Plane and Square
300 North Water Street
Petaluma, CA 94952
(707) 763-0159
Salvage old-growth woods.
Tosten Brothers
P.O. Box 156
Miranda, CA 95553
(707) 943-3093
Redwood and Douglas fir lumber.
Wild Iris Forestry
P.O. Box 1423
Redway, CA 95560
(707) 923-2344
Redwood, Douglas fir, madrone, tanoak, and
  other lumber; tongue-and-groove redwood
  paneling and tanoak flooring.

Appendix B: RECOMMENDED INSULATION LEVELS

To find the U.S. Department of Energy's recommended insulation levels for houses in your area, check the map for your insulation zone. For a more precise determination of your insulation zone, look for your zip code in table 2. Table 1 lists recommended R-values for ceilings, floors, exterior walls, and crawl-space walls in your insulation zone. These recommendations should be considered the *minimum acceptable* insulation levels.

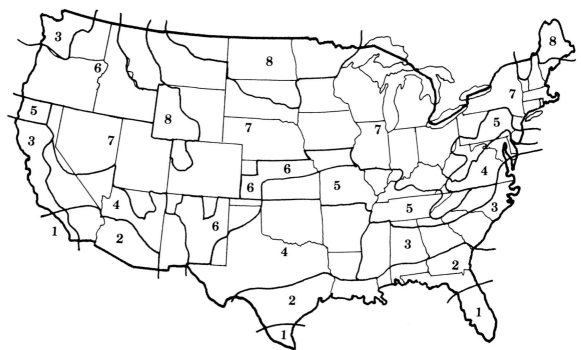

Table 1: Recommended Total R-Values for Houses in the Eight Insulation Zones[a]

Component	Ceilings below Ventilated Attics		Floors Over Unheated Crawl Spaces, Basements		Exterior Walls[b] (Wood Frame)		Crawl-Space Walls[c]	
Insulation Zone	Oil, Gas, Heat Pump	Electric Resistance	Oil, Gas, Heat Pump	Electric Resistance	Oil, Gas, Heat Pump	Electric Resistance	Oil, Gas, Heat Pump	Electric Resistance
1	19	30	0	0	0	11	11	11
2	30	30	0	0	11	11	19	19
3	30	38	0	19	11	11	19	19
4	30	38	19	19	11	11	19	19
5	38	38	19	19	11	11	19	19
6	38	38	19	19	11	11	19	19
7	38	49	19	19	11	11	19	19
8	49	49	19	19	11	11	19	19

[a] These recommendations are based on the assumption that no structural modifications are needed to accommodate the added insulation.
[b] R-value of full wall insulation, which is 3½ inches thick, will depend on material used. Range is R-11 to R-13. For new construction R-19 is recommended for exterior walls. Jamming an R-19 batt in a 3½ inch cavity will not yield R-19.
[c] Insulate crawl-space walls only if the crawl-space is dry all year, the floor above is not insulated, and all ventilation to the crawl-space is blocked. A vapor barrier (e.g., 4- or 6-mil polyethylene film) should be installed on the ground to reduce moisture migration into the crawl space.

Table 2: Zip Codes and Corresponding Insulation Zones*

Example: If your zip code begins with these 3 numbers: 010
your insulation zone is: 7

Zip Codes Beginning with 009		100			200			300		400			500
010 7	054 8	100 7	145 7	189 4	200 4	244 4	289 7	300 3	356 5	400 7	447 7	494 7	500 7
011 7	056 8	101 7	146 7	190 4	202 4	245 4	290 3	301 3	357 5	401 7	448 7	495 7	501 7
012 7	057 7	102 7	147 7	191 4	203 4	246 4	291 3	302 3	358 5	402 7	449 7	496 7	502 7
013 7	058 8	103 7	148 7	192 4	204 4	247 5	292 3	303 3	359 3	403 7	450 7	497 7	503 7
014 7	059 8	104 7	149 7	193 4	205 4	248 4	293 5	304 2	360 3	404 7	451 7	498 7	504 7
015 7	060 7	105 7	150 7	194 4	206 4	249 5	294 3	305 5	361 3	405 7	453 7	499 7	505 7
016 7	061 7	106 7	151 5	195 4	207 4	250 4	295 3	306 3	362 3	406 7	454 7		506 7
017 7	062 7	107 7	152 7	196 5	208 4	251 4	296 5	307 5	363 2	407 7	455 7		507 7
018 7	063 7	108 7	153 5	197 4	209 4	252 4	297 3	308 3	364 2	408 5	456 7		508 7
019 7	064 7	109 7	154 5	198 4	210 4	253 4	298 3	309 3	365 2	409 5	457 7		510 7
020 7	065 7	110 7	155 5	199 4	211 4	254 5	299 3	310 3	366 2	410 7	458 7		511 7
021 7	066 7	111 7	156 7		212 4	255 4		312 3	367 3	411 7	460 7		512 7
022 7	067 7	112 7	157 7		214 4	256 4		313 2	368 3	412 7	461 7		513 7
023 7	068 7	113 7	158 7		215 4	257 4		314 2	369 3	413 7	462 7		514 7
024 7	069 7	114 7	159 5		216 4	258 5		315 2	370 5	414 7	463 7		515 7
025 7	070 7	115 7	160 7		217 4	259 5		316 2	371 5	415 7	464 7		516 7
026 7	071 7	116 7	161 7		218 3	260 5		317 2	372 5	416 7	465 7		520 7
027 7	072 7	118 7	162 7		217 4	261 5		318 3	373 5	417 7	466 7		521 7
028 7	073 7	119 7	163 7		218 3	262 7		319 3	374 5	418 7	467 7		522 7
029 7	074 7	120 7	164 7		219 4	263 5		320 2	376 7	420 5	468 7		523 7
030 7	075 7	121 7	165 7		220 4	264 5		321 2	377 5	421 5	469 7		524 7
031 7	076 7	122 7	166 7		221 4	265 5		322 2	378 5	422 5	470 7		525 7
032 7	077 7	123 7	167 7		222 4	266 7		323 2	379 5	423 7	471 5		526 7
033 7	078 7	124 7	168 5		223 4	267 5		324 2	380 5	424 7	472 7		527 7
034 7	079 7	125 7	169 7		224 4	268 5		325 2	381 5	425 7	473 7		528 7
035 7	080 5	126 7	170 5		225 4	270 5		326 2	382 5	426 7	474 5		530 7
036 7	081 7	127 7	171 5		226 4	271 5		327 1	383 5	427 7	475 5		531 7
037 7	082 5	128 7	172 5		227 4	272 5		328 1	384 5	430 7	476 5		532 7
038 7	083 5	129 7	173 5		228 4	273 5		329 1	385 5	431 7	477 5		534 7
039 7	084 5	130 7	174 5		229 4	274 5		330 1	386 3	432 7	478 7		535 7
040 7	085 7	131 7	175 5		230 3	275 5		331 1	387 3	433 7	479 7		537 7
041 7	086 7	132 7	176 5		231 3	276 5		332 1	388 3	434 7	480 7		538 7
042 8	087 5	133 7	177 7		232 3	277 5		333 1	389 3	435 7	481 7		539 7
043 7	088 7	134 7	178 5		233 3	278 5		334 1	390 3	436 7	482 7		540 7
044 8	089 7	135 7	179 5		234 3	279 5		335 1	391 3	437 7	484 7		541 7
045 7		136 7	180 5		235 3	280 5		336 1	392 3	438 7	485 7		542 7
046 8		137 7	181 5		236 3	281 5		337 1	393 3	439 7	486 7		543 7
047 8		138 7	182 5		237 3	282 5		338 1	394 3	440 7	487 7		544 7
048 7		139 7	183 5		238 3	283 5		339 1	395 3	441 7	488 7		545 7
049 8		140 7	184 5		239 3	284 3		350 3	396 3	442 7	489 7		546 7
050 7		141 7	185 5		240 4	285 3		351 3	397 3	443 7	490 7		547 7
051 7		142 7	186 4		241 4	286 7		352 3		444 7	491 7		548 7
052 7		143 7	187 4		242 4	287 7		354 3		445 7	492 7		549 7
053 7		144 7	188 4		243 4	288 7		355 3		446 7	493 7		550 7

*For Hawaii, Puerto Rico, and the Virgin Islands, the insulation zone is 1.

GLOSSARY

Active solar: Home design that relies on collectors and mechanical systems to distribute solar heat throughout a house.

Bioshelter: A greenhouse designed to enable a family to produce a significant amount of food year-round. A bioshelter is more biologically diverse than a typical greenhouse garden: vegetables and fruits flourish in the structure's many microclimates, and fish are often raised in water-filled translucent tanks. The plants themselves are grown not in containers but rather in soil that is separated from the earth outside only by insulated walls extending below the frost line, making the bioshelter more hospitable to earthworms and other soil organisms.

Building envelope: The area within a home's interior and exterior walls and roof and ceilings. By increasing the amount of insulation in these areas, and controlling the amount of hot air that is vented from them, you can greatly improve a house's energy efficiency.

Clerestory window: A window or row of windows located high on a wall, near where it meets the ceiling. In some houses the roofline is bumped up to create a kind of upper extension into which the clerestory fits.

Drain field: An important part of a conventional home septic system, consisting of a series of perforated pipes buried in gravel-filled trenches. Wastewater flows into a septic tank, where solids settle and are broken down to some degree by bacteria. The cleaner wastewater at the top of the septic tank flows into the drain field, then percolates into the surrounding soil, where it is further purified by bacteria and other organisms.

Dripline: The area on the ground that corresponds to the horizontal reach of a tree's canopy or foliage.

Life-cycle cost: The full cost of an appliance or home improvement when the cost of the water or energy it uses over its lifetime is added to the purchase price. When the life-cycle cost is calculated, the savings on electric bills may quickly more than justify the higher initial cost of, for example, an energy-efficient air-conditioner.

Leach field: see **Drain field.**

Low-E (low-emissivity): The term used for energy-efficient glass that is coated with an atoms-thin layer of metal, which prevents heat loss in cool climates by reflecting the heat back into the room, and prevents heat gain in warm climates by reflecting it away from the house. Low-E windows are made with either coated glass or a coated plastic film suspended between panes of glass.

Off-gassing: Pollution caused by formaldehyde and other chemicals called volatile organic compounds, which volatilize, or become a gas, at room temperature.

Passive solar: Home design that relies on the orientation and building materials of the structure itself, not on mechanical systems, to heat and cool a house in natural, energy-conserving ways. The home is oriented on an east-west axis, for example, to increase the area available for solar heat gain through windows on the south side in winter. It is built with materials with thermal mass to store the solar heat, and is well insulated and tightly constructed to reduce heat loss.

Pleaching: Training the branches of trees along wires by entwining, interlacing, or grafting them together, usually to form a narrow hedge above bare trunks.

Radiant barrier: A layer of reinforced aluminum foil that is built into the walls and roofs of houses in hot climates to restrict the transfer of solar heat indoors by reflecting it back outdoors.

R-value (resistance value): The measure of a material's ability to keep heat from flowing into or out of a room. The higher the R-value of a type of glass or insulation, for example, the more energy-conserving it is.

Shading coefficient: The measure of a window's ability to transmit solar heat, a more important factor than R-value in hot climates, where overheating is the primary problem. In these areas, the lower a window's shading coefficient, the better. Low-E windows have low shading coefficients because their metallic coating deflects the sun's warming rays before they can enter the house.

Soffit: The underside of a roof overhang.

Superinsulation: An energy-efficient building technique that is especially economical in cool climates. A superinsulated house is so highly insulated and so tightly constructed (thereby minimizing drafts) that very little heating is necessary.

Thermal break: An insulating material that separates the inner and outer layers of a window frame, reducing conduction and therefore unwanted heat loss.

Thermal mass: The capacity of some construction materials, including brick, concrete, adobe, and stone, to store heat from the sun, furnace, or fireplace and slowly radiate it when needed to keep a house warm. Thermal mass is often incorporated in walls, chimneys, and floors.

Vent-skin construction: A building technique that is particularly effective in hot and humid climates because it expels heat from within a home's walls and roof before it can heat up the interior. Ridge vents (vents in the roof peak) exhaust hot air, which is replaced by cooler air that enters through soffit vents (vents at the bottom of the roof overhang) and screens at the foot of the vent-skin walls.

Whole-house fan: An effective means of ventilation in hot and humid climates with little wind, in densely developed neighborhoods, or in townhouses. A whole-house fan centrally located in an attic operates by pulling air in through opened windows and expelling it through larger-than-normal attic vents.

INDEX

PHOTO CREDITS

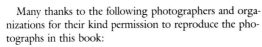

Many thanks to the following photographers and organizations for their kind permission to reproduce the photographs in this book:

Title page, Alan Weintraub; p. 3 top, Karen Bussolini; p. 3 bottom, Alan Weintraub; p. 4, Jerry Pavia; p. 6, William Turnbull Associates; p. 7 top, Obie Bowman; p. 7 bottom, Robert Perron; p. 8 top, Michael Anisfeld; p. 8 bottom left, David Cavagnaro; p. 8 bottom right, Cynthia Wright; p. 9, Karen Bussolini; p. 10 left, Photography by Marissa; p. 10 right, Peter J. Menzel; p. 11, Obie Bowman; p. 12, J. Randall Cotton; p. 13 left and right, James Brett; p. 14 left, William Turnbull Associates; p. 14 right, Donald Watson; p. 15 top, Rick Gardner; p. 15 bottom, Allen Maertz; p. 16 top, Design Guild; p. 16 bottom left and right, *Fine Homebuilding;* p. 17, Richard Gross; p. 18 top and bottom, Christian Staub; p. 19 top, Alan Weintraub; p. 20 left and right, Steve Martino; p. 21 top and right, Jerry Pavia; p. 22 top left and right, Michael Anisfeld; pp. 22 bottom and 23 top left and right, Karen Bussolini; p. 23 bottom center and right, Robert Kourik; pp. 24 and 25 top, Patrick Chassé; pp. 26 top and bottom and 27, Jane Stader; p. 28 left and right, Jonathan Poore, Architectural Designer; p. 30 left and right, Alan Weintraub; p. 31 center and bottom, Richard Gross; p. 33 top left, Robert Perron; p. 33 top right and bottom, Rick Gardner; p. 34 top, William Turnbull Associates; p. 34 bottom, Andrew Kramer; pp. 35 top and bottom left, Clifford Miller; pp. 35 bottom right and 36 and 37 top, Karen Bussolini; p. 37 bottom, Arne Bystrom; p. 38, Jerry Pavia; p. 39 top and bottom center, James Brett; p. 39 right, Rick Gardner; p. 40 top left and right, Alan Weintraub; p. 40 bottom, Karen Bussolini; p. 41, Robert Perron; p. 42 top, Karen Bussolini; p. 42 bottom, Photography by Marissa; p. 43, Michael J. Moreland;

p. 44 top left and right, Obie Bowman; p. 45 top, Obie Bowman; p. 45 bottom left, Peter Gisolfi Associates; p. 45 bottom right, Robert Perron; p. 46 top, Alan Weintraub; p. 46 bottom, Guy Mancuso; pp. 48, 49, and 50, Nick Wheeler/Wheeler Photographics; pp. 51, 52, and 53, Robert Perron; p. 54 top and bottom, Alan Weintraub; pp. 55 bottom and 56 left, Steve Badanes/Jersey Devil; p. 56 right, *Fine Homebuilding;* pp. 57, 58, and 59, Greg Hursley; pp. 60, 61, and 62, Lake/Flato Architects; p. 63, Robert M. Freund; p. 64, James Brett; p. 65, *Fine Homebuilding;* p. 66 top, James Brett; p. 66 center and bottom, *Fine Homebuilding;* p. 67 top and bottom, Robert Murase; pp. 68 and 69 top and bottom, Arne Bystrom; pp. 70, 71, and 72, Greg Hursley; p. 77, Robert Kourik; pp. 79, 80, 81, and 82, Obie Bowman; p. 83, Robert Perron; pp. 87 and 88, Biofire Inc.; pp. 90 and 91, Solar Design Associates; p. 99, Greg Hursley; p. 100, Steve Badanes/Jersey Devil; p. 104, Photography by Marissa; p. 109, Robert Perron; p. 113, Arne Bystrom; p. 115, Jennifer Lévy; p. 116, Richard Gross; p. 117, Jennifer Lévy; p. 121, Robert Perron; p. 122, Lake/Flato Architects; p. 129, Cynthia Wright; p. 131, Robert Perron; p. 136, Bosch; p. 137, Robert Perron; p. 142, Photography by Marissa; p. 144, Cynthia Wright; p. 150, Bill Wolverton; p. 152, Karen Bussolini; p. 154, Robert Perron; pp. 156 and 157, Robert Perron; p. 158, Jennifer Lévy; p. 159, Karen Bussolini; pp. 170 and 171, Robert Kourik; pp. 172 top and 174, Patrick Chassé; pp. 175, 176, and 177, Michael Anisfeld; pp. 178 and 179, Jane Stader; pp. 181 and 182, Steve Martino; pp. 184 and 185, Jerry Pavia; pp. 187 and 188, Karen Bussolini; pp. 190 and 191, Robert Kourik; p. 195, Jennifer Lévy; p. 197, Robert Kourik; pp. 202 and 203 top and center, Jerry Pavia; p. 207, Robert Kourik; p. 213, Gardener's Supply; p. 215, Robert Kourik; p. 218 top and bottom, Balcon, Inc.; p. 219, Robert Kourik.